LEARNING ASP.NET 4.0

LEARNING ASP.NET 4.0

Ramesh Bangia
B.Sc., Comp. Sc. (IIT - Delhi)
Formerly Managing Editor, Software Today
Formerly Incharge Computer Centre, Hindustan Copper Ltd., New Delhi

KHANNA BOOK PUBLISHING CO. (P) LTD.
DELHI

Learning ASP.NET 4 — Ramesh Bangia

First Edition 2012

Published by:
Khanna Book Publishing Co. (P) Ltd.
4C/4344, Ansari Road, Darya Ganj, New Delhi-110 002
Phone: 011-23244447, 23244448
E-mail: contact@khannabooks.com
Website: www.khannabooks.com

Regd. Off: 1694-95, 1st Floor, Nai Sarak, Delhi-110006 (India)
Phone: 011-23283211, 23256658
Fax: 011-23256658

Printed in India by SPS Printers and Binders, Delhi

PREFACE

Learning of a software is both easy and difficult. It depends upto what level you are planning to learn. If you are learning only for the working use, then it is very easy. But, when you try to go deep into it, then you realise how difficult it is to master it.

This book has been written in mind to make you aware of the options available in the software and how they can be used. It is like telling the child about the steps and stairs. You are the one who is to climb the stair. This book will just guide you how to use the stairs.

I am indeed debited to my publishers Khanna Book Publishing Co. Pvt. Ltd. for their suggestions and encouragement given in producing this book.

Suggestions for improvement of the book are indeed welcome.

Author

CONTENTS

CHAPTER 1

Introduction to ASP.NET 4.0

In this chapter you will read about:

- Introduction to ASP.NET Framework.
- Understanding ASP.NET Controls
- Using the Standard Controls.
- Understanding HTML Controls
- Understanding ASP.NET Controls.
- Installing ASP.NET

Installing ASP.NET

The easiest way to install ASP.NET Framework is to install Visual Web Developer Express. You can download the latest version of Visual Web Developer from www.ASP.net, which is the official Microsoft ASP.NET website.

Installing Visual Web Developer Express also installs the following components:

- Microsoft .NET Framework version 4
- SQL Server Express

Visual Web Developer Express is compatible with the following operating systems:

- Windows XP (x86) Service Pack 3
- Windows XP (x64) Service Pack 2
- Windows Server 2003 Service Pack 2
- Windows Server 2003 R2
- Windows Server 2008 Service Pack 2
- Windows Server 2008 R2
- Windows Vista
- Windows 7

You can install Visual Web Developer Express on a computer that already has other versions of Visual Studio or Visual Web Developer installed. Different versions of the development environments can coexist peacefully. Furthermore, the same web server can serve ASP.NET 1.1 pages, ASP.NET 2.0 pages, ASP.NET 3.0 pages, ASP.NET 3.5 pages, and ASP.NET 4 pages. Each version of .NET Framework is installed in the following folder:

```
C:\WINDOWS\Microsoft.NET\Framework
```

For example, on my computer, I have the following six versions of .NET Framework installed (version 1.0, version 1.1, version 2.0, version 3.0, version 3.5, and version 4):

```
C:\WINDOWS\Microsoft.NET\Framework\v1.0.3705
C:\WINDOWS\Microsoft.NET\Framework\v1.1.4322
C:\WINDOWS\Microsoft.NET\Framework\v2.0.50727
C:\WINDOWS\Microsoft.NET\Framework\v3.0
C:\WINDOWS\Microsoft.NET\Framework\v3.5
C:\WINDOWS\Microsoft.NET\Framework\v4.0.30128
```

Note: The Framework directory contains the 32-bit (x86) version of .NET. If you are running on a 64-bit (x64) operating system, you also have another directory named Framework64.

All the folders except for v3.0 and v3.5 include a command-line tool named aspnet_regiis.exe. You can use this tool to associate a particular virtual directory on your machine with a particular version of .NET Framework.

For example, executing the following command from a command prompt located in the v1.0.3705, v1.1.4322, v2.0.50727, or v4.0.30128 folders enables the 1.0, 1.1, 2.0, or 4 version of ASP.NET for a virtual directory named MyApplication:

```
aspnet_regiis -s W3SVC/1/ROOT/MyApplication
```

By executing the aspnet_regiis.exe tool located in the different .NET Framework version folders, you can map a particular virtual directory to any version of ASP.NET Framework.

The .NET Frameworks 3.0 and 3.5 work differently than earlier versions. The 3.0 and 3.5 versions build on top of the existing .NET Framework 2.0. To use these versions of .NET Framework, you need to add the correct assembly references to your website and use the correct versions of the C# or VB.NET compilers.

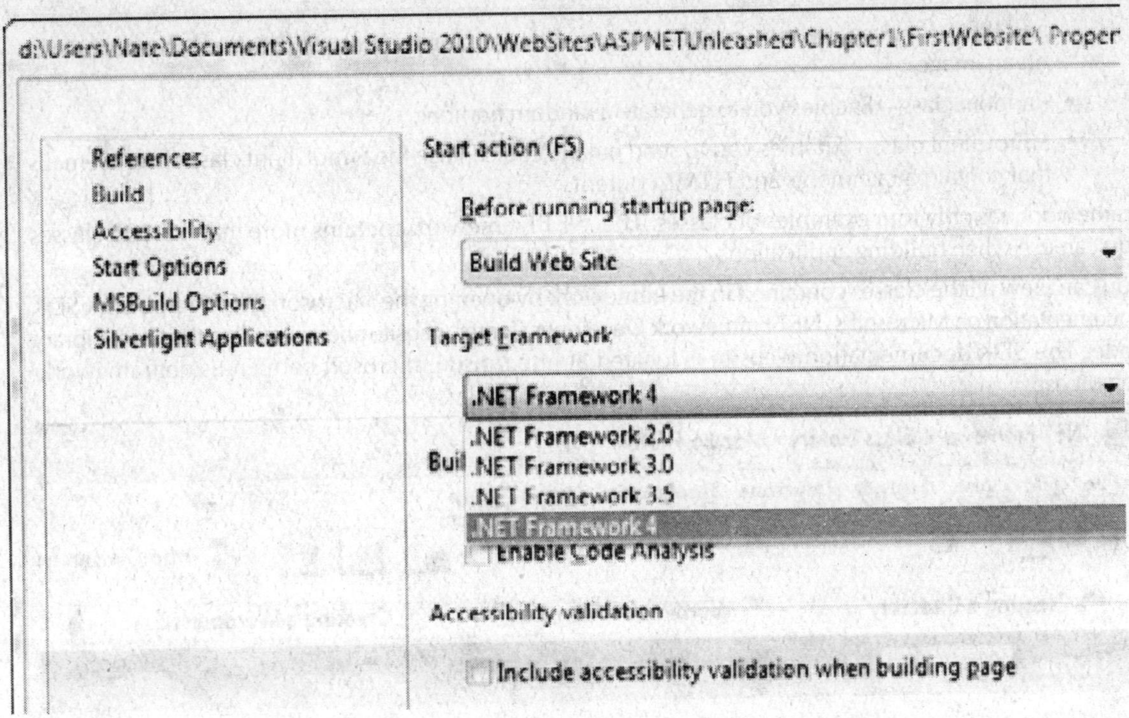

Figure Targeting a particular version of .NET Framework.

You reference these assemblies and configure the compiler within your application's web.config file. When you create a new website in Visual Web Developer, the necessary configuration settings are included in your web.config file automatically. The .NET Framework 4 is the first version since 2.0 that does not build off of a previous version.

You also have the option of targeting a particular version of .NET Framework. To do this, select Website, Start Options and select the Build tab. You can choose to target .NET Framework 2.0, .NET Framework 3.0, .NET Framework 3.5, or .NET Framework 4.

Note: If you load an existing ASP.NET 2.0, 3.0, or 3.5 website into Visual Web Developer 2010, Visual Web Developer prompts you to upgrade the website to ASP.NET 4. When Visual Web Developer upgrades your website, it modifies your web.config file.

Introduction

ASP.NET is part of the Microsoft .NET Framework. To build ASP.NET pages, you need to take advantage of the features of .NET Framework, which consists of two parts: the Framework Class Library and the Common Language Runtime.

Understanding the Framework Class Library

The .NET Framework contains thousands of classes that you can use when building an application. Framework Class Library was designed to make it easier to perform the most common programming tasks. Following are just a few examples of the classes in the framework:

- File class— Enables you to represent a file on your hard drive. You can use the File class to check whether a file exists, create a new file, delete a file, and perform many other file-related tasks.
- Graphics class— Enables you to work with different types of images such as GIF, PNG, BMP,

and JPEG. You can use the Graphics class to draw rectangles, arcs, ellipses, and other elements on an image

- Random class— Enables you to generate a random number.
- SmtpClient class— Enables you to send email. You can use the SmtpClient class to send emails that contain attachments and HTML content.

Framework has only four examples of classes. The .NET Framework contains more than 13,000 classes you can use when building applications.

You can view all the classes contained in the framework by opening the Microsoft .NET Framework SDK documentation on Microsoft's .NET Framework Developer Center website and expanding the Class Library node. The SDK documentation website is located at http://msdn.microsoft.com/en-us/netframework/default.aspx.

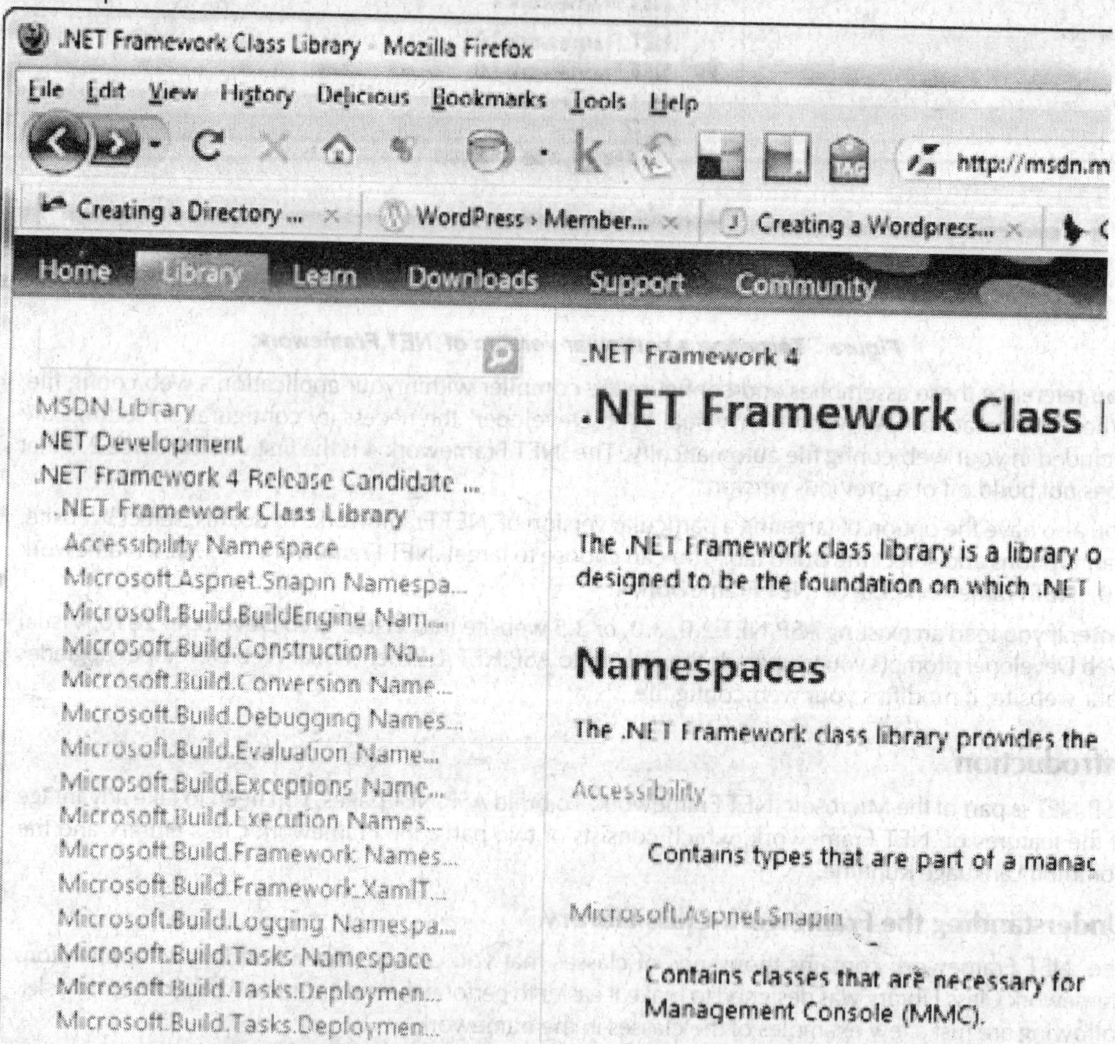

The online Microsoft .NET Framework SDK documentation.

Each class in the Framework can include properties, methods, and events. The properties, methods, and events exposed by a class are the members of a class. For example, following is a partial list of the members of the SmtpClient class:

- Properties
  - o Host— The name or IP address of your email server
  - o Port— The number of the port to use when sending an email message
- Methods
  - o Send— Enables you to send an email message synchronously
  - o SendAsync— Enables you to send an email message asynchronously
- Events
  - o SendCompleted— Raised when an asynchronous send operation completes

If you know the members of a class, you know everything that you can do with a class. For example, the SmtpClient class includes two properties named Host and Port, which enable you to specify the email server and port to use when sending an email message.

The SmtpClient class also includes two methods you can use to send an email: Send() and SendAsync(). The Send method blocks further program execution until the send operation is completed. The SendAsync() method, on the other hand, sends the email asynchronously. Unlike the Send() method, the SendAsync() method does not wait to check whether the send operation was successful.

Finally, the SmtpClient class includes an event named SendCompleted, which is raised when an asynchronous send operation completes. You can create an event handler for the SendCompleted event that displays a message when the email has been successfully sent.

The page in the following listing sends an email by using the SmtpClient class and calling its Send() method.

```
<%@ Import Namespace="System.Net.Mail" %>
<!DOCTYPE html PUBLIC "-//W3C//DTD XHTML 1.0 Transitional//EN"
"http://www.w3.org/TR/xhtml1/DTD/xhtml1-transitional.dtd">
<script runat="server">

    void Page_Load()
    {
        SmtpClient client = new SmtpClient();
        client.Host = "localhost";
        client.Port = 25;
        client.Send("nate@somewhere", "nate@exclaimcomputing.com",
            "Beware!", "Watch out for zombies!");
    }

</script>
<html xmlns="http://www.w3.org/1999/xhtml" >
<head id="Head1" runat="server">
    <title>Send Mail</title>
</head>
<body>
    <form id="form1" runat="server">
    <div>
    Email sent!

    </div>
    </form>
</body>
</html>
```

The page in above listing calls the SmtpClient Send() method to send the email. The first parameter is the from: address; the second parameter is the to: address; the third parameter is the subject; and the final parameter is the body of the email.

Understanding Namespaces

There are more than 13,000 classes in .NET Framework. This is an overwhelming number. If Microsoft simply jumbled all the classes together, you would never find anything. Fortunately, Microsoft divided the classes in the framework into separate namespaces.

A namespace is simply a category. For example, all the classes related to working with the file system are located in the System.IO namespace. All the classes for working a Microsoft SQL Server database are located in the System.Data.SqlClient namespace.

Before you can use a class in a page, you must indicate the namespace associated with the class. There are multiple ways of doing this.

First, you can fully qualify a class náme with its namespace. For example, because the File class is contained in the System.IO namespace, you can use the following statement to check whether a file exists:

```
System.IO.File.Exists("SomeFile.txt")
```

Specifying a namespace every time you use a class can quickly become tedious. (It involves a lot of typing.) A second option is to import a namespace.

You can add an <$I<%@ Import % directive><%@ Import %> directive to a page to import a particular namespace. In the listing, we imported the System.Net.Mail namespace because the SmtpClient is part of this namespace. The page in the listing includes the following directive near the top of the page:

```
<%@ Import Namespace="System.Net.Mail" %>
```

After you import a particular namespace, you can use all the classes in that namespace without qualifying the class names.

Finally, if you discover that you use a namespace in multiple pages in your application, you can configure all the pages in your application to recognize the namespace.

If you add the web configuration file in following listing to your application, you do not need to import the System.Net.Mail namespace in a page to use the classes from this namespace. For example, if you include the Web.config file in your project, you can remove the <%@ Import %> directive from the page in earlier listing.

```
<?xml version="1.0"?>
<configuration>
    <system.web>
        <pages>
            <namespaces>
                <add namespace="System.Net.Mail"/>
            </namespaces>
        </pages>
    </system.web>
</configuration>
```

Web.Config

You don't have to import every namespace. ASP.NET gives you the most commonly used namespaces for free:

- System
- System.Collections

- System.Collections.Generic
- System.Collections.Specialized
- System.ComponentModel.DataAnnotations
- System.Configuration
- System.Data.Entity.Linq
- System.Data.Linq
- System.Text
- System.Text.RegularExpressions
- System.Web
- System.Web.Caching
- System.Web.DynamicData
- System.Web.SessionState
- System.Web.Security
- System.Web.Profile
- System.Web.UI
- System.Web.UI.WebControls
- System.Web.UI.WebControls.WebParts
- System.Web.UI.HtmlControls
- System.Xml.Linq

The default namespaces are listed inside the pages element in the root web configuration file located at the following path:

```
\Windows\Microsoft.NET\Framework\v4.0.30128\Config\Web.Config
```

Understanding Assemblies

An assembly is the actual .dll file on your hard drive in which the classes in .NET Framework are stored. For example, all the classes contained in the ASP.NET Framework are located in an assembly named System.Web.dll.

More accurately, an assembly is the primary unit of deployment, security, and version control in .NET Framework. Because an assembly can span multiple files, an assembly is often referred to as a "logical" dll. The two types of assemblies are private and shared. A private assembly can be used by only a single application. A shared assembly, on the other hand, can be used by all applications located on the same server.

Shared assemblies are located in the Global Assembly Cache (GAC). For example, the System.Web.dll assembly and all the other assemblies included with .NET Framework are located in the Global Assembly Cache. Before you can use a class contained in an assembly in your application, you must add a reference to the assembly. By default, an ASP.NET 4 application references the most common assemblies contained in the Global Assembly Cache:

- mscorlib.dll
- Microsoft.CSharp
- System.dll
- System.Configuration.dll
- System.Web.dll

- System.Data.dll
- System.Web.Services.dll
- System.Xml.dll
- System.Drawing.dll
- System.EnterpriseServices.dll
- System.IdentityModel.dll
- System.Runtime.Serialization.dll
- System.ServiceModel.dll
- System.ServiceModel.Activation.dll
- System.ServiceModel.Web.dll
- System.Activities.dll
- System.ServiceModel.Activities.dll
- System.WorkflowServices.dll
- System.Core.dll
- System.Web.Extensions.dll
- System.Data.DataSetExtensions.dll
- System.Xml.Linq.dll
- System.ComponentModel.DataAnnotations.dll
- System.Web.DynamicData.dll
- System.Data.Entity.dll
- System.Web.Entity.dll
- System.Data.Linq.dll
- System.Data.Entity.Design.dll
- System.Web.ApplicationServices.dll

All these assemblies are part of .NET 4 Framework. Websites created on previous versions of .NET referenced a different set of assemblies.

To use any particular class in .NET Framework, you must do two things. First, your application must reference the assembly that contains the class. Second, your application must import the namespace associated with the class. In most cases, you won't worry about referencing the necessary assembly because the most common assemblies are referenced automatically. However, if you need to use a specialized assembly, you need to add a reference explicitly to the assembly. For example, if you need to interact with Active Directory by using the classes in the System.DirectoryServices namespace, you need to add a reference to the System.DirectoryServices.dll assembly to your application.

Each class entry in .NET Framework SDK documentation lists the assembly and namespace associated with the class. For example, if you look up the MessageQueue class in the documentation, you discover that this class is located in the System.Messaging namespace located in the System.Messaging.dll assembly.

If you use Visual Web Developer, you can add a reference to an assembly explicitly by selecting Web Site, Add Reference, and the name of the assembly that you need to reference. For example, adding a reference to the System.Messaging.dll assembly results in the web configuration file in listing 1.4 being added to your application.

```
<?xml version="1.0"?>
<configuration>
<system.web>
 <compilation>
 <assemblies>
  <add
   assembly="System.Messaging, Version=4.0.0.0,
   Culture=neutral, PublicKeyToken=B03F5F7F11D50A3A"/>
 </assemblies>
 </compilation>
</system.web>
</configuration>
```

Web.Config

If you prefer not to use Visual Web Developer, you can add the reference to the System.Messaging.dll assembly by creating the file in above listing manually.

Understanding the Common Language Runtime

The second part of .NET Framework is the Common Language Runtime (CLR). The CLR is responsible for executing your application code. When you write an application for .NET Framework with a language such as C# or Visual Basic .NET, your source code is never compiled directly into machine code. Instead, the C# or Visual Basic compiler converts your code into a special language named Microsoft Intermediate Language (MSIL).

MSIL looks like an object-oriented assembly language; however, unlike a typical assembly language, it is not CPU-specific. MSIL is a low-level and platform-independent language. When your application actually executes, the MSIL code is just-in-time compiled into machine code by the JITTER (the Just-In-Time compiler). Normally, your entire application is not compiled from MSIL into machine code. Instead, only the methods actually called during execution are compiled.

In reality, .NET Framework understands only one language: MSIL. However, you can write applications using languages such as Visual Basic .NET and C# for .NET Framework because .NET Framework includes compilers for these languages that enable you to compile your code into MSIL.

You can write code for .NET Framework using any one of dozens of different languages, including

- Ada
- Apl
- Caml
- COBOL
- Eiffel
- Forth
- Fortran
- JavaScript
- Oberon
- PERL
- Pascal
- PHP
- Python

- RPG
- Ruby
- Scheme
- Small Talk

The vast majority of developers building ASP.NET applications write the applications in either C# or Visual Basic .NET. Many of the other .NET languages in the preceding list are academic experiments. Once upon a time, if you wanted to become a developer, you concentrated on becoming proficient at a particular language. For example, you became a C++ programmer, a COBOL programmer, or a Visual Basic Programmer.

For .NET Framework, however, knowing a particular language is not particularly important. The choice of which language to use when building a .NET application is largely a preference choice. If you like case-sensitivity and curly braces, you should use the C# programming language. If you want to be lazy about casing and you don't like semicolons, write your code with Visual Basic .NET.

All the real action in .NET Framework happens in the Framework Class Library. If you want to become a good programmer using Microsoft technologies, you need to learn how to use the methods, properties, and events of the 13,000 classes included in the Framework. From the point of view of .NET Framework, it doesn't matter whether you use these classes from a Visual Basic .NET or C# application.

Understanding ASP.NET Controls

ASP.NET controls are the heart of ASP.NET Framework. An ASP.NET control is a .NET class that executes on the server and renders certain content to the browser. For example, in the first ASP.NET page created at the beginning of this chapter, a Label control was used to display the current date and time. The ASP.NET framework includes more than 90 controls, which enable you to do everything from displaying a list of database records to displaying a randomly rotating banner advertisement.

This section provides an overview of the controls included in ASP.NET Framework. You also learn how to handle events raised by controls and how to take advantage of View State.

Overview of ASP.NET Controls

The ASP.NET Framework contains more than 90 controls. These controls can be divided into seven groups:

- Standard Controls— Enable you to render standard form elements such as buttons, input fields, and labels.
- Validation Controls— Enable you to validate form data before you submit the data to the server. For example, you can use a RequiredFieldValidator control to check whether a user entered a value for a required input field.
- Rich Controls— Enable you to render things such as calendars, file upload buttons, rotating banner advertisements, and multistep wizards.
- Data Controls— Enable you to work with data such as database data. For example, you can use these controls to submit new records to a database table or display a list of database records.
- Navigation Controls— Enable you to display standard navigation elements such as menus, tree views, and bread crumb trails.
- Login Controls— Enables you to display login, change password, and registration forms.
- HTML Controls— Enable you to convert any HTML tag into a server-side control.

With the exception of the HTML controls, you declare and use all ASP.NET controls in a page in exactly the same way. For example, if you want to display a text input field in a page, you can declare a TextBox control like this:

```
<asp:TextBox id="TextBox1" runat="Server" />
```

This control declaration looks like the declaration for an HTML tag. Remember, however, unlike an HTML tag, a control is a .NET class that executes on the server and not in the web browser. When the TextBox control is rendered to the browser, it renders the following content:

```
<input name="TextBox1" type="text" id="TextBox1" />
```

The first part of the control declaration, the asp: prefix, indicates the namespace for the control. All the standard ASP.NET controls are contained in the System.Web.UI.WebControls namespace. The prefix asp: represents this namespace.

Next, the declaration contains the name of the control being declared. In this case, a TextBox control is declared. This declaration also includes an ID attribute. You use the ID to refer to the control in the page within your code. Every control must have a unique ID. The declaration also includes a runat="Server" attribute. This attribute marks the tag as representing a server-side control. If you neglect to include this attribute, the TextBox tag would be passed, without being executed, to the browser. The browser would simply ignore the tag.

Finally, notice that the tag ends with a forward slash. The forward slash is shorthand for creating a closing </asp:TextBox> tag. You can, if you prefer, declare the TextBox control like this:

```
<asp:TextBox id="TextBox1" runat="server"></asp:TextBox>
```

In this case, the opening tag does not contain a forward slash and an explicit closing tag is included.

Understanding HTML Controls

You declare HTML controls in a different way than you declare standard ASP.NET controls. The ASP.NET Framework enables you to take any HTML tag (real or imaginary) and add a runat="server" attribute to the tag. The runat="server" attribute converts the HTML tag into a server-side ASP.NET control.

For example, the page in follwoing listing contains a <span> tag, which has been converted into an ASP.NET control.

```
<!DOCTYPE html PUBLIC "-//W3C//DTD XHTML 1.0 Transitional//EN"
"http://www.w3.org/TR/xhtml1/DTD/xhtml1-transitional.dtd">
<script runat="server">

   void Page_Load()
   {
       spanNow.InnerText = DateTime.Now.ToString("T");
   }

</script>
<html xmlns="http://www.w3.org/1999/xhtml" >
<head id="Head1" runat="server">
    <title>HTML Controls</title>
</head>
<body>
    <form id="form1" runat="server">
    <div>

    At the tone, the time will be:
```

```
    <span id="spanNow" runat="server" />

    </div>
    </form>
</body>
</html>
```

HtmlControls.aspx

The <span> tag in the above listing looks just like a normal HTML <span> tag except for the addition of the runat="server" attribute. Because the <span> tag in above listing is a server-side HTML control, you can program against it. In the listing, the current date and time are assigned to the <span> tag in the Page_Load() method.

The HTML controls are included in ASP.NET Framework to make it easier to convert existing HTML pages to use ASP.NET Framework. I rarely use the HTML controls in this book because, in general, the standard ASP.NET controls provide all the same functionality and more.

Understanding and Handling Control Events

The majority of ASP.NET controls support one or more events. For example, the ASP.NET Button control supports the Click event. The Click event is raised on the server after you click the button rendered by the Button control in the browser.

The page listing illustrates how you can write code that executes when a user clicks the button rendered by the Button control (in other words, it illustrates how you can create a Click event handler):

```
<!DOCTYPE html PUBLIC "-//W3C//DTD XHTML 1.0 Transitional//EN"
"http://www.w3.org/TR/xhtml1/DTD/xhtml1-transitional.dtd">
<script runat="server">
    protected void btnSubmit_Click(object sender, EventArgs e)
     {
         Label1.Text = "Thanks!";
     }
</script>
<html xmlns="http://www.w3.org/1999/xhtml" >
<head id="Head1" runat="server">
    <title>Show Button Click</title>
</head>
<body>
    <form id="form1" runat="server">
     <div>

    <asp:Button
         id="btnSubmit"
         Text="Click Here"
         OnClick="btnSubmit_Click"
         Runat="server" />

    <br /><br />

    <asp:Label
         id="Label1"
         Runat="server" />
```

```
        </div>
        </form>
    </body>
    </html>
```

listing ShowButtonClick.aspx

Notice that the Button control in above listing includes an OnClick attribute. This attribute points to a subroutine named btnSubmit_Click(). The btnSubmit_Click() subroutine is the handler for the Button Click event. This subroutine executes whenever you click the button.

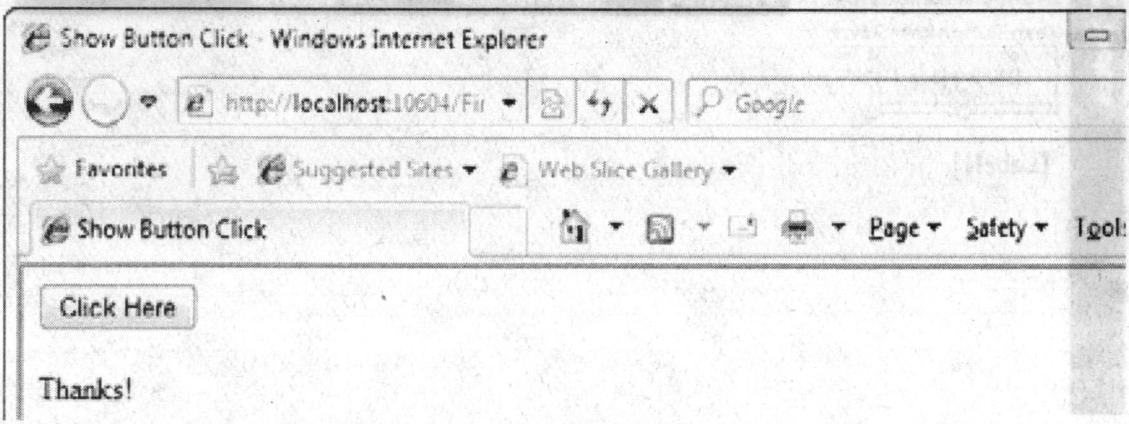

Raising a Click event.

You can add an event handler automatically to a control in multiple ways when using Visual Web Developer. In Source view, add a handler by selecting a control from the top-left drop-down list and selecting an event from the top-right drop-down list. The event handler code is added to the page automatically.

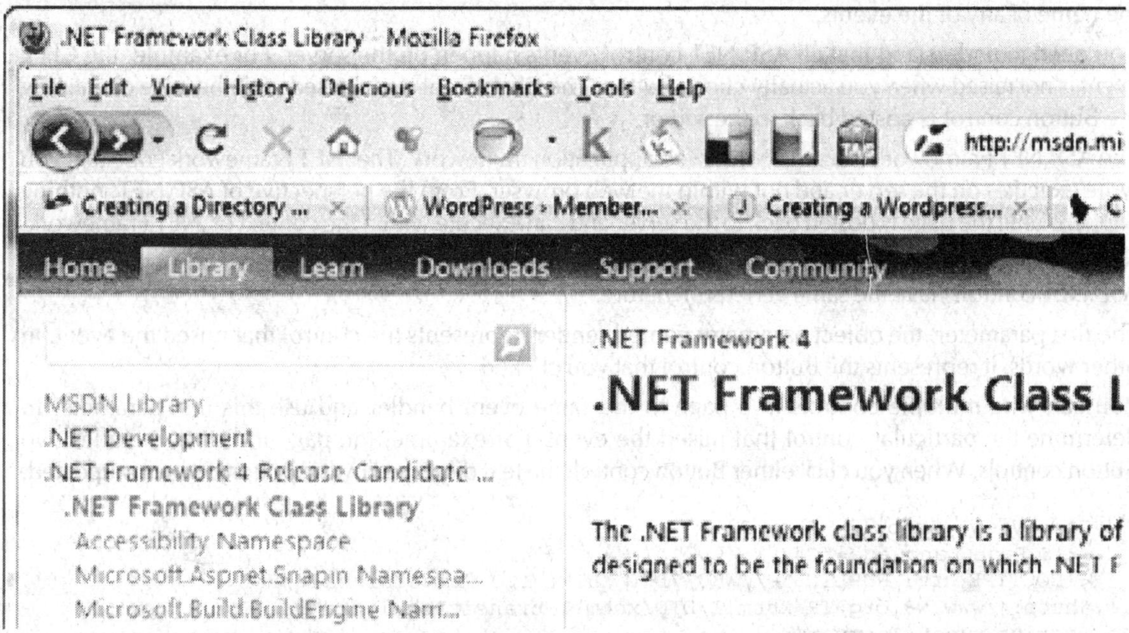

Adding an event handler from Source view.

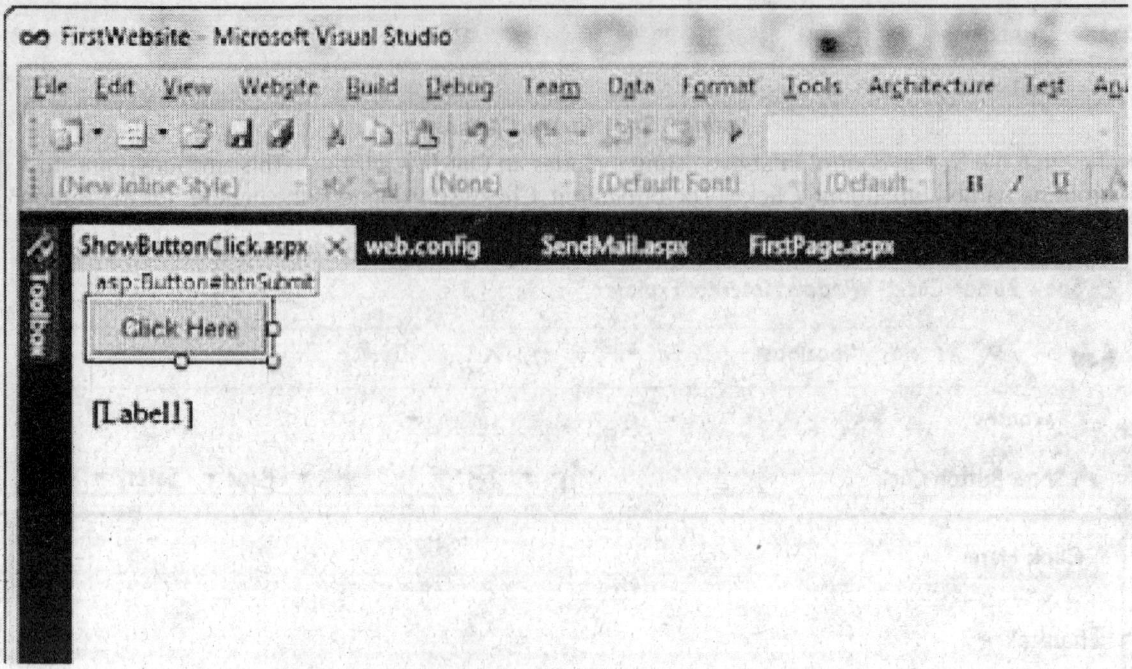

Adding an event handler from the Properties window.

In Design view, you can double-click a control to add a handler for the control's default event. Double-clicking a control switches you to Source view and adds the event handler.

Finally, from Design view, after selecting a control on the designer surface, you can add an event handler from the Properties window by clicking the Events button (the lightning bolt) and double-clicking next to the name of any of the events.

You need to understand that all ASP.NET control events happen on the server. For example, the Click event is not raised when you actually click a button. The Click event is not raised until the page containing the Button control is posted back to the server.

The ASP.NET Framework is a server-side web application framework. The .NET Framework code that you write executes on the server and not within the web browser. From the perspective of ASP.NET, nothing happens until the page is posted back to the server and can execute within the context of .NET Framework.

Notice that two parameters are passed to the btnSubmit_Click() handler in listing. All event handlers for ASP.NET controls have the same general signature.

The first parameter, the object parameter named sender, represents the control that raised the event. In other words, it represents the Button control that you clicked.

You can wire multiple controls in a page to the same event handler and use this first parameter to determine the particular control that raised the event. For example, the page in listing includes two Button controls. When you click either Button control, the text displayed by the Button control is updated.

```
Code View: Scroll / Show All
 <%@ Page Language="C#" %>
<!DOCTYPE html PUBLIC "-//W3C//DTD XHTML 1.0 Transitional//EN"
"http://www.w3.org/TR/xhtml1/DTD/xhtml1-transitional.dtd">
<script runat="server">
```

```
    protected void Button_Click(object sender, EventArgs e)
    {
        Button btn = (Button)sender;
        btn.Text = (Int32.Parse(btn.Text) + 1).ToString();
    }
</script>
<html xmlns="http://www.w3.org/1999/xhtml" >
<head id="Head1" runat="server">
    <title>Button Counters</title>
</head>
<body>
    <form id="form1" runat="server">
    <div>

    First Counter:
    <asp:Button
        id="Button1"
        Text="0"
        OnClick="Button_Click"
        Runat="server" />

    <br /><br />

    Second Counter:
    <asp:Button
        id="Button2"
        Text="0"
        OnClick="Button_Click"
        Runat="server" />

    </div>
    </form>
</body>
</html>
```

ButtonCounters.aspx

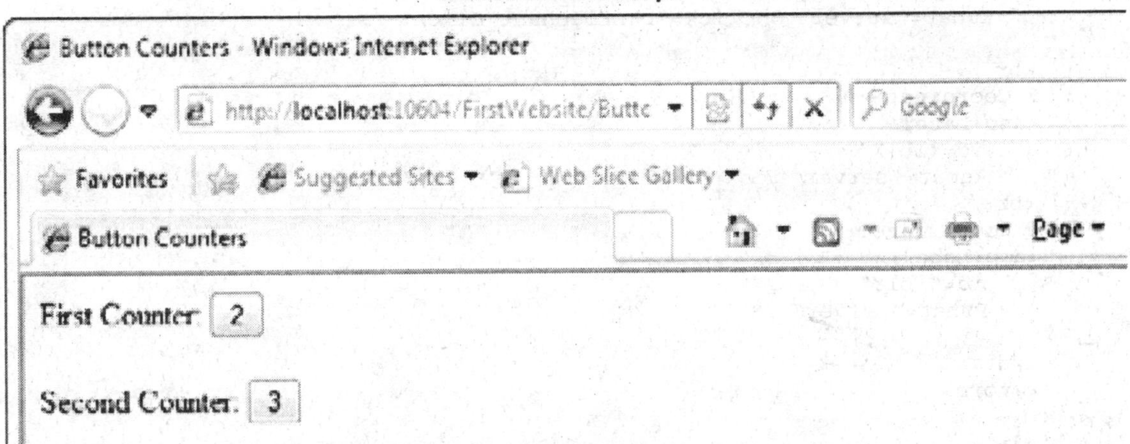

Handling two Button controls with one event handler.

The second parameter passed to the Click event handler, the EventArgs parameter named e, represents any additional event information associated with the event. No additional event information is associated with clicking a button, so this second parameter does not represent anything useful in either of the listings.

CHAPTER 1

When you click an ImageButton control instead of a Button control, on the other hand, additional event information is passed to the event handler. When you click an ImageButton control, the X and Y coordinates of where you clicked are passed to the handler.

The page in next listing contains an ImageButton control that displays a picture. When you click the picture, the X and Y coordinates of the spot you clicked display in a Label control.

Figure Clicking an ImageButton.

```
Code View: Scroll / Show All
<%@ Page Language="C#" %>
<!DOCTYPE html PUBLIC "-//W3C//DTD XHTML 1.0
Transitional//EN"
"http://www.w3.org/TR/xhtml1/DTD/xhtml1-
transitional.dtd">
<script runat="server">

    protected void btnElephant_Click(object
sender, ImageClickEventArgs e)
    {
        lblX.Text = e.X.ToString();
        lblY.Text = e.Y.ToString();
    }
</script>
<html xmlns="http://www.w3.org/1999/xhtml" >
<head id="Head1" runat="server">
    <title>Show EventArgs</title>
</head>
<body>
    <form id="form1" runat="server">
    <div>

    <asp:ImageButton
        id="btnElephant"
        ImageUrl="Elephant.jpg"
       Runat="server" OnClick="btnElephant_Click" />

    <br />
    X Coordinate:
    <asp:Label
        id="lblX"
        Runat="server" />
    <br />
    Y Coordinate:
    <asp:Label
        id="lblY"
        Runat="server" />

    </div>
    </form>
</body>
</html>
```

ShowEventArgs.aspx

The second parameter passed to the btnElephant_Click() method is an ImageClickEventArgs parameter. Whenever the second parameter is not the default EventArgs parameter, you know that additional event information is passed to the handler.

Understanding View State

The HTTP protocol, the fundamental protocol of the World Wide Web, is a stateless protocol. Each time you request a web page from a website, from the website's perspective, you are a completely new person.

The ASP.NET Framework, however, manages to transcend this limitation of the HTTP protocol. For example, if you assign a value to a Label control's Text property, the Label control retains this value across multiple page requests.

Consider the page in next listing. This page contains a Button control and a Label control. Each time you click the Button control, the value displayed by the Label control is incremented by 1. How does the Label control preserve its value across postbacks to the web server?

```
Code View: Scroll / Show All
<%@ Page Language="C#" %>
<!DOCTYPE html PUBLIC "-//W3C//DTD XHTML 1.0 Transitional//EN"
"http://www.w3.org/TR/xhtml1/DTD/xhtml1-transitional.dtd">
<script runat="server">

    protected void btnAdd_Click(object sender, EventArgs e)
    {
        lblCounter.Text = (Int32.Parse(lblCounter.Text) + 1).ToString();
    }
</script>
<html xmlns="http://www.w3.org/1999/xhtml" >
<head id="Head1" runat="server">
    <title>Show View State</title>
</head>
<body>
    <form id="form1"
runat="server">
    <div>

    <asp:Button
        id="btnAdd"
        Text="Add"
        OnClick="btnAdd_Click"
        Runat="server" />

    <asp:Label
        id="lblCounter"
        Text="0"
        Runat="server" />

    </div>
    </form>
</body>
</html>
```

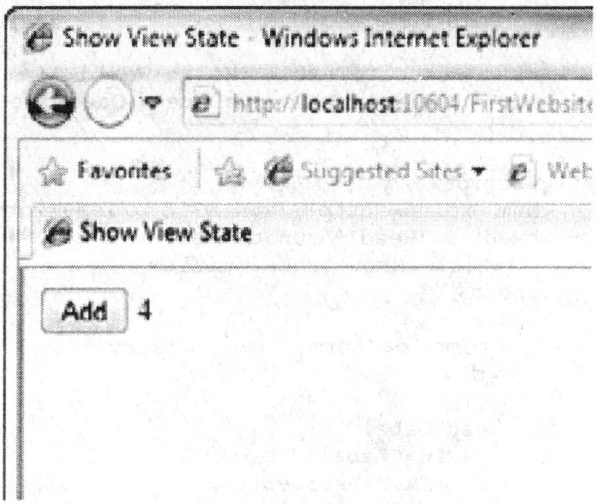

Preserving state between postbacks.

ShowViewState.aspx

The ASP.NET Framework uses a trick called View State. If you open the page in next listing in your browser and select View Source, you notice that the page includes a hidden form field named __VIEWSTATE that looks like this:

```
<input type="hidden" name="__VIEWSTATE" id="__
 VIEWSTATE" value="/wEPDwUKLTc2ODE1OTYxNw9kFgICBA9kFgIC
 Aw8PFgIeBFRleHQFATFkZGT3tMnThg9KZpGak55p367vfInj1w==" />
```

This hidden form field contains the value of the Label control's Text property (and the values of any other control properties stored in View State). When the page is posted back to the server, ASP.NET Framework rips apart this string and re-creates the values of all the properties stored in View State. In this way, ASP.NET Framework preserves the state of control properties across postbacks to the web server.

By default, View State is enabled for every control in ASP.NET Framework. If you change the background color of a Calendar control, the new background color is remembered across postbacks. If you change the selected item in a DropDownList, the selected item is remembered across postbacks. The values of these properties are automatically stored in View State.

View State is a good thing, but sometimes it can be too much of a good thing. The __VIEWSTATE hidden form field can become large. Stuffing too much data into View State can slow down the rendering of a page because the contents of the hidden field must be pushed back and forth between the web server and web browser.

You can determine how much View State each control contained in a page is consuming by enabling tracing for a page. The page in next listing includes a Trace="true" attribute in its <%@ Page %> directive, which enables tracing.

```
Code View: Scroll / Show All
<%@ Page Language="C#" Trace="true" %>
<!DOCTYPE html PUBLIC "-//W3C//DTD XHTML 1.0 Transitional//EN"
"http://www.w3.org/TR/xhtml1/DTD/xhtml1-transitional.dtd">
<script runat="server">

    void Page_Load()
    {
        Label1.Text = "Hello World!";
        Calendar1.TodaysDate = DateTime.Now;
    }

</script>
<html xmlns="http://www.w3.org/1999/xhtml" >
<head id="Head1" runat="server">
    <title>Show Trace</title>
</head>
<body>
    <form id="form1" runat="server">
    <div>

    <asp:Label
        id="Label1"
        Runat="server" />
    <asp:Calendar
        id="Calendar1"
        TodayDayStyle-BackColor="Yellow"
        Runat="server" />

    </div>
    </form>
</body>
</html>
```

ShowTrace.aspx

When you open the page in listing, additional information about the page is appended to the bottom of the page. The Control Tree section displays the amount of View State used by each ASP.NET control contained in the page.

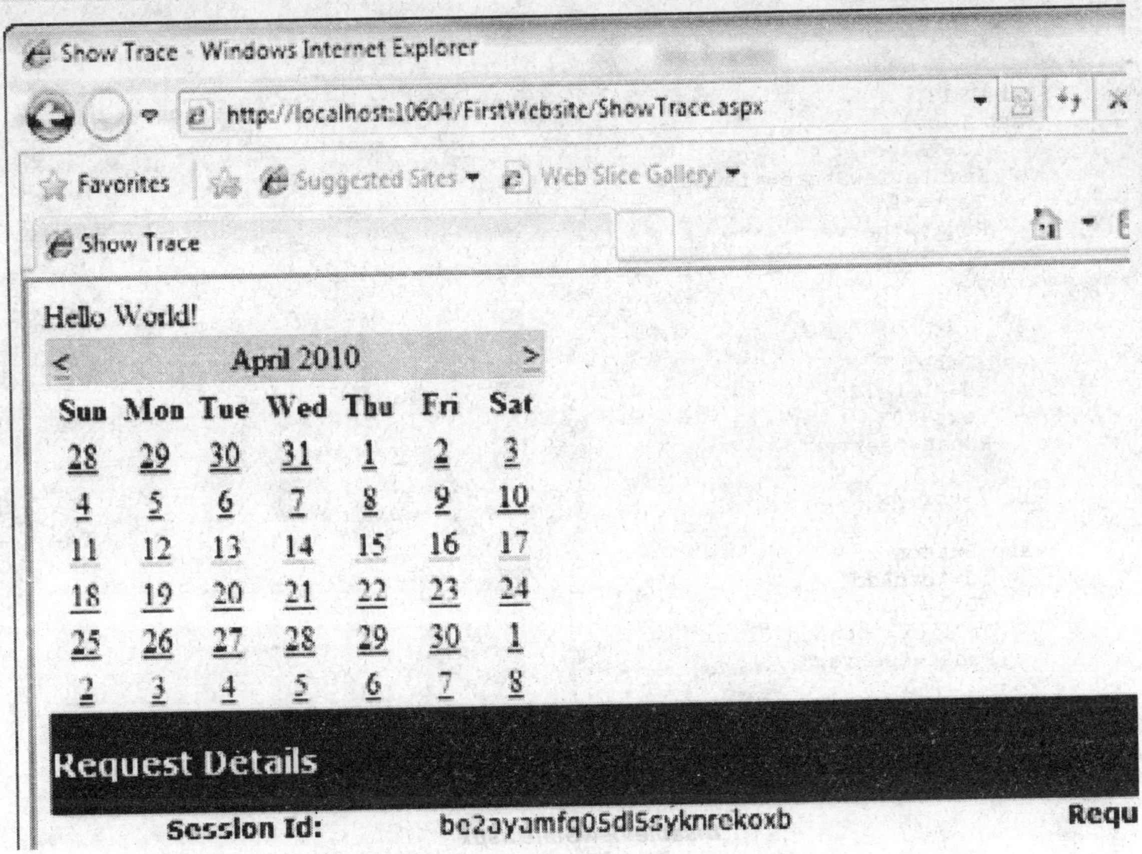

Viewing View State size for each control.

Every ASP.NET control includes a property named EnableViewState. If you set this property to the value False, View State is disabled for the control. In that case, the values of the control properties are not remembered across postbacks to the server.

For example, the page in next listing contains two Label controls and a Button control. The first Label has View State disabled, and the second Label has View State enabled. When you click the button, only the value of the second Label control is incremented past 1.

```
Code View: Scroll / Show All
<%@ Page Language="C#" %>
<!DOCTYPE html PUBLIC "-//W3C//DTD XHTML 1.0 Transitional//EN"
"http://www.w3.org/TR/xhtml1/DTD/xhtml1-transitional.dtd">
<script runat="server">

    protected void btnAdd_Click(object sender, EventArgs e)
    {
        Label1.Text = (Int32.Parse(Label1.Text) + 1).ToString();
        Label2.Text = (Int32.Parse(Label2.Text) + 1).ToString();
    }
</script>
<html xmlns="http://www.w3.org/1999/xhtml" >
<head id="Head1" runat="server">
  <title>Disable View State</title>
</head>
<body>
```

```
    <form id="form1" runat="server">
    <div>

    Label 1:
    <asp:Label
        id="Label1"
        EnableViewState="false"
        Text="0"
        Runat="server" />

    <br />

    Label 2:
    <asp:Label
        id="Label2"
        Text="0"
        Runat="server" />

    <br /><br />

    <asp:Button
        id="btnAdd"
        Text="Add"
        OnClick="btnAdd_Click"
        Runat="server" />

    </div>
    </form>
</body>
</html>
```

DisableViewState.aspx

Sometimes, you might want to disable View State even when you aren't concerned with the size of the __VIEWSTATE hidden form field. For example, if you use a Label control to display a form validation error message, you might want to start from scratch each time the page is submitted. In that case, simply disable View State for the Label control.

Note

The ASP.NET Framework version 2.0 introduced a new feature called Control State, which is similar to View State except that it is used to preserve only critical state information. For example, the GridView control uses Control State to store the selected row. Even if you disable View State, the GridView control remembers which row is selected.

Understanding ASP.NET Pages

This section examines ASP.NET pages in more detail. You learn about dynamic compilation and code-behind files. We also discuss the events supported by the Page class.

Understanding Dynamic Compilation

Strangely enough, when you create an ASP.NET page, you are actually creating the source code for a .NET class. You are creating a new instance of the System.Web.UI.Page class. The entire contents of an ASP.NET page, including all script and HTML content, are compiled into a .NET class.

When you request an ASP.NET page, ASP.NET Framework checks for a .NET class that corresponds to the page. If a corresponding class does not exist, the Framework automatically compiles the page into a new class and stores the compiled class (the assembly) in the Temporary ASP.NET Files folder located at the following path:

```
\WINDOWS\Microsoft.NET\Framework\v4.0.30128\Temporary ASP.NET Files
```

The next time anyone requests the same page in the future, the page is not compiled again. The previously compiled class is executed, and the results are returned to the browser.

Even if you unplug your web server, move to Borneo for 3 years, and start up your web server again, the next time someone requests the same page, the page does not need to be recompiled. The compiled class is preserved in the Temporary ASP.NET Files folder until the source code for your application is modified.

When the class is added to the Temporary ASP.NET Files folder, a file dependency is created between the class and the original ASP.NET page. If the ASP.NET page is modified in any way, the corresponding .NET class is automatically deleted. The next time someone requests the page, the Framework automatically compiles the modified page source into a new .NET class.

This process is called dynamic compilation, which enables ASP.NET applications to support thousands of simultaneous users. Unlike an ASP Classic page, for example, an ASP.NET page does not need to be parsed and compiled every time it is requested. An ASP.NET page is compiled only when an application is modified.

Disabling compilation is useful when you have thousands of pages in a website and you don't want to load too many assemblies into memory. When the CompilationMode attribute is set to the value Never, the page is never compiled, and an assembly is never generated for the page. The page is interpreted at runtime.

You cannot disable compilation for pages that include server-side code. In particular, a no compile page cannot include a server-side <script>...</script> block. On the other hand, a no compile page can contain ASP.NET controls and databinding expressions.

If you are curious, I've included the source code for the class that corresponds to the FirstPage.aspx page in listing. (I cleaned up the code and made it shorter to save space.) I copied this file from the Temporary ASP.NET Files folder after enabling debugging for the application.

```
Code View: Scroll / Show All
namespace ASP
{
    using System.Web.Security;
    using System.Web;
    using System.Web.SessionState;
    using System.Text;
    using System.Collections.Specialized;
    using System.Web.Profile;
    using System.Net.Mail;
    using System.Collections;
    using System.Web.UI.WebControls.WebParts;
    using System.Configuration;
    using System;
    using System.Web.Caching;
    using System.Web.UI;
    using System.Text.RegularExpressions;
    using System.Web.UI.WebControls;
    using System.Web.UI.HtmlControls;

    [System.Runtime.CompilerServices.CompilerGlobalScopeAttribute()]
    public class firstpage_aspx : global::System.Web.UI.Page,
```

CHAPTER 1

```
System.Web.SessionState.IRequiresSessionState, System.Web.IHttpHandler
    {
        protected global::System.Web.UI.WebControls.Label lblServerTime;
        protected global::System.Web.UI.HtmlControls.HtmlForm form1;
        private static bool @__initialized;
        private static object @__fileDependencies;

        void Page_Load()
        {
            lblServerTime.Text = DateTime.Now.ToString();
        }

        public firstpage_aspx()
        {
            string[] dependencies;
            ((global::System.Web.UI.Page)(this)).AppRelativeVirtualPath = "~/
FirstPage.aspx";
            if ((global::ASP.firstpage_aspx.@__initialized == false))
            {
                dependencies = new string[1];
                dependencies[0] = "~/FirstPage.aspx";
                global::ASP.firstpage_aspx.@__fileDependencies =
this.GetWrappedFileDependencies(dependencies);
                global::ASP.firstpage_aspx.@__initialized = true;
            }
            this.Server.ScriptTimeout = 30000000;
        }

        protected System.Web.Profile.DefaultProfile Profile
        {
            get
            {
                return
((System.Web.Profile.DefaultProfile)(this.Context.Profile));
            }
        }

        protected System.Web.HttpApplication ApplicationInstance
        {
            get
            {
                return
((System.Web.HttpApplication)(this.Context.ApplicationInstance));
            }
        }

        private global::System.Web.UI.WebControls.Label
@__BuildControllblServerTime()
        {
        ...code...
        }

        private global::System.Web.UI.HtmlControls.HtmlForm
@__BuildControlform1()
        {
        ...code...
        }
```

```
        private void @__BuildControlTree(firstpage_aspx @__ctrl)
        {
        ...code...
        }

        protected override void FrameworkInitialize()
        {
            base.FrameworkInitialize();
            this.@__BuildControlTree(this);
        this.AddWrappedFileDependencies(global::ASP.firstpage_aspx.@__fileDependencies);
            this.Request.ValidateInput();
        }

        public override int GetTypeHashCode()
        {
            return 243955639;
        }

        public override void ProcessRequest(System.Web.HttpContext context)
        {
            base.ProcessRequest(context);
        }
    }
}
```

FirstPage.aspx Source

The class in above listing inherits from the System.Web.UI.Page class. The ProcessRequest() method is called by ASP.NET Framework when the page is displayed. This method builds the page's control tree, which is the subject of the next section.

Understanding Control Trees

In the previous section, you learned that an ASP.NET page is actually the source code for a .NET class. Alternatively, you can think of an ASP.NET page as a bag of controls. More accurately, because some controls might contain child controls, you can think of an ASP.NET page as a control tree.

For example, the page in next listing contains a DropDownList control and a Button control. Furthermore, because the < %@ Page % > directive has the Trace="true" attribute, tracing is enabled for the page.

```
Code View: Scroll / Show All
<%@ Page Language="C#" Trace="true" %>
<!DOCTYPE html PUBLIC "-//W3C//DTD XHTML 1.0 Transitional//EN"
"http://www.w3.org/TR/xhtml1/DTD/xhtml1-transitional.dtd">
<html xmlns="http://www.w3.org/1999/xhtml" >
<head id="Head1" runat="server">
    <title>Show Control Tree</title>
</head>
<body>
    <form id="form1" runat="server">
    <div>

    <asp:DropDownList
        id="DropDownList1"
        Runat="server">
        <asp:ListItem Text="Oranges" />
        <asp:ListItem Text="Apples" />
```

```
        </asp:DropDownList>

        <asp:Button
            id="Button1"
            Text="Submit"
            Runat="server" />

        </div>
        </form>
    </body>
    </html>
```

ShowControlTree.aspx

When you open the page in above listing in your browser, you can see the control tree for the page appended to the bottom of the page. It looks like this:

```
__Page ASP.showcontroltree_aspx
    ctl02 System.Web.UI.LiteralControl
    ctl00 System.Web.UI.HtmlControls.HtmlHead
        ctl01 System.Web.UI.HtmlControls.HtmlTitle
    ctl03 System.Web.UI.LiteralControl
    form1 System.Web.UI.HtmlControls.HtmlForm
        ctl04 System.Web.UI.LiteralControl
        DropDownList1 System.Web.UI.WebControls.DropDownList
        ctl05 System.Web.UI.LiteralControl
        Button1 System.Web.UI.WebControls.Button
        ctl06 System.Web.UI.LiteralControl
    ctl07
```

The root node in the control tree is the page itself. The page has an ID of __Page. The page class contains all the other controls in its child controls collection. The control tree also contains an instance of the HtmlForm class named form1. This control is the server-side form tag contained in the page. It contains all the other form controls—the DropDownList and Button controls—as child controls.

Several LiteralControl controls are interspersed between the other controls in the control tree. What are these controls?

Remember that everything in an ASP.NET page is converted into a .NET class, including any HTML or plain text content in a page. The LiteralControl class represents the HTML content in the page (including any carriage returns between tags).

Using Code-Behind Pages

The ASP.NET Framework (and Visual Web Developer) enables you to create two different types of ASP.NET pages. You can create both single-file and two-file ASP.NET pages.

All the code samples in this book are written as single-file ASP.NET pages. In a single-file ASP.NET page, a single file contains both the page code and page controls. The page code is contained in a <script runat="server"> tag.

As an alternative to a single-file ASP.NET page, you can create a two-file ASP.NET page. A two-file ASP.NET page is normally referred to as a code-behind page. In a code-behind page, the page code is contained in a separate file.

For example, the next two listing Listings contain the two halves of a code-behind page.

Code View: Scroll / Show All

```
<%@ Page Language="C#" AutoEventWireup="true"
CodeFile="FirstPageCodeBehind.aspx.cs
"Inherits="FirstPageCodeBehind" %>
<!DOCTYPE html PUBLIC "-//W3C//DTD XHTML 1.0 Transitional//EN"
"http://www.w3.org/TR/xhtml1/DTD/xhtml1-transitional.dtd">
<html xmlns="http://www.w3.org/1999/xhtml" >
<head id="Head1" runat="server">
    <title>First Page Code-Behind</title>
</head>
<body>
    <form id="form1" runat="server">
    <div>

    <asp:Button
        id="Button1"
        Text="Click Here"
        OnClick="Button1_Click"
        Runat="server" />

    <br /><br />

    <asp:Label
        id="Label1"
        Runat="server" />

    </div>
    </form>
</body>
</html>
```

FirstPageCodeBehind.aspx

```
using System;
using System.Collections.Generic;
using System.Web;
using System.Web.UI;
using System.Web.UI.WebControls;

public partial class FirstPageCodeBehind : System.Web.UI.Page
{
    protected void Page_Load(object sender, EventArgs e)
    {
        Label1.Text = "Click the Button";
    }

    protected void Button1_Click(object sender, EventArgs e)
    {
        Label1.Text - "Thanks!";
    }
}
```

FirstPageCodeBehind.aspx.cs

The page in first listing is called the presentation page. It contains a Button control and a Label control. However, the page does not contain any code. All the code is contained in the code-behind file. The code-behind the file in second listing contains the Page_Load() and Button1_Click() handlers. The code-behind file in second listing does not contain any controls. Notice that the page in first listing includes both a CodeFile and Inherits attribute in its <%@ Page %> directive. These attributes link the page to its code-behind file.

How Code-Behind Works: The Ugly Details

In the early versions of ASP.NET Framework (ASP.NET 1.x), two classes were generated by a code-behind page. One class corresponded to the presentation page, and one class corresponded to the code-behind file. These classes were related to one another through class inheritance. The presentation page class inherited from the code-behind file class.

The problem with this method of associating presentation pages with their code-behind files was that it was brittle. Inheritance is a one-way relationship. Anything that is true of the mother is true of the daughter, but not the other way around. Any control that you declared in the presentation page was required to be declared in the code-behind file. Furthermore, the control had to be declared with exactly the same ID. Otherwise, the inheritance relationship would be broken and events raised by a control could not be handled in the code-behind file.

In the beta version of ASP.NET 2.0, a completely different method of associating presentation pages with their code-behind files was used. This new method was far less brittle. The two halves of a code-behind page were no longer related through inheritance, but through a new technology supported by .NET 2.0 Framework called partial classes.

Partial classes enable you to declare a class in more than one physical file. When the class is compiled, one class is generated from all the partial classes. Any members of one partial class—including any private fields, methods, and properties—are accessible to any other partial classes of the same class. This makes sense because partial classes are combined eventually to create one final class.

The advantage of using partial classes is that you don't need to worry about declaring a control in both the presentation page and code-behind file. Anything that you declare in the presentation page is available automatically in the code-behind file, and anything you declare in the code-behind file is available automatically in the presentation page.

The beta version of ASP.NET 2.0 Framework used partial classes to relate a presentation page with its code-behind file. However, certain advanced features of ASP.NET 1.x Framework were not compatible with using partial classes. To support these advanced features, a more complex method of associating presentation pages with code-behind files is used in the final release of ASP.NET 2.0 Framework. This method is still the standard in ASP.NET 4.

Since version 2.0 of ASP.NET, the framework uses a combination of inheritance and partial classes to relate presentation pages and code-behind files. Three classes are generated whenever you create a code-behind page.

The first two classes correspond to the presentation page. For example, when you create the FirstPageCodeBehind.aspx page, the following two classes are generated automatically in the Temporary ASP.NET Files folder:

```
public partial class FirstPageCodeBehind
{
   protected System.Web.UI.WebControls.Button Button1;
   protected System.Web.UI.WebControls.Label Label1;

    ... additional code ...
}

public class firstpagecodebehind_aspx : FirstPageCodeBehind
{
    ... additional code ...
}
```

A third class is generated that corresponds to the code-behind file. Corresponding to the FirstPageCodeBehind.aspx.cs file, the following class is generated:

```
public partial class FirstPageCodeBehind : System.Web.UI.Page
{
    protected void Page_Load(object sender, EventArgs e)
    {
        Label1.Text = "Click the Button";
    }

    protected void Button1_Click(object sender, EventArgs e)
    {
        Label1.Text = "Thanks!";
    }
}
```

The firstpagecodebehind_aspx class is executed when the FirstPageCodeBehind.aspx page is requested from a browser. This class inherits from the FirstPageCodeBehind class. The FirstPageCodeBehind class is a partial class. It gets generated twice: once by the presentation page and once by the code-behind file.

The ASP.NET Framework uses a combination of partial classes and inheritance to relate presentation pages and code-behind files. Because the page and code-behind classes are partial classes, unlike the previous version of ASP.NET, you no longer need to declare controls in both the presentation and code-behind page. Any control declared in the presentation page is accessible in the code-behind file automatically. Because the page class inherits from the code-behind class, ASP.NET Framework continues to support advanced features of ASP.NET 1.x Framework, such as custom base Page classes.

Deciding Between Single-File and Code-Behind Pages

So, when should you use single-file ASP.NET pages and when should you use code-behind pages? This decision is a preference choice. There are intense arguments over this topic contained in blogs spread across the Internet.

I've heard it argued that code-behind pages are superior to single-file pages because code-behind pages enable you to more cleanly separate your user interface from your application logic. The problem with this argument is that the normal justification for separating your user interface from your application logic is code reuse. Building code-behind pages doesn't promote code reuse. A better way to reuse application logic across multiple pages is to build separate component libraries. (Part IV of this book explores this topic.)

Ultimately, it is a personal preference. The majority of enterprise projects that we have worked on utilize code-behind pages, but single-file pages are perfectly acceptable under the right circumstances.

Handling Page Events

Whenever you request an ASP.NET page, a particular set of events is raised in a particular sequence. This sequence of events is called the page execution lifecycle.

For example, we have already used the Page Load event in previous code samples. You normally use the Page Load event to initialize the properties of controls contained in a page. However, the Page Load event is only one event supported by the Page class.

Following is the sequence of events raised whenever you request a page:

1. PreInit
2. Init

3. InitComplete
4. PreLoad
5. Load
6. LoadComplete
7. PreRender
8. PreRenderComplete
9. SaveStateComplete
10. Unload

Why so many events? Different things happen and different information is available at different stages in the page execution lifecycle.

For example, View State is not loaded until after the InitComplete event. Data posted to the server from a form control, such as a TextBox control, is also not available until after this event.

Ninety-nine percent of the time, you won't handle any of these events except for the Load and the PreRender events. The difference between these two events is that the Load event happens before any control events, and the PreRender event happens after any control events.

The page in next listing illustrates the difference between the Load and PreRender events. The page contains three event handlers: one for the Load event, one for the Button Click event, and one for the PreRender event. Each handler adds a message to a Label control.

```
Code View: Scroll / Show All
<%@ Page Language="C#" %>
<!DOCTYPE html PUBLIC "-//W3C//DTD XHTML 1.0 Transitional//EN"
"http://www.w3.org/TR/xhtml1/DTD/xhtml1-transitional.dtd">
<script runat="server">

    void Page_Load(object sender, EventArgs e)
    {
        Label1.Text = "Page Load";
    }

    void Button1_Click(object sender, EventArgs e)
    {
        Label1.Text += "<br />Button Click";
    }
```

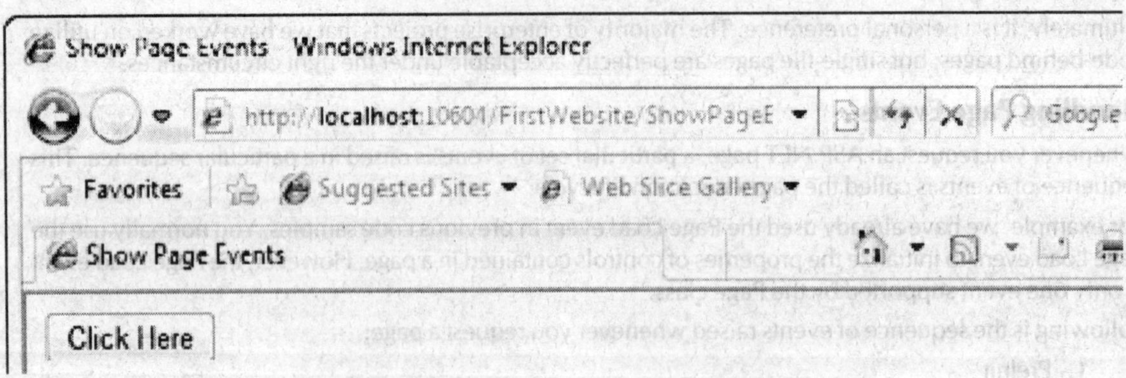

Viewing the sequence of page events.

```
    void Page_PreRender()
    {
        Label1.Text += "<br />Page PreRender";
    }
</script>
<html xmlns="http://www.w3.org/1999/xhtml" >
<head id="Head1" runat="server">
    <title>Show Page Events</title>
</head>
<body>
    <form id="form1" runat="server">
    <div>

    <asp:Button
        id="Button1"
        Text="Click Here"
        OnClick="Button1_Click"
        Runat="server" />

    <br /><br />

    <asp:Label
        id="Label1"
        Runat="server" />

    </div>
    </form>
</body>
</html>
```

ShowPageEvents.aspx

When you click the Button control, the Click event does not happen on the server until after the Load event and before the PreRender event.

The other thing you should notice about the page in above listing is the way the event handlers are wired to the Page events. ASP.NET pages support a feature named AutoEventWireUp, which is enabled by default. If you name a subroutine Page_Load(), the subroutine automatically handles the Page Load event; if you name a subroutine Page_PreRender(), the subroutine automatically handles the Page PreRender event, and so on.

Using the Page.IsPostBack Property

The Page class includes a property called the IsPostBack property, which you can use to detect whether the page has already been posted back to the server. Because of View State, when you initialize a control property, you do not want to initialize the property every time a page loads. Because View State saves the state of control properties across page posts, you typically initialize a control property only once, when the page first loads. Many controls don't work correctly if you reinitialize the properties of the control with each page load. In these cases, you must use the IsPostBack property to detect whether the page has been posted.

The page in next listing illustrates how you can use the Page.IsPostBack property when adding items to a DropDownList control.

```
Code View: Scroll / Show All
<%@ Page Language="C#" %>
```

```
<!DOCTYPE html PUBLIC "-//W3C//DTD XHTML 1.0 Transitional//EN"
"http://www.w3.org/TR/xhtml1/DTD/xhtml1-transitional.dtd">
<script runat="server">

    void Page_Load()
    {
        if (!Page.IsPostBack)
        {
            // Create collection of items
            ArrayList items = new ArrayList();
            items.Add("Apples");
            items.Add("Oranges");

            // Bind to DropDownList
            DropDownList1.DataSource = items;
            DropDownList1.DataBind();
        }
    }

    protected void Button1_Click(object sender, EventArgs e)
    {
        Label1.Text = DropDownList1.SelectedItem.Text;
    }
</script>
<html xmlns="http://www.w3.org/1999/xhtml" >
<head id="Head1" runat="server">
    <title>Show IsPostBack</title>
</head>
<body>
    <form id="form1" runat="server">
    <div>

    <asp:DropDownList
        id="DropDownList1"
        Runat="server" />

    <asp:Button
        id="Button1"
        Text="Select"
        OnClick="Button1_Click"
        Runat="server" />

    <br /><br />

    You selected:
    <asp:Label
        id="Label1"
        Runat="server" />
    </div>
    </form>
</body>
</html>
```

ShowIsPostBack.aspx

In above listing, the code in the Page_Load() event handler executes only once when the page first loads. When you post the page again, the IsPostBack property returns True and the code contained in the Page_Load() handler is skipped.

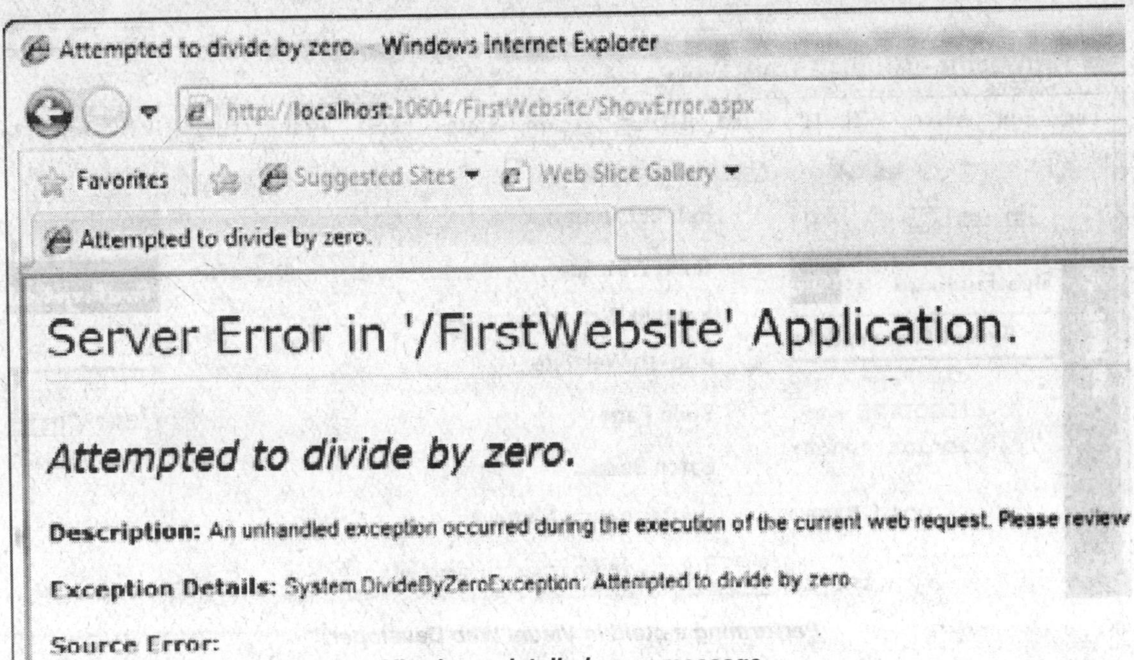

Viewing a detailed error message.

If you remove the IsPostBack check from the Page_Load() method, you get a strange result. The DropDownList always displays its first item as the selected item. Binding the DropDownList to a collection of items reinitializes the DropDownList control. Therefore, you want to bind the DropDownList control only once, when the page first loads.

Debugging and Tracing ASP.NET Pages

The sad fact of life is that you spend the majority of your development time when building applications debugging the application. In this section, you learn how to get detailed error messages when developing ASP.NET pages. You also learn how you can display custom trace messages that you can use when debugging a page.

Debugging ASP.NET Pages

If you need to view detailed error messages when you execute a page, you need to enable debugging for either the page or your entire application. You can enable debugging for a page by adding a Debug="true" attribute to the < %@ Page % > directive. For example, the page in next listing has debugging enabled.

```
Code View: Scroll / Show All
<%@ Page Language="C#" Debug="true" %>
<!DOCTYPE html PUBLIC "-//W3C//DTD XHTML 1.0 Transitional//EN"
"http://www.w3.org/TR/xhtml1/DTD/xhtml1-transitional.dtd">
<script runat="server">

    void Page_Load()
    {
        int zero = 0;
        Label1.Text = (1 / zero).ToString();
    }

</script>
```

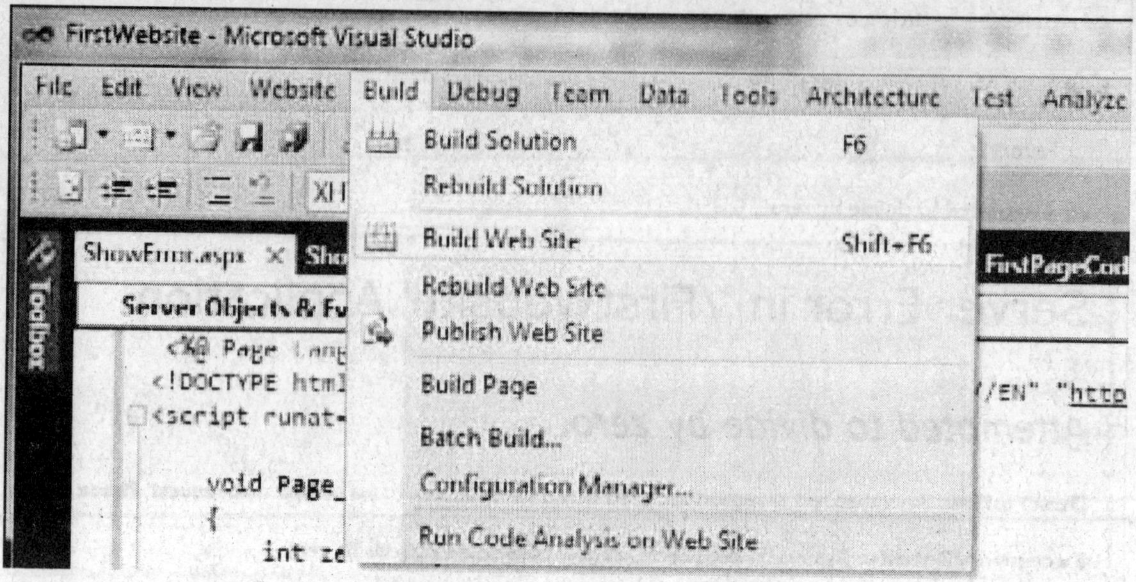

Performing a build in Visual Web Developer.

```
<html xmlns="http://www.w3.org/1999/xhtml" >
<head id="Head1" runat="server">
    <title>Show Error</title>
</head>
<body>
    <form id="form1" runat="server">
    <div>

    <asp:Label
        id="Label1"
        Runat="server" />

    </div>
    </form>
</body>
</html>
```

ShowError.aspx

When you open the page in above listing in your web browser, a detailed error message displays.

Warning: Make sure that you disable debugging before placing your application into production. When an application is compiled in debug mode, the compiler can't make certain performance optimizations.

Rather than enable debugging for a single page, you can enable debugging for an entire application by adding the web configuration file in next listing to your application.

```
<?xml version="1.0"?>
<configuration>
<system.web>
  <compilation debug="true" />
</system.web>
</configuration>
```

listing Web.Config

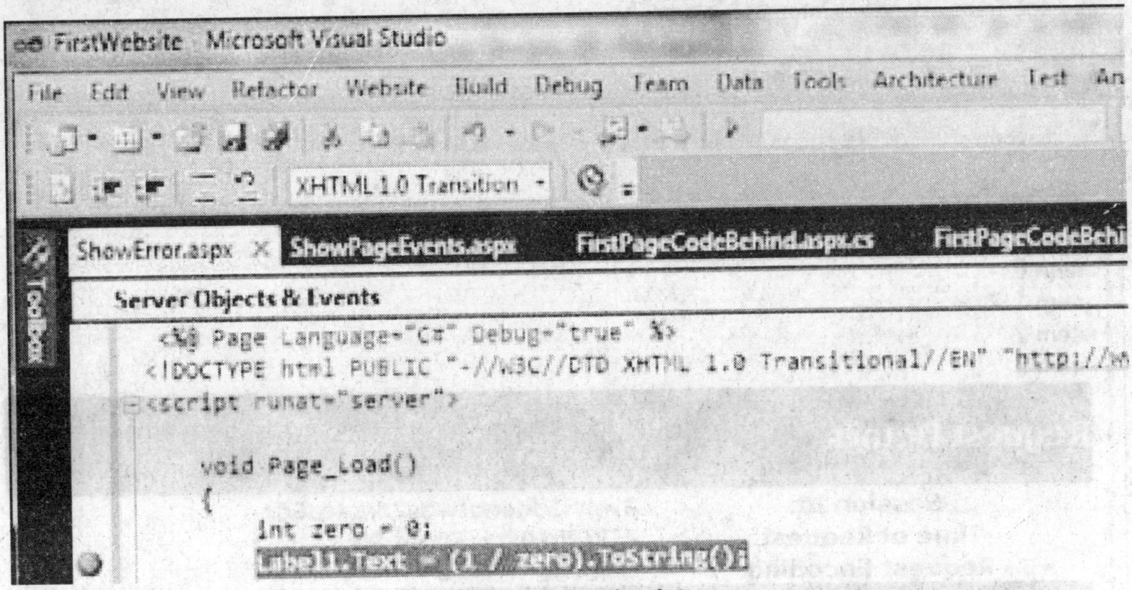

Setting a breakpoint.

When debugging an ASP.NET application located on a remote web server, you need to disable custom errors. For security reasons, by default, ASP.NET Framework doesn't display error messages when you request a page from a remote machine. When custom errors are enabled, you don't see errors on a remote machine. The modified web configuration file in next listing disables custom errors.

```
<?xml version="1.0"?>
<configuration>
<system.web>
  <compilation debug="true" />
  <customErrors mode="Off" />
</system.web>
</configuration>
```

Web.Config

On your production server, add the following element inside the system.web section of your machine.config file:

```
<deployment retail="true"/>
```

Adding this element disables debug mode, enables remote custom errors, and disables trace. You should add this element to the machine.config file located on all your production servers.

Debugging Pages with Visual Web Developer

If you use Visual Web Developer, you can display compilation error messages by performing a build on a page or an entire website. Select Build, Build Page or Build, Build Web Site. A list of compilation error messages and warnings appears in the Error List window. You can double-click any of the errors to navigate directly to the code that caused the error.

If you need to perform more advanced debugging, you can use the Visual Web Developer's debugger. The debugger enables you to set breakpoints and step line by line through your code. You set a breakpoint by double-clicking the left-most column in Source view. When you add a breakpoint, a red circle appears.

After you set a breakpoint, run your application by selecting Debug, Start Debugging. Execution stops when the breakpoint is hit. At that point, you can hover your mouse over any variable or control property to view the current value of the variable or control property.

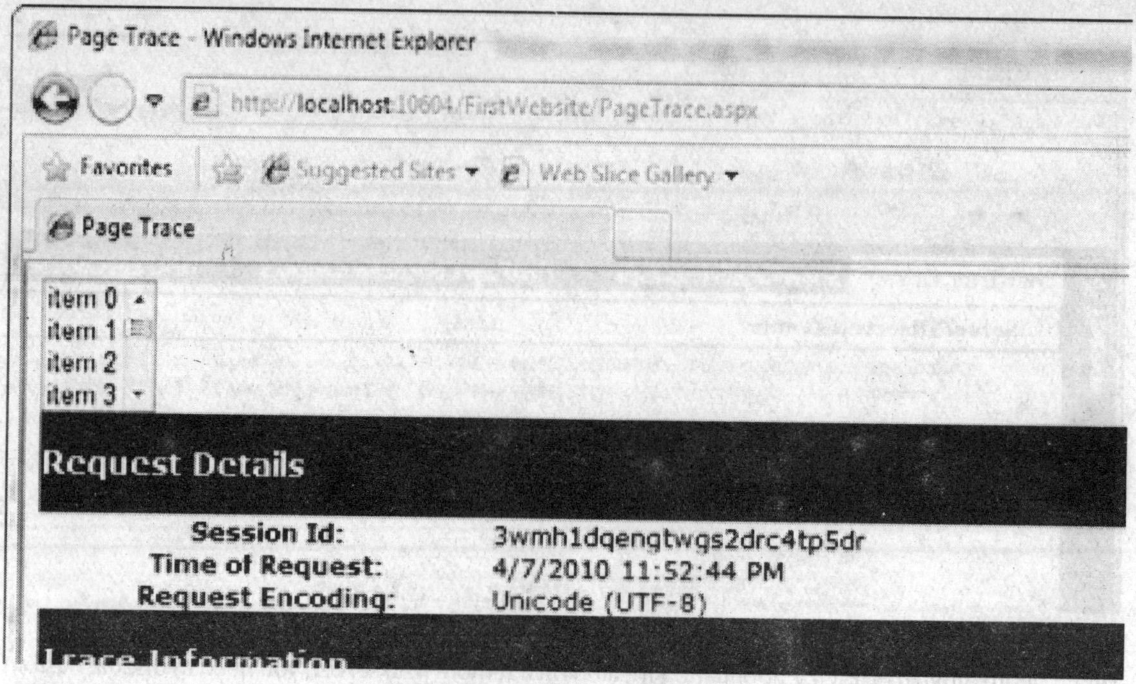

Viewing page trace information.

You can designate one of the pages in your application as the Start Page. That way, whenever you run your application, the Start Page is executed regardless of the page that you have open. Set the Start Page by right-clicking a page in the Solution Explorer window and selecting Set As Start Page.

After you hit a breakpoint, you can continue execution by selecting Step Into, Step Over, or Step Out from the Debug menu or the toolbar. Here's an explanation of each of these options:

- Step Into— Executes the next line of code
- Step Over— Executes the next line of code without leaving the current method
- Step Out— Executes the next line of code and returns to the method that called the current method

When you finish debugging a page, you can continue, stop, or restart your application by selecting a particular option from the Debug menu or the toolbar.

Tracing Page Execution

If you want to output trace messages while a page executes, you can enable tracing for a particular page or an entire application. The ASP.NET Framework supports both page-level tracing and application-level tracing.

The page in next listing illustrates how you can take advantage of page-level tracing.

Code View: Scroll / Show All

```
<%@ Page Language="C#" Trace="true" %>
<!DOCTYPE html PUBLIC "-//W3C//DTD XHTML 1.0 Transitional//EN"
"http://www.w3.org/TR/xhtml1/DTD/xhtml1-transitional.dtd">
<script runat="server">

   void Page_Load()
   {
```

```
        for (int counter = 0; counter < 10; counter++)
        {
          ListBox1.Items.Add("item " + counter.ToString());
           Trace.Warn("counter=" + counter.ToString());
        }
    }

</script>
<html xmlns="http://www.w3.org/1999/xhtml" >
<head id="Head1" runat="server">
    <title>Page Trace</title>
</head>
<body>
    <form id="form1" runat="server">
    <div>

    <asp:ListBox
        id="ListBox1"
        Runat="server" />

    </div>
    </form>
</body>
</html>
```

PageTrace.aspx

The <%@ Page %> directive in above listing includes a trace="true" attribute. This attribute enables tracing and causes a Trace Information section to be appended to the bottom of the page.

Notice, furthermore, that the Page_Load() handler uses the Trace.Warn() method to write messages to the Trace Information section. You can output any string to the Trace Information section that you want. In above listing, the current value of a variable named counter displays. You need to take advantage of page tracing when you want to determine exactly what is happening when a page executes. You can call the Trace.Warn() method wherever you need in your code. Because the Trace Information section appears even when an error exists on your page, you can use tracing to diagnose the causes of any page errors.

One disadvantage of page tracing is that everyone in the world gets to see your trace information. You can get around this problem by taking advantage of application-level tracing. When application-level tracing is enabled, trace information appears only when you request a special page named Trace.axd.

To enable application-level tracing, you need to add the web configuration file in next listing to your application.

```
<?xml version="1.0"?>
<configuration>
<system.web>
    <trace enabled="true" />
</system.web>
</configuration>
```

Web.Config

After you add the Web.Config file in above listing 1.22 to your application, you can request the Trace.axd page in your browser. The last 10 page requests made after application-level tracing is enabled display.

By default, the Trace.axd page cannot be requested from a remote machine. If you need to access the Trace.axd page remotely, you need to add a localOnly="false" attribute to the trace element in the web configuration file.

If you click the View Details link next to any of the listed page requests, you can view all the trace messages outputted by the page. Messages written with the Trace.Warn() method display by the Trace.axd page even when page-level tracing is disabled.

You can use the new writeToDiagnosticsTrace attribute of the trace element to write all trace messages to the Output window of Visual Web Developer when you run an application. You can use the new mostRecent attribute to display the last 10 page requests rather than the 10 page requests after tracing was enabled.

If you don't enable the mostRecent attribute when application level tracing is enabled, tracing stops after 10 pages.

CHAPTER 2

Understanding the Standard Controls

In this chapter you will read about:

- Using the Literal Control
- Using the TextBox Control.
- Using the CheckBox Control.
- Using the RadioButton Control.
- Using the LinkButton Control.
- Using the ImageButton Control.
- Using the Client Scripts with Button Control.
- Using the Image Control.
- Using the ImageMap Control.
- Using the Panel Control.
- Using the HyperLink Control.

Introduction

Now, you learn how to use the core controls contained in ASP.NET 4 Framework. These are controls you use in just about any ASP.NET application that you build. You learn how to display information to users by using the Label and Literal controls. You learn how to accept user input with the TextBox, CheckBox, and RadioButton controls. You also learn how to submit forms with the button controls.

Displaying Information

The ASP.NET Framework includes two controls you can use to display text in a page: the Label control and the Literal control. Whereas the Literal control simply displays text, the Label control supports several additional formatting properties.

Using the Label Control

Whenever you need to modify the text displayed in a page dynamically, you can use the Label control. For example, the page in next listing dynamically modifies the value of a Label control's Text property to display the current time.

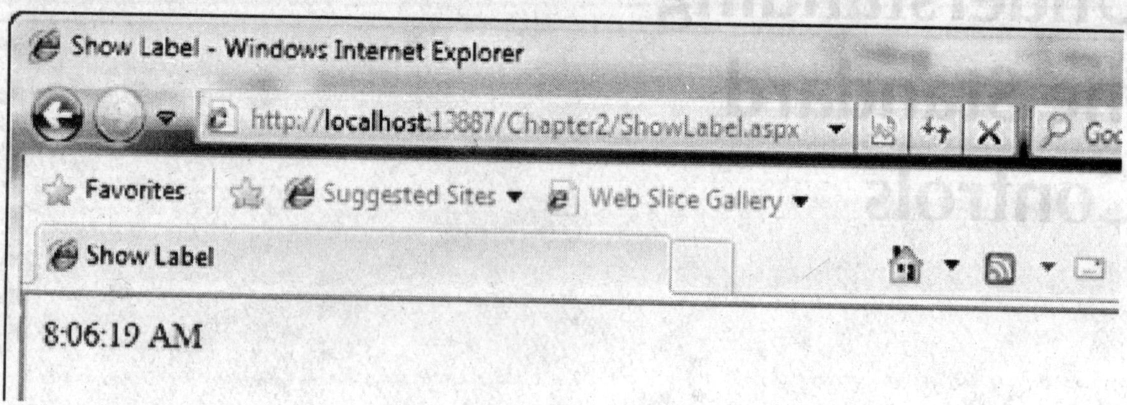

Displaying the time with a Label control.

```
Code View: Scroll / Show All
<%@ Page Language="C#" %>
<!DOCTYPE html PUBLIC "-//W3C//DTD XHTML 1.0 Transitional//EN"
"http://www.w3.org/TR/xhtml1/DTD/xhtml1-transitional.dtd">
<script runat="server">

    void Page_Load()
    {
        lblTime.Text = DateTime.Now.ToString("T");
    }
</script>
<html xmlns="http://www.w3.org/1999/xhtml" >
<head id="Head1" runat="server">
   <title>Show Label</title>
</head>
<body>
   <form id="form1" runat="server">
   <div>

   <asp:Label
```

```
        id="lblTime"
        Runat="server" />

    </div>
    </form>
</body>
</html>
```

showLabel.aspx

Any string that you assign to the Label control's Text property is displayed by the Label when the control is rendered. You can assign simple text to the Text property, or you can assign HTML content. As an alternative to assigning text to the Text property, you can place the text between the Label control's opening and closing tags.

Any text that you place before the opening and closing tags is assigned to the Text property. By default, a Label control renders its contents in an HTML <span> tag. Whatever value you assign to the Text property is rendered to the browser enclosed in a <span> tag.

The Label control supports several properties you can use to format the text displayed by the Label (this is not a complete list):

- **BackColor**— Enables you to change the background color of the label.
- **BorderColor**— Enables you to set the color of a border rendered around the label.
- **BorderStyle**— Enables you to display a border around the label. Possible values are NotSet, None, Dotted, Dashed, Solid, Double, Groove, Ridge, Inset, and Outset.
- **BorderWidth**— Enables you to set the size of a border rendered around the label.
- **CssClass**— Enables you to associate a Cascading Style Sheet class with the label.
- **Font**— Enables you to set the label's font properties.
- **ForeColor**— Enables you to set the color of the content rendered by the label.
- **Style**— Enables you to assign style attributes to the label.
- **ToolTip**— Enables you to set a label's title attribute. (In Microsoft Internet Explorer, the title attribute displays as a floating tooltip.)

The page in next listing contains two Label controls: The first is formatted with properties and the second is formatted with a Cascading Style Sheet.

```
Code View: Scroll / Show All
<%@ Page Language="C#" %>
<!DOCTYPE html PUBLIC "-//W3C//DTD XHTML 1.0 Transitional//EN"
 "http://www.w3.org/TR/xhtml1/DTD/xhtml1-transitional.dtd">
<html xmlns="http://www.w3.org/1999/xhtml" >
<head id="Head1" runat="server">
    <style type="text/css">
        div
        {
            padding:10px;
        }
        .labelStyle
        {
            color:red;
            background-color:yellow;
            border:Solid 2px Red;
        }
```

```
    </style>
    <title>Format Label</title>
</head>
<body>
    <form id="form1" runat="server">
    <div>

    <asp:Label
        id="lblFirst"
        Text="First Label"
        ForeColor="Red"
        BackColor="Yellow"
        BorderStyle="Solid"
        BorderWidth="2"
        BorderColor="red"
        Runat="server" />

    <br /><br />

    <asp:Label
        id="lblSecond"
        Text="Second Label"
        CssClass="labelStyle"
        Runat="server" />

    </div>
    </form>
</body>
</html>
```

FormatLabel.aspx

You should use a Label control when labeling the fields in an HTML form. The Label control includes a property named the AssociatedControlID property. You can set this property to point at an ASP.NET control that represents a form field. For example, the page in next listing contains a simple form that contains fields for entering a first and last name. Label controls label the two TextBox controls.

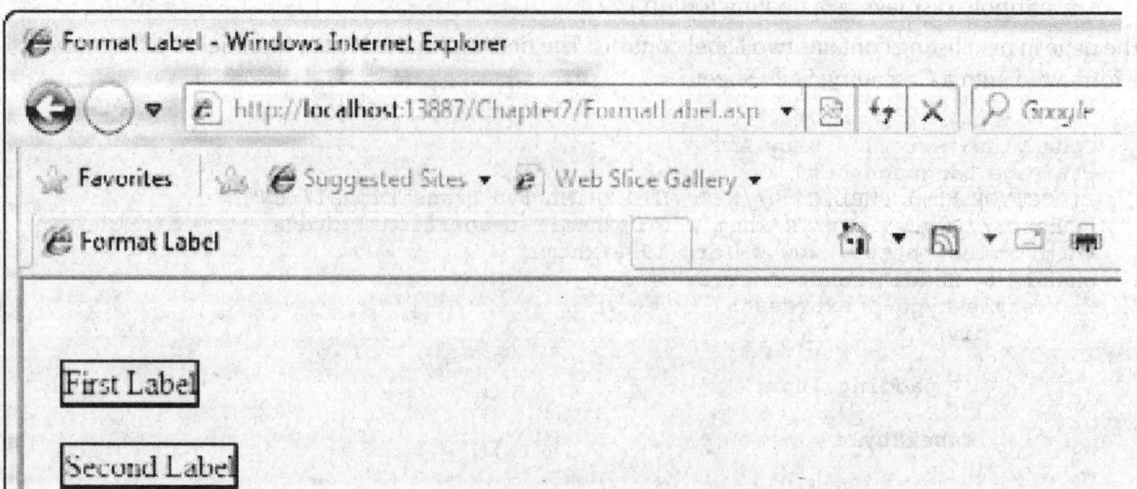

Formatting a label

Code View: Scroll / Show All

```
<%@ Page Language="C#" %>
<!DOCTYPE html PUBLIC "-//W3C//DTD XHTML 1.0 Transitional//EN"
"http://www.w3.org/TR/xhtml1/DTD/xhtml1-transitional.dtd">
<html xmlns="http://www.w3.org/1999/xhtml" >
<head id="Head1" runat="server">
    <title>Label Form</title>
</head>
<body>
    <form id="form1" runat="server">
    <div>

    <asp:Label
        id="lblFirstName"
        Text="First Name:"
       AssociatedControlID="txtFirstName"
        Runat="server" />
    <br />
    <asp:TextBox
        id="txtFirstName"
        Runat="server" />

    <br /><br />

    <asp:Label
        id="lblLastName"
        Text="Last Name:"
       AssociatedControlID="txtLastName"
        Runat="server" />
    <br />
    <asp:TextBox
        id="txtLastName"
        Runat="server" />

    </div>
    </form>
</body>
</html>
```

LabelForm.aspx

When you provide a Label control with an AssociatedControlID property, the Label control is rendered as an HTML <label> tag instead of an HTML <span> tag. For example, if you select View Source on your web browser, you see that the first Label in above listing renders the following content to the browser:

```
<label for="txtFirstName" id="lblFirstName">First Name:</label>
```

Always use a Label control with an AssociatedControlID property when labeling form fields. This is important when you need to make your website accessible to persons with disabilities. If someone uses an assistive device, such as a screen reader, to interact with your website, the AssociatedControlID property enables the assistive device to associate the correct label with the correct form field. A side benefit of using the AssociatedControlID property is that clicking a label when this property is set automatically changes the form focus to the associated form input field.

Web Standards Note: Both the WCAG 1.0 and Section 508 accessibility guidelines require you to use the <label for> tag when labeling form fields. For more information, see http://www.w3.org/wai and http://www.Section508.gov.

Using the Literal Control

The Literal control is similar to the Label control. You can use the Literal control to display text or HTML content in a browser. However, unlike the Label control, the Literal control does not render its content inside of a <span> tag. For example, the page in next listing uses a Literal control in the page's <head> tag to dynamically modify the title displayed in the browser title bar. The current date displays in the Literal control.

Modifying the browser title with a Literal control.

```
<%@ Page Language="C#" %>
<!DOCTYPE html PUBLIC "-//W3C//DTD XHTML 1.0 Transitional//EN"
"http://www.w3.org/TR/xhtml1/DTD/xhtml1-transitional.dtd">
<script runat="server">
    void Page_Load()
    {
        ltlTitle.Text = DateTime.Now.ToString("D");
    }
</script>
<html xmlns="http://www.w3.org/1999/xhtml" >
<head>
   <title><asp:Literal id="ltlTitle" Runat="Server" /></title>
</head>
<body>
    <form id="form1" runat="server">
    <div>

    <h1>Look in the title bar</h1>

    </div>
    </form>
</body>
</html>
```

ShowLiteral.aspx

If you used a Label control in above listing instead of a Literal control, the uninterpreted <span> tags would appear in the browser title bar. The page in above listing uses a format specifier to format the date before assigning the date to the Label control. The D format specifier causes the date to be formatted in a long format. You can use several standard format specifiers with the ToString() method to format dates, times, currency amounts, and numbers. For a list of these format specifiers, look up the Format Specifiers topic in the index of the Microsoft .NET Framework SDK Documentation.

Because the contents of a Literal control are not contained in a <span> tag, the Literal control does not support any of the formatting properties supported by the <span> tag. For example, the Literal control does not support either the CssClass or BackColor properties.

The Literal control does support one property not supported by the Label control: the Mode property. The Mode property enables you to encode HTML content and accepts any of the following three values:

- **PassThrough**— Displays the contents of the control without encoding.
- **Encode**— Displays the contents of the control after HTML encoding the content.
- **Transform**— Displays the contents of the control after stripping markup not supported by the requesting device.

For example, the page in next listing contains three Literal controls set to the three possible values of the Mode property.

Code View: Scroll / Show All

```
<%@ Page Language="C#" %>
<!DOCTYPE html PUBLIC "-//W3C//DTD XHTML 1.0 Transitional//EN"
"http://www.w3.org/TR/xhtml1/DTD/xhtml1-transitional.dtd">
<html xmlns="http://www.w3.org/1999/xhtml" >
<head id="Head1" runat="server">
    <title>Show Literal Mode</title>
</head>
<body>
    <form id="form1" runat="server">
    <div>

    <asp:Literal
        id="ltlFirst"
        Mode="PassThrough"
        Text="<hr />"
        Runat="server" />

    <br /><br />

    <asp:Literal
        id="ltlSecond"
        Mode="Encode"
        Text="<hr />"
        Runat="server" />

    <br /><br />

    <asp:Literal
        id="ltlThird"
        Mode="Transform"
        Text="<hr />"
        Runat="server" />

    </div>
    </form>
</body>
</html>
```

ShowLiteralMode.aspx

When you request the page in above listing with a web browser, the first Literal control displays a horizontal rule; the second Literal control displays the uninterpreted <hr /> tag; and the final Literal control displays another horizontal rule. If you request the page from a device (such as a WML cell phone) that does not support the <hr> tag, the third <hr /> tag is stripped.

Accepting User Input

The ASP.NET Framework includes several controls that you can use to gather user input. In this section, you learn how to use the TextBox, CheckBox, and RadioButton controls. These controls correspond to the standard types of HTML input tags.

Using the TextBox Control

You can use the TextBox control to display three different types of input fields depending on the value of its TextMode property. The TextMode property accepts the following three values:

- **SingleLine**— Displays a single-line input field.
- **MultiLine**— Displays a multiline input field.
- **Password**— Displays a single-line input field in which the text is hidden.

The page in next listing contains three TextBox controls that illustrate all three of the TextMode values.

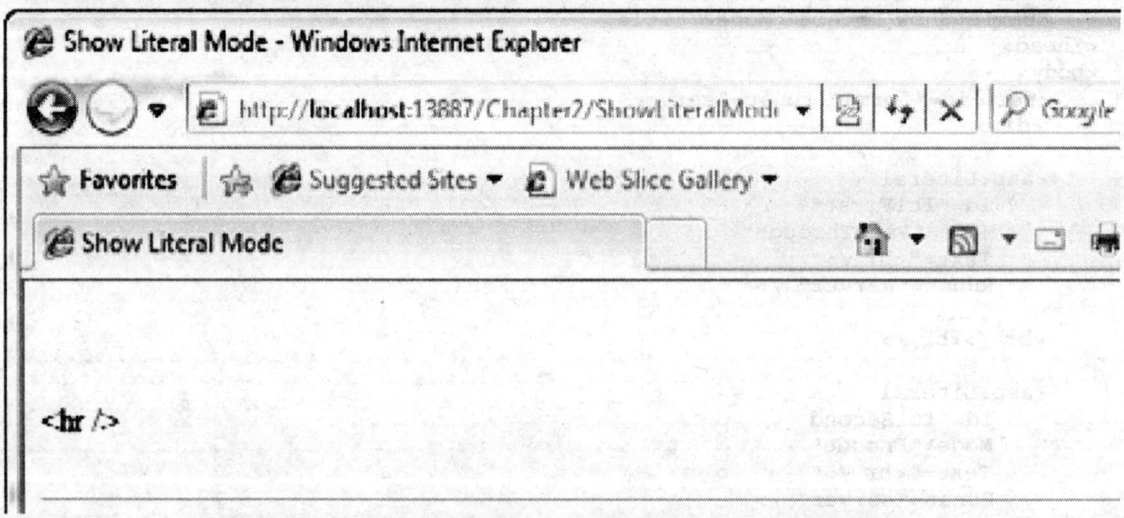

Displaying TextBox controls with different values for TextMode.

```
Code View: Scroll / Show All
<%@ Page Language="C#" %>
<!DOCTYPE html PUBLIC "-//W3C//DTD XHTML 1.0 Transitional//EN"
"http://www.w3.org/TR/xhtml1/DTD/xhtml1-transitional.dtd">
<html xmlns="http://www.w3.org/1999/xhtml" >
<head id="Head1" runat="server">
    <title>Show TextBox</title>
</head>
<body>
    <form id="form1" runat="server">
    <div>

    <asp:TextBox
        id="txtUserName"
```

```
        TextMode="SingleLine"
        Runat="server" />

    <br /><br />

    <asp:TextBox
        id="txtPassword"
        TextMode="Password"
        Runat="server" />

    <br /><br />

    <asp:TextBox
        id="txtComments"
        TextMode="MultiLine"
        Runat="server" />

    </div>
    </form>
</body>
</html>
```

ShowTextBox.aspx

You can use the following properties to control the rendering characteristics of the TextBox control (this is not a complete list):

- **AccessKey**— Enables you to specify a key that navigates to the TextBox control.
- **AutoCompleteType**— Enables you to associate an AutoComplete class with the TextBox control.

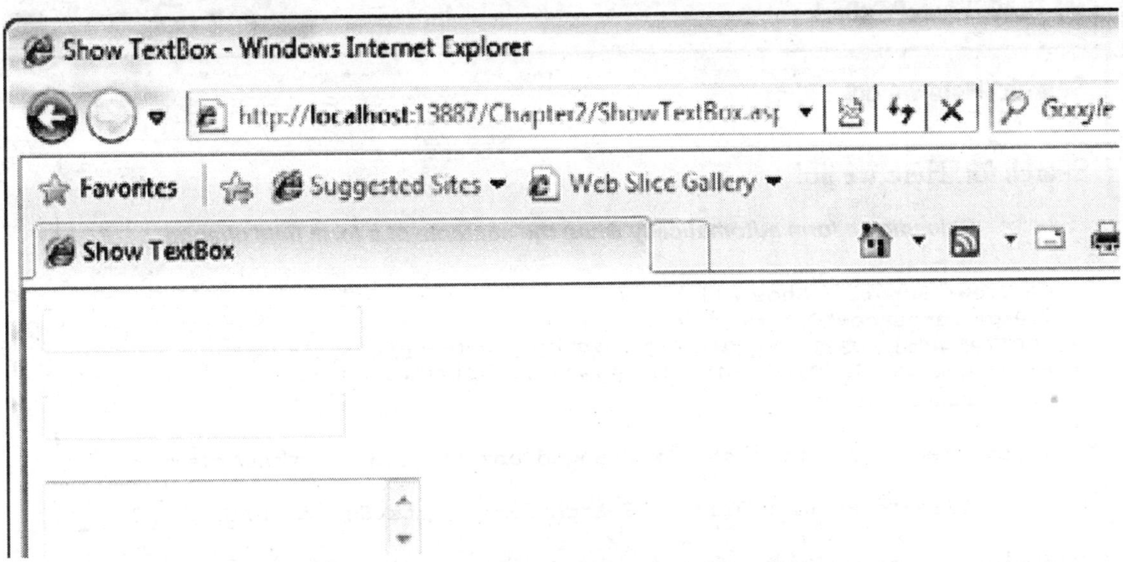

Three values of the Literal control's Mode property.

- **AutoPostBack**— Enables you to post the form containing the TextBox back to the server automatically when the contents of the TextBox is changed.
- **Columns**— Enables you to specify the number of columns to display.
- **Enabled**— Enables you to disable the text box.

- **MaxLength**— Enables you to specify the maximum length of data that a user can enter in a text box. (This does not work when TextMode is set to Multiline.)
- **ReadOnly**— Enables you to prevent users from changing the text in a text box.
- **Rows**— Enables you to specify the number of rows to display.
- **TabIndex**— Enables you to specify the tab order of the text box.
- **Wrap**— Enables you to specify whether text word-wraps when the TextMode is set to Multiline.

The TextBox control also supports the following method:

- **Focus**— Enables you to set the initial form focus to the text box.

And, the TextBox control supports the following event:

- **TextChanged**— Raised on the server when the contents of the text box are changed.

When the AutoPostBack property has the value True, the form containing the TextBox is automatically posted back to the server when the contents of the TextBox changes. For example, the page in next listing contains a simple search form. If you modify the contents of the text box and tab out of the TextBox control, the form is automatically posted back to the server, and the contents of the TextBox display.

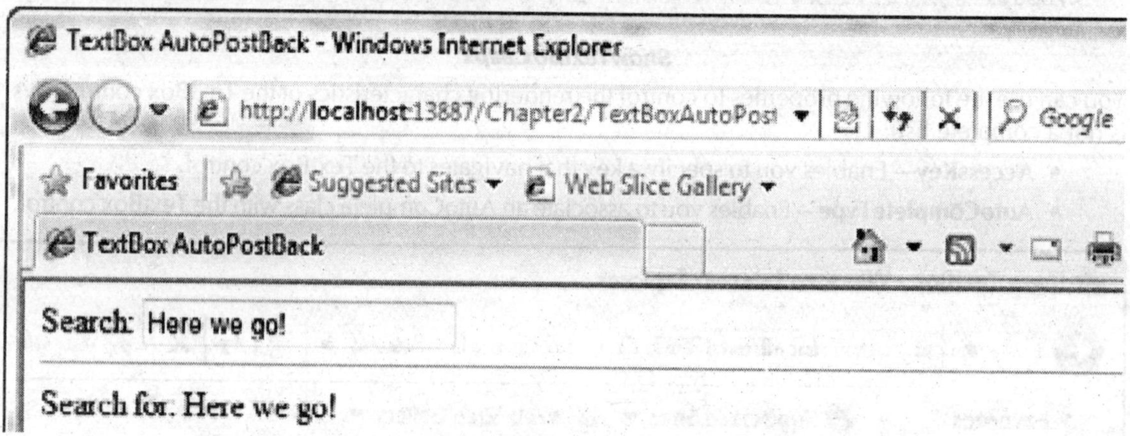

Reloading a form automatically when the contents of a form field change.

Code View: Scroll / Show All

```
<%@ Page Language="C#" %>
<!DOCTYPE html PUBLIC "-//W3C//DTD XHTML 1.0 Transitional//EN"
"http://www.w3.org/TR/xhtml1/DTD/xhtml1-transitional.dtd">
<script runat="server">

    protected void txtSearch_TextChanged(object sender, EventArgs e)
    {
        lblSearchResults.Text = "Search for: " + txtSearch.Text;
    }
</script>
<html xmlns="http://www.w3.org/1999/xhtml" >
<head id="Head1" runat="server">
    <title>TextBox AutoPostBack</title>
</head>
<body>
    <form id="form1" runat="server">
     <div>
```

```
    <asp:Label
        id="lblSearch"
        Text="Search:"
        Runat="server" />
    <asp:TextBox
        id="txtSearch"
        AutoPostBack="true"
       OnTextChanged="txtSearch_TextChanged"
        Runat="server" />

    <hr />

    <asp:Label
        id="lblSearchResults"
        Runat="server" />

    </div>
    </form>
</body>
</html>
```

TextBoxAutoPostBack.aspx

In above listing, the TextBox control's TextChanged event is handled. This event is raised on the server when the contents of the TextBox have been changed. You can handle this event even when you don't use the AutoPostBack property.

Web Standards Note

You should avoid using the AutoPostBack property for accessibility reasons. Creating a page that automatically reposts the server can be confusing to someone using an assistive device such as a screen reader. A better way to send data back to the server and dynamically update the page without a PostBack is to utilize features of Microsoft AJAX, JavaScript, or jQuery. This approach often results in a cleaner, faster page.

Notice that the TextBox control also includes a property that enables you to associate the TextBox with a particular AutoComplete class. When AutoComplete is enabled, the user does not need to reenter common information—such as a first name, last name, or phone number—in a form field. If the user has not disabled AutoComplete on his browser, his browser prompts him to enter the same value that he entered previously for the form field (even if the user entered the value for a form field at a different website).

You can disable auto-complete by adding an AutoComplete="Off" attribute to the TextBox. This is useful when you want to use ASP.NET AJAX Control Toolkit AutoComplete control, and you don't want the browser auto complete to interfere with the Ajax auto-complete.

For example, the page in next listing asks for your first name, last name, and phone number. Each TextBox control is associated with a particular AutoComplete class. The AutoComplete class specifies the type of information associated with the form field. After you complete the form once, if you return to the same form in the future, you are prompted to enter the same responses.

```
Code View: Scroll / Show All
<%@ Page Language="C#" %>
<!DOCTYPE html PUBLIC "-//W3C//DTD XHTML 1.0 Transitional//EN"
"http://www.w3.org/TR/xhtml1/DTD/xhtml1-transitional.dtd">
<html xmlns="http://www.w3.org/1999/xhtml" >
<head id="Head1" runat="server">
    <title>Show AutoComplete</title>
```

```
</head>
<body>
   <form id="form1" runat="server">
   <div>

   <asp:Label
       id="lblFirstName"
       Text="First Name:"
      AssociatedControlID="txtFirstName"
       Runat="server" />
   <br />
   <asp:TextBox
       id="txtFirstName"
      AutoCompleteType="FirstName"
       Runat="server" />
   <br /><br />
   <asp:Label
       id="lblLastname"
       Text="Last Name:"
      AssociatedControlID="txtLastName"
       Runat="server" />
   <br />
   <asp:TextBox
       id="txtLastName"
      AutoCompleteType="LastName"
       Runat="server" />
   <br /><br />
   <asp:Button
       id="btnSubmit"
       Text="Submit"
       Runat="server" />
   </div>
   </form>
</body>
</html>
```

ShowAutoComplete.aspx

Note: When using Internet Explorer, you can configure AutoComplete by selecting Tools, Internet Options, Content, and clicking the AutoComplete button. The ASP.NET Framework does not support AutoComplete for other browsers such as FireFox or Opera. Finally, the TextBox control supports the Focus() method. You can use the Focus() method to shift the initial form focus to a particular TextBox control. By default, no form field has focus when a page first opens. If you want to make it easier for users to complete a form, you can set the focus automatically to a particular TextBox control contained in a form.

For example, the page in next listing sets the focus to the first of two form fields.

Code View: Scroll / Show All

```
<%@ Page Language="C#" %>
<!DOCTYPE html PUBLIC "-//W3C//DTD XHTML 1.0 Transitional//EN"
"http://www.w3.org/TR/xhtml1/DTD/xhtml1-transitional.dtd">
<script runat="server">

   void Page_Load()
   {
      txtFirstName.Focus();
   }
```

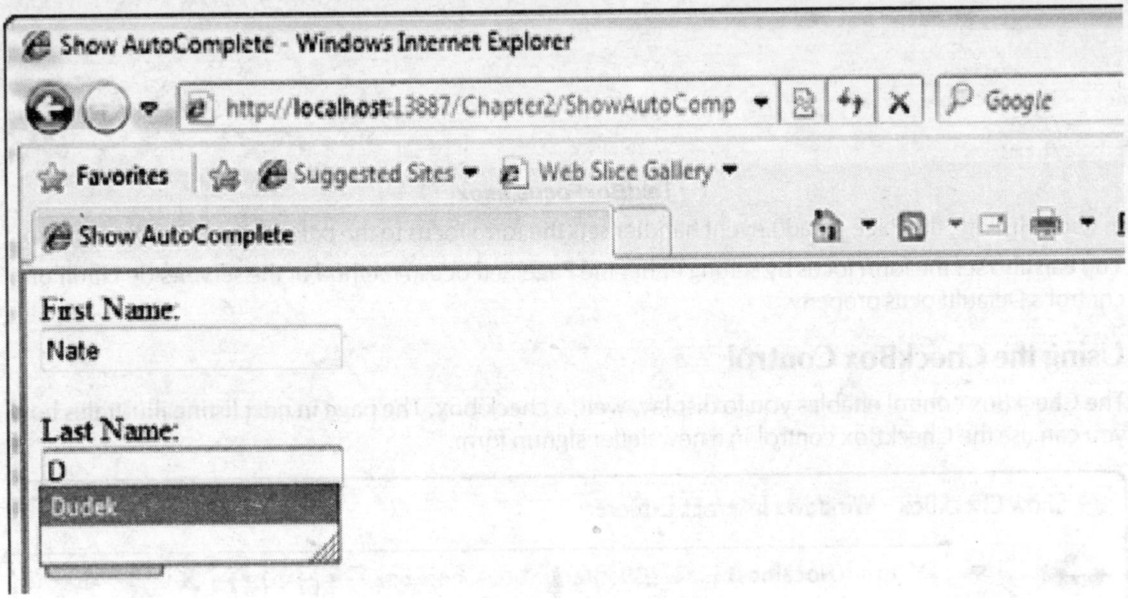

Using AutoComplete with the TextBox control.

```
</script>
<html xmlns="http://www.w3.org/1999/xhtml" >
<head id="Head1" runat="server">
   <title>TextBox Focus</title>
</head>
<body>
   <form id="form1" runat="server">
    <div>

    <asp:Label
        id="lblFirstName"
        Text="First Name:"
       AssociatedControlID="txtFirstName"
        Runat="server" />
    <br />
    <asp:TextBox
        id="txtFirstName"
       AutoCompleteType="FirstName"
        Runat="server" />
    <br /><br />
    <asp:Label
        id="lblLastname"
        Text="Last Name:"
       AssociatedControlID="txtLastName"
        Runat="server" />
    <br />
    <asp:TextBox
        id="txtLastName"
       AutoCompleteType="LastName"
        Runat="server" />
    <br /><br />
    <asp:Button
        id="btnSubmit"
        Text="Submit"
```

```
            Runat="server" />

        </div>
        </form>
    </body>
    </html>
```

TextBoxFocus.aspx

In above listing , the Page_Load() event handler sets the form focus to the txtFirstName TextBox control. You can also set the form focus by setting either the Page.SetFocus() method or the server-side HtmlForm control's DefaultFocus property.

Using the CheckBox Control

The CheckBox control enables you to display, well, a check box. The page in next listing illustrates how you can use the CheckBox control in a newsletter signup form.

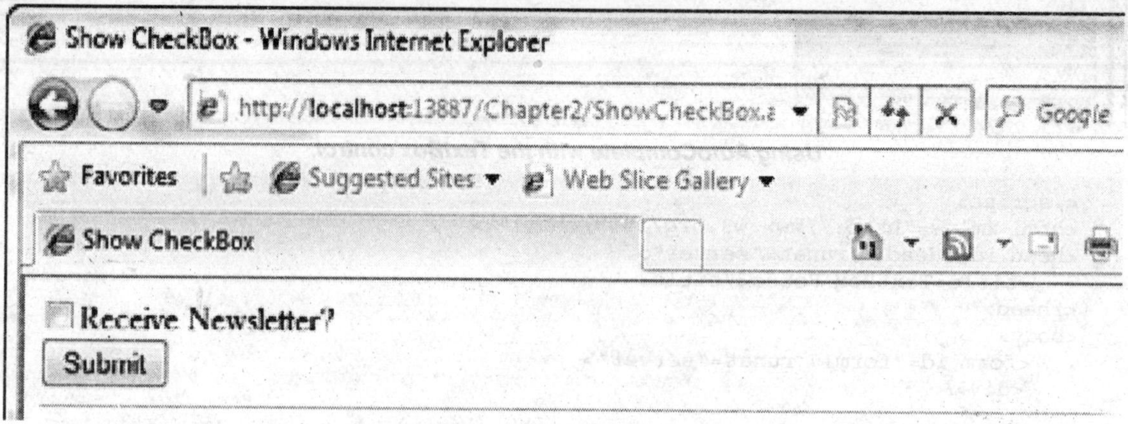

Displaying a CheckBox control.

```
Code View: Scroll / Show All
<%@ Page Language="C#" %>
<!DOCTYPE html PUBLIC "-//W3C//DTD XHTML 1.0 Transitional//EN"
"http://www.w3.org/TR/xhtml1/DTD/xhtml1-transitional.dtd">
<script runat="server">

    protected void btnSubmit_Click(object sender, EventArgs e)
    {
        lblResult.Text = chkNewsletter.Checked.ToString();
    }
</script>
<html xmlns="http://www.w3.org/1999/xhtml" >
<head id="Head1" runat="server">
    <title>Show CheckBox</title>
</head>
<body>
    <form id="form1" runat="server">
    <div>

    <asp:CheckBox
        id="chkNewsletter"
        Text="Receive Newsletter?"
```

```
        Runat="server" />
    <br />
    <asp:Button
        id="btnSubmit"
        Text="Submit"
        OnClick="btnSubmit_Click"
        Runat="server" />
    <hr />

    <asp:Label
        id="lblResult"
        Runat="server" />

    </div>
    </form>
</body>
</html>
```

ShowCheckBox.aspx

In above listing, the Checked property determines whether the user has checked the check box. Notice that the CheckBox includes a Text property that labels the CheckBox. If you use this property, the proper (accessibility standards-compliant) HTML <label> tag is generated for the TextBox.

The CheckBox control supports the following properties (this is not a complete list):

- **AccessKey**— Enables you to specify a key that navigates to the TextBox control.
- **AutoPostBack**— Enables you to post the form containing the CheckBox back to the server automatically when the CheckBox is checked or unchecked.
- **Checked**— Enables you to get or set whether the CheckBox is checked.
- **Enabled**— Enables you to disable the TextBox.
- **TabIndex**— Enables you to specify the tab order of the check box.
- **Text**— Enables you to provide a label for the check box.
- **TextAlign**— Enables you to align the label for the check box. Possible values are Left and Right.

The CheckBox control also supports the following method:

- **Focus**— Enables you to set the initial form focus to the check box.

And the CheckBox control supports the following event:

- **CheckedChanged**— Raised on the server when the check box is checked or unchecked.

Notice that the CheckBox control, like the TextBox control, supports the AutoPostBack property. The page in next listing illustrates how you can use the AutoPostBack property to post the form containing the check box back to the server automatically when the check box is checked or unchecked.

```
Code View: Scroll / Show All
<%@ Page Language="C#" %>
<!DOCTYPE html PUBLIC "-//W3C//DTD XHTML 1.0 Transitional//EN"
"http://www.w3.org/TR/xhtml1/DTD/xhtml1-transitional.dtd">
<script runat="server">

    protected void chkNewsletter_CheckedChanged(object sender, EventArgs e)
    {
        lblResult.Text = chkNewsletter.Checked.ToString();
    }
</script>
```

CHAPTER 2

```
<html xmlns="http://www.w3.org/1999/xhtml" >
<head id="Head1" runat="server">
   <title>CheckBox AutoPostBack</title>
</head>
<body>
   <form id="form1" runat="server">
    <div>

    <asp:CheckBox
        id="chkNewsletter"
        Text="Receive Newsletter?"
        AutoPostBack="true"
       OnCheckedChanged="chkNewsletter_CheckedChanged"
        Runat="server" />
    <hr />

    <asp:Label
        id="lblResult"
        Runat="server" />

    </div>
    </form>
</body>
</html>
```

CheckBoxAutoPostBack.aspx

The ASP.NET Framework also includes the CheckBoxList control that enables you to display a list of check boxes automatically.

Using the RadioButton Control

You always use the RadioButton control in a group. Only one radio button in a group of RadioButton controls can be checked at a time.

For example, the page in next listing contains three RadioButton controls.

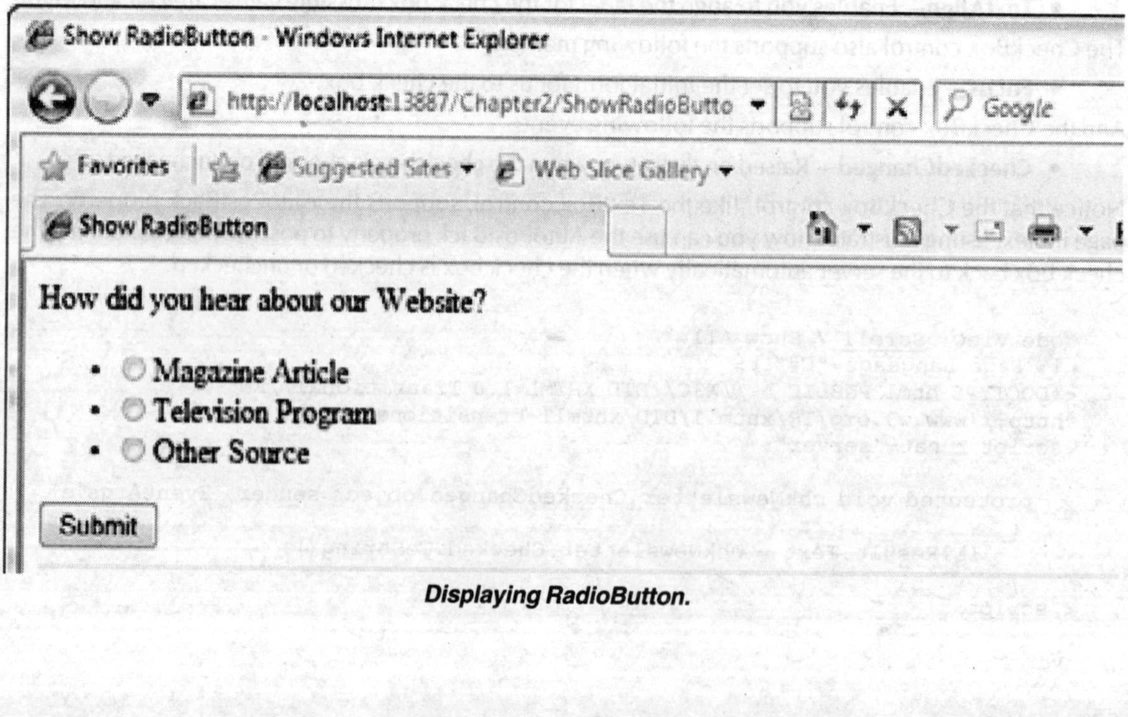

Displaying RadioButton.

Code View: Scroll / Show All

```
 <%@ Page Language="C#" %>
<!DOCTYPE html PUBLIC "-//W3C//DTD XHTML 1.0 Transitional//EN"
"http://www.w3.org/TR/xhtml1/DTD/xhtml1-transitional.dtd">
<script runat="server">

   protected void btnSubmit_Click(object sender, EventArgs e)
    {
       if (rdlMagazine.Checked)
          lblResult.Text = rdlMagazine.Text;
      if (rdlTelevision.Checked)
          lblResult.Text = rdlTelevision.Text;
       if (rdlOther.Checked)
          lblResult.Text = rdlOther.Text;
    }
 </script>
<html xmlns="http://www.w3.org/1999/xhtml" >
<head id="Head1" runat="server">
   <title>Show RadioButton</title>
</head>
<body>
   <form id="form1" runat="server">
    <div>

    How did you hear about our Website?

    <ul>
        <li>
       <asp:RadioButton
           id="rdlMagazine"
           Text="Magazine Article"
           GroupName="Source"
           Runat="server" />
        </li>
        <li>
       <asp:RadioButton
           id="rdlTelevision"
           Text="Television Program"
           GroupName="Source"
           Runat="server" />
        </li>
        <li>
       <asp:RadioButton
           id="rdlOther"
           Text="Other Source"
           GroupName="Source"
           Runat="server" />
        </li>
    </ul>

    <asp:Button
        id="btnSubmit"
        Text="Submit"
       Runat="server" OnClick="btnSubmit_Click" />

    <hr />

    <asp:Label
```

```
            id="lblResult"
            Runat="server" />

        </div>
        </form>
    </body>
    </html>
```

ShowRadioButton.aspx

The RadioButton controls in above listing are grouped together with the RadioButton control's GroupName property. Only one of the three RadioButton controls can be checked at a time.

The RadioButton control supports the following properties (this is not a complete list):

- **AccessKey**— Enables you to specify a key that navigates to the RadioButton control.
- **AutoPostBack**— Enables you to post the form containing the RadioButton back to the server automatically when the radio button is checked or unchecked.
- **Checked**— Enables you to get or set whether the RadioButton control is checked.
- **Enabled**— Enables you to disable the RadioButton.
- **GroupName**— Enables you to group RadioButton controls.
- **TabIndex**— Enables you to specify the tab order of the RadioButton control.
- **Text**— Enables you to label the RadioButton control.
- **TextAlign**— Enables you to align the RadioButton label. Possible values are Left and Right.

The RadioButton control supports the following method:

- **Focus**— Enables you to set the initial form focus to the RadioButton control.

Finally, the RadioButton control supports the following event:

- **CheckedChanged**— Raised on the server when the RadioButton is checked or unchecked.

The page in next listing demonstrates how you can use the AutoPostBack property with a group of RadioButton controls and detect which RadioButton control is selected.

```
Code View: Scroll / Show All
<%@ Page Language="C#" %>
<!DOCTYPE html PUBLIC "-//W3C//DTD XHTML 1.0 Transitional//EN"
"http://www.w3.org/TR/xhtml1/DTD/xhtml1-transitional.dtd">
<script runat="server">

    protected void RadioButton_CheckedChanged(object sender, EventArgs e)
    {
        RadioButton selectedRadioButton = (RadioButton)sender;
        lblResult.Text = selectedRadioButton.Text;
    }
</script>
<html xmlns="http://www.w3.org/1999/xhtml" >
<head id="Head1" runat="server">
    <title>RadioButton AutoPostBack</title>
</head>
<body>
    <form id="form1" runat="server">
    <div>

    How did you hear about our Website?
```

```
<ul>
    <li>
    <asp:RadioButton
        id="rdlMagazine"
        Text="Magazine Article"
        GroupName="Source"
        AutoPostBack="true"
       OnCheckedChanged="RadioButton_CheckedChanged"
        Runat="server" />
    </li>
    <li>
    <asp:RadioButton
        id="rdlTelevision"
        Text="Television Program"
        GroupName="Source"
        AutoPostBack="true"
       OnCheckedChanged="RadioButton_CheckedChanged"
        Runat="server" />
    </li>
    <li>
    <asp:RadioButton
        id="rdlOther"
        Text="Other Source"
        GroupName="Source"
        AutoPostBack="true"
       OnCheckedChanged="RadioButton_CheckedChanged"
        Runat="server" />
    </li>
</ul>

<hr />

<asp:Label
    id="lblResult"
    Runat="server" />

</div>
</form>
</body>
</html>
```

RadioButtonAutoPostBack.aspx

In above listing, when you select a RadioButton control, the page is automatically posted back to the server, and the value of the Text property of the selected RadioButton control displays. Notice that all three of the RadioButton controls are associated with the same CheckedChanged event handler. The first parameter passed to the handler represents the particular RadioButton that was changed.

Submitting Form Data

The ASP.NET Framework includes three controls you can use to submit a form to the server: Button, LinkButton, and ImageButton. These controls have the same function, but each control has a distinct appearance.

Using the Button Control

The Button control renders a push button that you can use to submit a form to the server. For example, the page in next listing contains a Button control. When you click the Button control, the time displayed by a Label control is updated.

```
Code View: Scroll / Show All
<%@ Page Language="C#" %>
<!DOCTYPE html PUBLIC "-//W3C//DTD XHTML 1.0 Transitional//EN"
"http://www.w3.org/TR/xhtml1/DTD/xhtml1-transitional.dtd">
<script runat="server">

    protected void btnSubmit_Click(object sender, EventArgs e)
    {
        lblTime.Text = DateTime.Now.ToString("T");
    }
</script>
<html xmlns="http://www.w3.org/1999/xhtml" >
<head id="Head1" runat="server">
    <title>Show Button</title>
</head>
<body>
    <form id="form1" runat="server">
    <div>

    <asp:Button
        id="btnSubmit"
        Text="Submit"
        OnClick="btnSubmit_Click"
        Runat="server" />

    <br /><br />

    <asp:Label
        id="lblTime"
        Runat="server" />

    </div>
    </form>
</body>
</html>
```

ShowButton.aspx

The Button control supports the following properties (this is not a complete list):

- **AccessKey**— Enables you to specify a key that navigates to the Button control.
- **CommandArgument**— Enables you to specify a command argument passed to the Command event.
- **CommandName**— Enables you to specify a command name passed to the Command event.
- **Enabled**— Enables you to disable the Button control.
- **OnClientClick**— Enables you to specify a client-side script that executes when the button is clicked.
- **PostBackUrl**— Enables you to post a form to a particular page.
- **TabIndex**— Enables you to specify the tab order of the Button control.
- **Text**— Enables you to label the Button control.
- **UseSubmitBehavior**— Enables you to use JavaScript to post a form.

The Button control also supports the following method:

- **Focus**— Enables you to set the initial form focus to the Button control.

The Button control also supports the following two events:

- **Click**— Raised when the Button control is clicked.
- **Command**— Raised when the Button control is clicked. The CommandName and CommandArgument are passed to this event.

Using the LinkButton Control

The LinkButton control, like the Button control, enables you to post a form to the server. Unlike a Button control, however, the LinkButton control renders a link instead of a push button.

The page in next listing contains a simple form. The form includes a LinkButton control that enables you to submit the form to the server and display the contents of the form fields.

```
Code View: Scroll / Show All
<%@ Page Language="C#" %>
<!DOCTYPE html PUBLIC "-//W3C//DTD XHTML 1.0 Transitional//EN"
"http://www.w3.org/TR/xhtml1/DTD/xhtml1-transitional.dtd">
<script runat="server">

    protected void lnkSubmit_Click(object sender, EventArgs e)
    {
        lblResults.Text = "First Name: " + txtFirstName.Text;
        lblResults.Text += "<br />Last Name: " + txtLastName.Text;
    }
</script>
<html xmlns="http://www.w3.org/1999/xhtml" >
<head id="Head1" runat="server">
    <title>Show LinkButton</title>
</head>
<body>
    <form id="form1" runat="server">
    <div>

    <asp:Label
        id="lblFirstName"
        Text="First Name:"
        AssociatedControlID="txtFirstName"
        Runat="server" />
    <br />
    <asp:TextBox
        id="txtFirstName"
        Runat="server" />
    <br /><br />
    <asp:Label
        id="lblLastName"
        Text="Last Name:"
        AssociatedControlID="txtLastName"
        Runat="server" />
    <br />
    <asp:TextBox
        id="txtLastName"
        Runat="server" />
    <br /><br />
    <asp:LinkButton
        id="lnkSubmit"
        Text="Submit"
```

CHAPTER 2

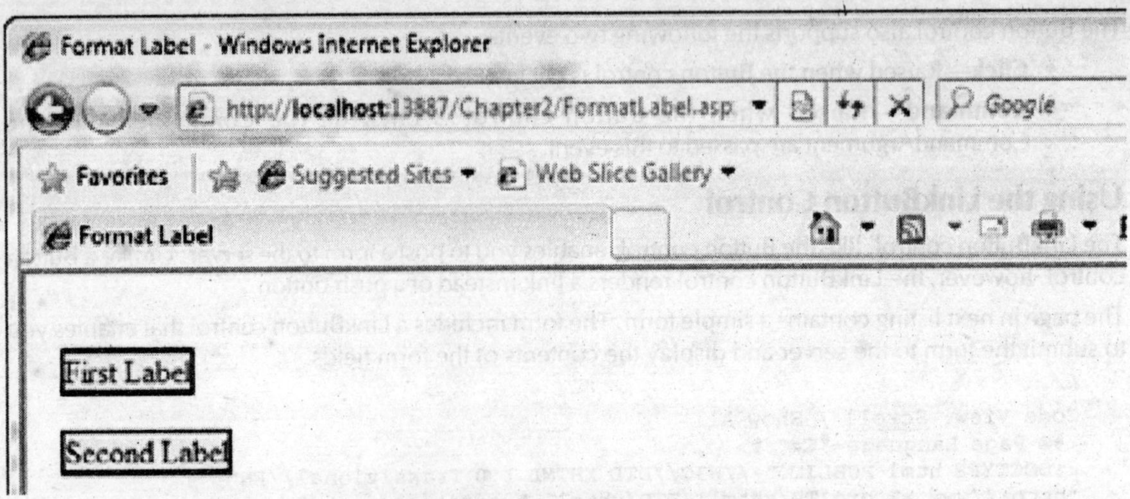

Displaying a LinkButton control.

```
        OnClick="lnkSubmit_Click"
        Runat="server" />

    <br /><br />

    <asp:Label
        id="lblResults"
        Runat="server" />

    </div>
    </form>
</body>
</html>
```

ShowLinkButton.aspx

Behind the scenes, the LinkButton control uses JavaScript to post the form back to the server. The hyperlink rendered by the LinkButton control looks like this:

```
<a id="lnkSubmit" href="javascript:__doPostBack('lnkSubmit','')">Submit</a>
```

Clicking the LinkButton invokes the JavaScript __doPostBack() method, which posts the form to the server. When the form is posted, the values of all the other form fields in the page are also posted to the server.

The LinkButton control supports the following properties (this is not a complete list):

- **AccessKey**— Enables you to specify a key that navigates to the Button control.
- **CommandArgument**— Enables you to specify a command argument passed to the Command event.
- **CommandName**— Enables you to specify a command name passed to the Command event.
- **Enabled**— Enables you to disable the LinkButton control.
- **OnClientClick**— Enables you to specify a client-side script that executes when the LinkButton is clicked.
- **PostBackUrl**— Enables you to post a form to a particular page.
- **TabIndex**— Enables you to specify the tab order of the LinkButton control.
- **Text**— Enables you to label the LinkButton control.

The LinkButton control also supports the following method:

- **Focus**— Enables you to set the initial form focus to the LinkButton control

The LinkButton control also supports the following two events:

- **Click**— Raised when the LinkButton control is clicked.
- **Command**— Raised when the LinkButton control is clicked. The CommandName and CommandArgument are passed to this event.

CHAPTER 2

Using the ImageButton Control

The ImageButton control, like the Button and LinkButton controls, enables you to post a form to the server. However, the ImageButton control always displays an image.

The page in next listing contains an ImageButton control that posts a simple form back to the server.

```
Code View: Scroll / Show All
<%@ Page Language="C#" %>
<!DOCTYPE html PUBLIC "-//W3C//DTD XHTML 1.0 Transitional//EN"
"http://www.w3.org/TR/xhtml1/DTD/xhtml1-transitional.dtd">
<script runat="server">

    protected void btnSubmit_Click(object sender, ImageClickEventArgs e)
    {
        lblResults.Text = "First Name: " + txtFirstName.Text;
        lblResults.Text += "<br />Last Name: " + txtLastName.Text;
    }
</script>
<html xmlns="http://www.w3.org/1999/xhtml" >
<head id="Head1" runat="server">
    <title>Show ImageButton</title>
</head>
<body>
    <form id="form1" runat="server">
    <div>

    <asp:Label
        id="lblFirstName"
        Text="First Name:"
        AssociatedControlID="txtFirstName"
        Runat="server" />
    <br />
    <asp:TextBox
        id="txtFirstName"
        Runat="server" />
    <br /><br />
    <asp:Label
        id="lblLastName"
        Text="Last Name:"
        AssociatedControlID="txtLastName"
        Runat="server" />
    <br />
    <asp:TextBox
        id="txtLastName"
        Runat="server" />
    <br /><br />
    <asp:ImageButton
```

```
            id="btnSubmit"
            ImageUrl="Submit.gif"
            AlternateText="Submit Form"
            Runat="server" OnClick="btnSubmit_Click" />

        <br /><br />
        <asp:Label
            id="lblResults"
            Runat="server" />

        </div>
        </form>
    </body>
    </html>
```

ShowImageButton.aspx

The ImageButton in above listing includes both an ImageUrl and AlternateText property. The ImageUrl contains the path to the image that the ImageButton displays. The AlternateText property provides alternate text for the image used by screen readers and text-only browsers.

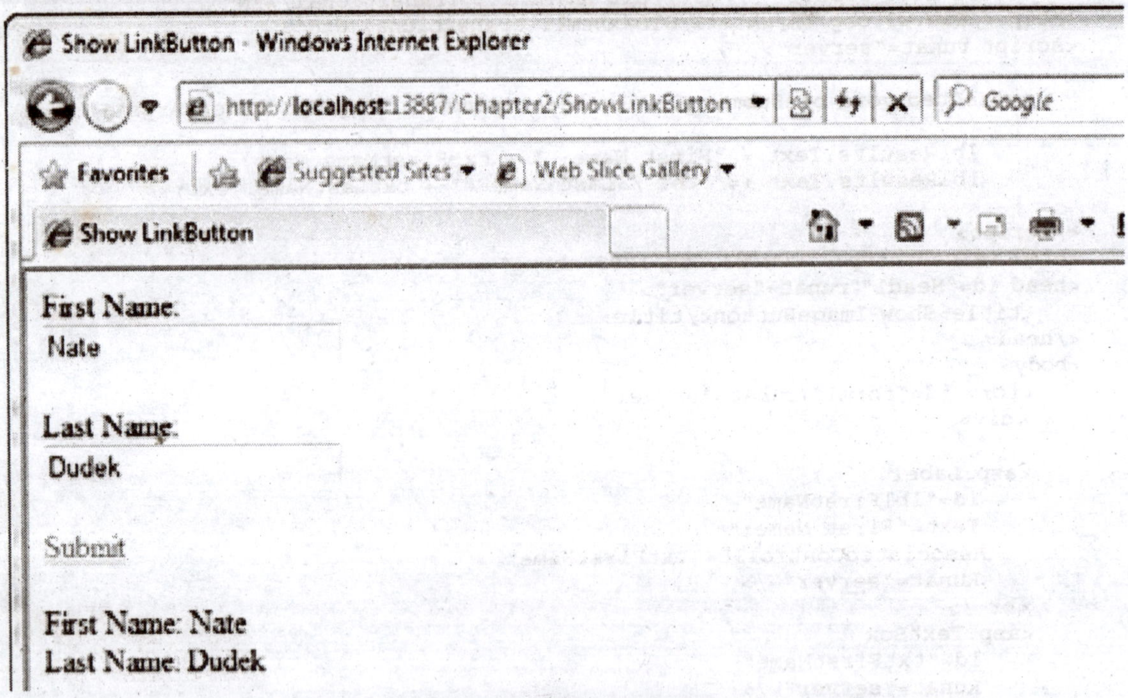

Displaying a Button control.

Web Standards Note

Always include alternate text for any image. The accessibility guidelines require it. Furthermore, remember that some people turn off images in their browsers for a faster surfing experience.

The event handler for an Image control's Click event is different than that for the other button controls. The second parameter passed to the event handler is an instance of the ImageClickEventArgs class. This class has the following properties:

- X— The x coordinate relative to the image the user clicked.

- Y— The y coordinate relative to the image the user clicked.

You can use the ImageButton control to create a simple image map. For example, the page in next listing contains an ImageButton that displays an image of a target. If you click the center of the target, a success message is displayed.

```
Code View: Scroll / Show All
<%@ Page Language="C#" %>
<!DOCTYPE html PUBLIC "-//W3C//DTD XHTML 1.0 Transitional//EN"
"http://www.w3.org/TR/xhtml1/DTD/xhtml1-transitional.dtd">
<script runat="server">

    protected void btnTarget_Click(object sender, ImageClickEventArgs e)
    {
        if ((e.X > 90 && e.X < 110) && (e.Y > 90 && e.Y < 110))
            lblResult.Text = "You hit the target!";
        else
            lblResult.Text = "You missed!";
    }
</script>
<html xmlns="http://www.w3.org/1999/xhtml" >
<head id="Head1" runat="server">
    <title>ImageButton Target</title>
</head>
<body>
    <form id="form1" runat="server">
    <div>

    <asp:ImageButton
        id="btnTarget"
        ImageUrl="Target.gif"
       Runat="server" OnClick="btnTarget_Click" />

    <br /><br />

    <asp:Label
        id="lblResult"
        Runat="server" />

    </div>
    </form>
</body>
</html>
```

ImageButtonTarget.aspx

Web Standards Note

The ImageButton can create a server-side image map. Server-side image maps are not accessible to persons with disabilities. A better method for creating an ImageMap is to use the ImageMap control, which enables you to create a client-side image map.

The ImageButton control supports the following properties (this is not a complete list):

- **AccessKey**— Enables you to specify a key that navigates to the ImageButton control.
- **AlternateText**— Enables you to provide alternate text for the image (required for accessibility).
- **DescriptionUrl**— Enables you to provide a link to a page that contains a detailed description of the image (required to make a complex image accessible).

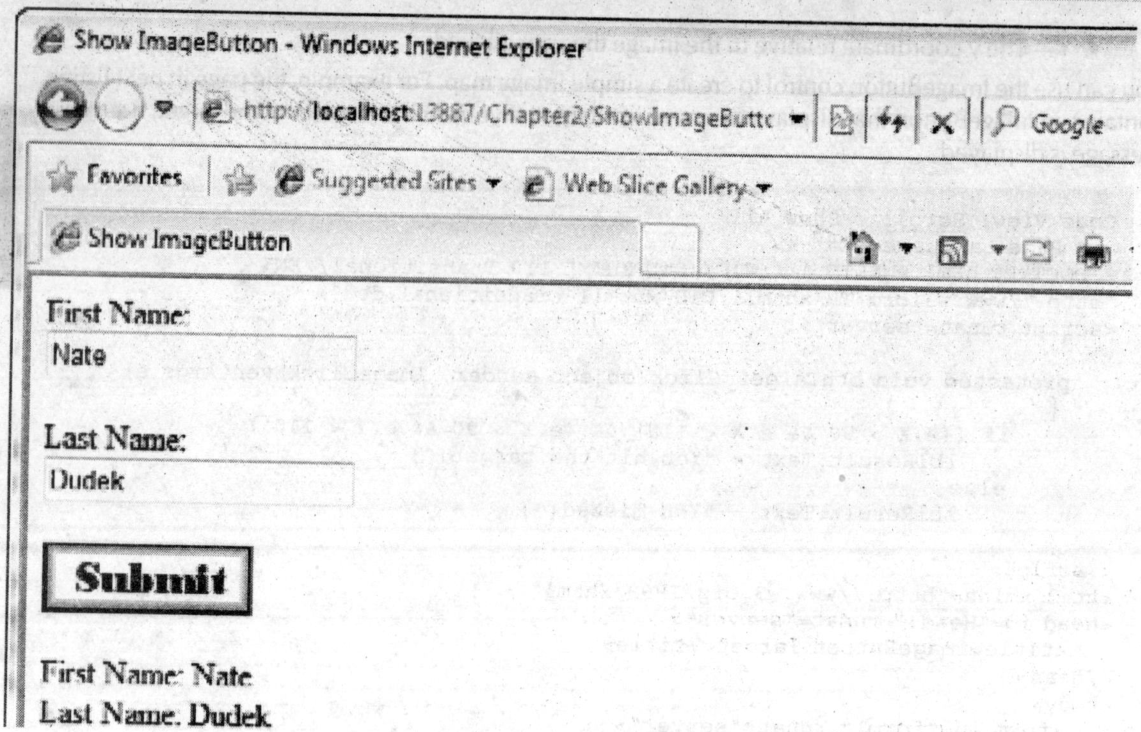

Figure Displaying an ImageButton control.

- **CommandArgument**— Enables you to specify a command argument that is passed to the Command event.
- **CommandName**— Enables you to specify a command name passed to the Command event.
- **Enabled**— Enables you to disable the ImageButton control.
- **GenerateEmptyAlternateText**— Enables you to set the AlternateText property to an empty string.
- **ImageAlign**— Enables you to align the image relative to other HTML elements in the page. Possible values are AbsBottom, AbsMiddle, Baseline, Bottom, Left, Middle, NotSet, Right, TextTop, and Top.
- **ImageUrl**— Enables you to specify the URL to the image.
- **OnClientClick**— Enables you to specify a client-side script that executes when the ImageButton is clicked.
- **PostBackUrl**— Enables you to post a form to a particular page.
- **TabIndex**— Enables you to specify the tab order of the ImageButton control.

The ImageButton control also supports the following method:

- **Focus**— Enables you to set the initial form focus to the ImageButton control.

The ImageButton control also supports the following two events:

- **Click**— Raised when the ImageButton control is clicked.
- **Command**— Raised when the ImageButton control is clicked. The CommandName and CommandArgument are passed to this event.

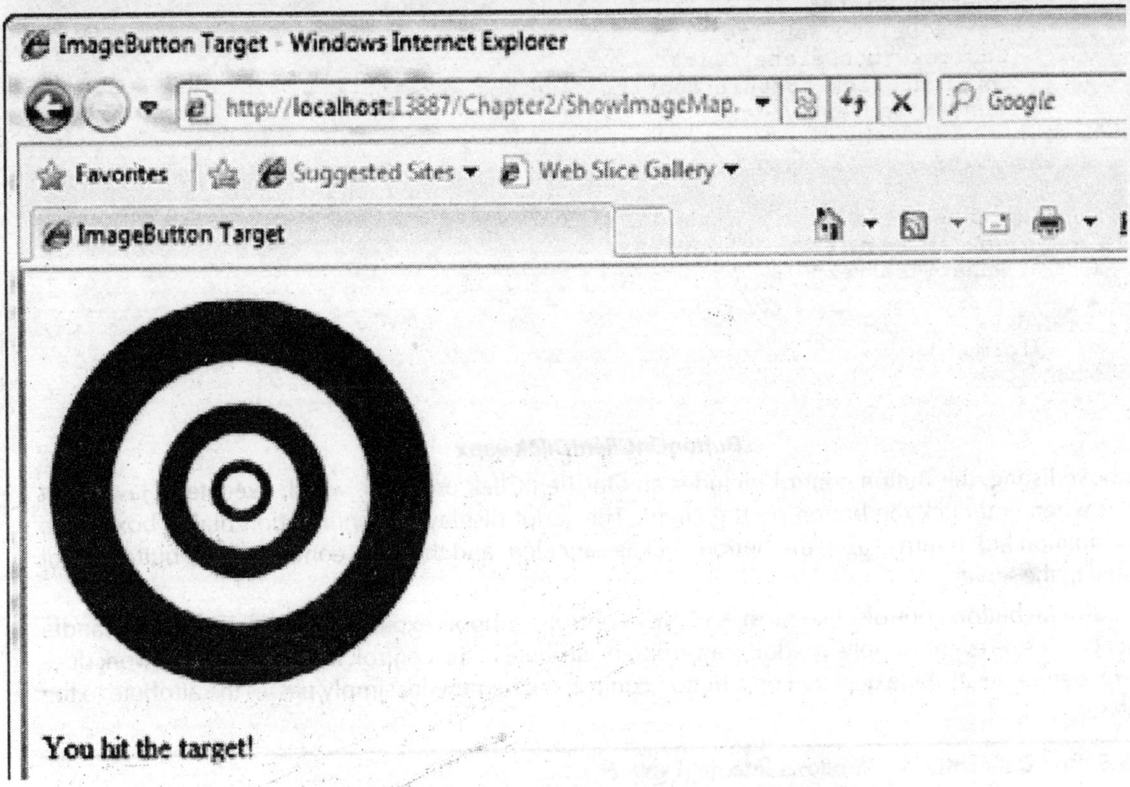

Retrieving X and Y coordinates from an ImageButton.

Using Client Scripts with Button Controls

All three Button controls support an OnClientClick property. You can use this property to execute any client-side code that you need when a button is clicked. The page in next listing illustrates how you can use the OnClientClick property to display a confirmation dialog box.

```
Code View: Scroll / Show All
<%@ Page Language="C#" %>
<!DOCTYPE html PUBLIC "-//W3C//DTD XHTML 1.0 Transitional//EN"
"http://www.w3.org/TR/xhtml1/DTD/xhtml1-transitional.dtd">
<script runat="server">

   protected void btnDelete_Click(object sender, EventArgs e)
    {
        lblResult.Text = "All pages deleted!";
    }
</script>
<html xmlns="http://www.w3.org/1999/xhtml" >
<head id="Head1" runat="server">
   <title>Button OnClientClick</title>
</head>
<body>
   <form id="form1" runat="server">
    <div>

    <asp:Button
```

```
            id="btnDelete"
            Text="Delete Website"
            OnClick="btnDelete_Click"
            OnClientClick="return confirm('Are you sure?');"
            Runat="server" />

        <br /><br />

        <asp:Label
            id="lblResult"
            Runat="server" />

        </div>
        </form>
    </body>
    </html>
```

ButtonOnClientClick.aspx

In above listing, the Button control includes an OnClientClick property, which executes a JavaScript script when you click the button on the client. The script displays a confirmation dialog box. If the confirmation box returns False, the button click is canceled, and the form containing the button is not posted to the server.

Because the button controls, like most ASP.NET controls, support expando attributes, you can handle other client-side events simply by adding an arbitrary attribute to the control. If ASP.NET Framework does not recognize an attribute declared on a button control, the framework simply passes the attribute to the browser.

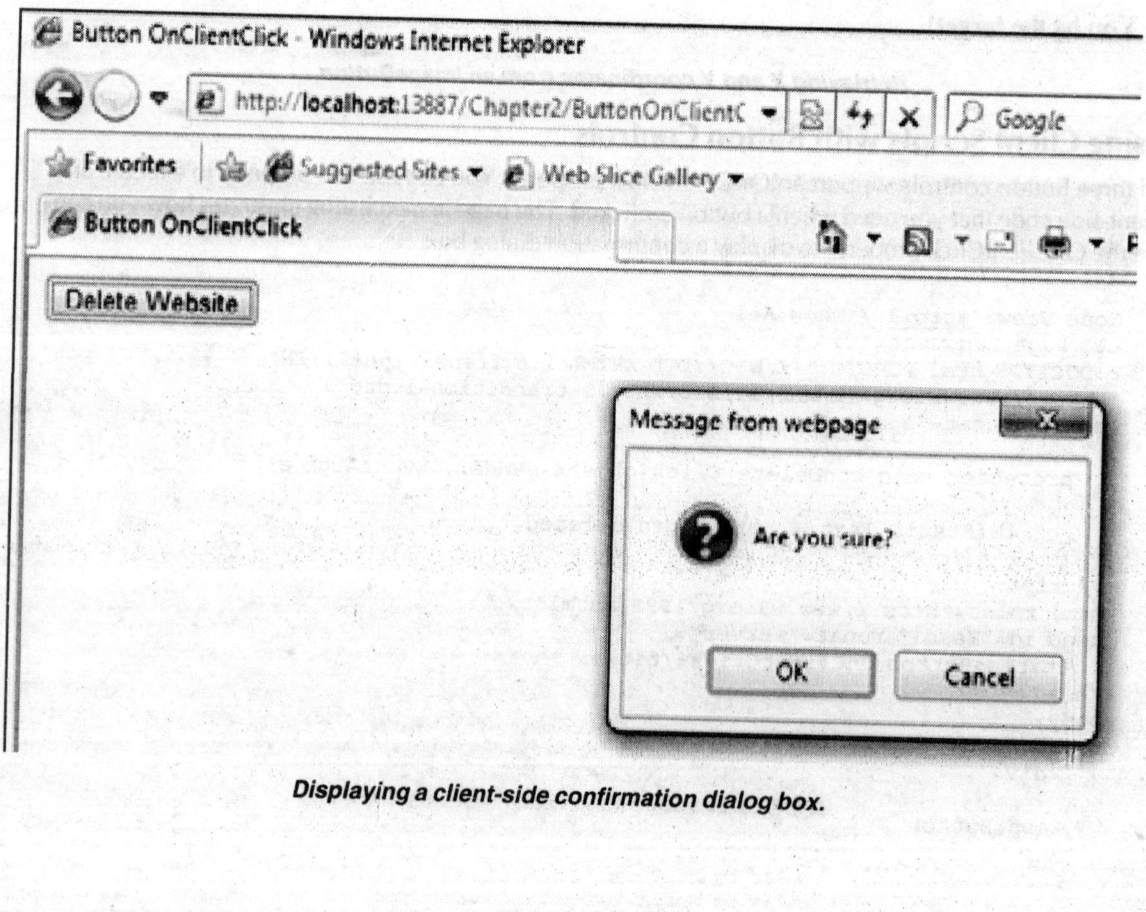

Displaying a client-side confirmation dialog box.

For example, the page in next listing contains a button control that includes onmouseover and onmouseout attributes. When you hover your mouse over the button, the text displayed in the button is changed.

```
<%@ Page Language="C#" %>
<!DOCTYPE html PUBLIC "-//W3C//DTD XHTML 1.0 Transitional//EN"
"http://www.w3.org/TR/xhtml1/DTD/xhtml1-transitional.dtd">
<html xmlns="http://www.w3.org/1999/xhtml" >
<head id="Head1" runat="server">
    <title>Button Expando</title>
</head>
<body>
    <form id="form1" runat="server">
    <div>

    <asp:Button
        id="btnSubmit"
        Text="Submit"
        onmouseover="this.value='Click Here!'"
        onmouseout="this.value='Submit'"
        Runat="server" />


    </div>
    </form>
</body>
</html>
```

ButtonExpando.aspx

Performing Cross-Page Posts

By default, if you click a button control, the page containing the control is posted back to itself, and the same page is reloaded. However, you can use the PostBackUrl property to post form data to another page.

For example, the page in next listing includes a search form. The Button control in the page posts the form to another page named ButtonSearchResults.aspx. The ButtonSearchResults.aspx page is contained in next listing.

```
Code View: Scroll / Show All
<%@ Page Language="C#" %>
<!DOCTYPE html PUBLIC "-//W3C//DTD XHTML 1.0 Transitional//EN"
"http://www.w3.org/TR/xhtml1/DTD/xhtml1-transitional.dtd">
<html xmlns="http://www.w3.org/1999/xhtml" >
<head id="Head1" runat="server">
    <title>Button Search</title>
</head>
<body>
    <form id="form1" runat="server">
    <div>

    <asp:Label
        id="lblSearch"
        Text="Search:"
        Runat="server" />
    <asp:TextBox
        id="txtSearch"
        Runat="server" />
```

```
        <asp:Button
            id="btnSearch"
             Text="Go!"
           PostBackUrl="ButtonSearchResults.aspx"
            Runat="server" />
        </div>
        </form>
</body>
</html>
```

ButtonSearch.aspx

```
Code View: Scroll / Show All
<%@ Page Language="C#" %>
<!DOCTYPE html PUBLIC "-//W3C//DTD XHTML 1.0 Transitional//EN"
"http://www.w3.org/TR/xhtml1/DTD/xhtml1-transitional.dtd">
<script runat="server">

    void Page_Load()
    {
        if (PreviousPage != null)
        {
            TextBox txtSearch =
(TextBox)PreviousPage.FindControl("txtSearch");
            lblSearch.Text = String.Format("Search For: {0}",
txtSearch.Text);
        }
    }

</script>
<html xmlns="http://www.w3.org/1999/xhtml" >
<head id="Head1" runat="server">
    <title>Button Search Results</title>
</head>
<body>
    <form id="form1" runat="server">
    <div>

    <asp:Label
        id="lblSearch"
        Runat="server" />

    </div>
    </form>
</body>
</html>
```

ButtonSearchResults.aspx

In the Page_Load event handler in second listing, the PreviousPage property gets a reference to the previous page (the ButtonSearch.aspx page in first listing). Next, the FindControl() method retrieves the txtSearch TextBox control from the previous page. Finally, the value entered into the TextBox displays in a label on the page. As an alternative to using the FindControl() method to retrieve a particular control from the previous page, you can expose the control through a page property. The page in first listing exposes the txtSearch TextBox through a property named SearchString. The page posts the form data to a page named ButtonSearchResultsTyped.aspx, contained in second listing.

```
Code View: Scroll / Show All
<%@ Page Language="C#" %>
<!DOCTYPE html PUBLIC "-//W3C//DTD XHTML 1.0 Transitional//EN"
"http://www.w3.org/TR/xhtml1/DTD/xhtml1-transitional.dtd">
<script runat="server">

    public string SearchString
    {
        get { return txtSearch.Text; }
    }

</script>
<html xmlns="http://www.w3.org/1999/xhtml" >
<head id="Head1" runat="server">
    <title>Button Search Typed</title>
</head>
<body>
    <form id="form1" runat="server">
    <div>

    <asp:Label
        id="lblSearch"
        Text="Search:"
        Runat="server" />
    <asp:TextBox
        id="txtSearch"
        Runat="server" />
    <asp:Button
        id="btnSearch"
        Text="Go!"
        PostBackUrl="ButtonSearchResultsTyped.aspx"
        Runat="server" />
    </div>
    </form>
</body>
</html>
```

ButtonSearchTyped.aspx

```
Code View: Scroll / Show All
<%@ Page Language="C#" %>
<%@ PreviousPageType VirtualPath="~/ButtonSearchTyped.aspx" %>
<!DOCTYPE html PUBLIC "-//W3C//DTD XHTML 1.0 Transitional//EN"
"http://www.w3.org/TR/xhtml1/DTD/xhtml1-transitional.dtd">
<script runat="server">

    void Page_Load()
    {
        if (Page.PreviousPage != null)
        {
            lblSearch.Text = String.Format("Search For: {0}",
PreviousPage.SearchString);
        }
    }

</script>
<html xmlns="http://www.w3.org/1999/xhtml" >
<head id="Head1" runat="server">
```

```
    <title>Button Search Results Typed</title>
</head>
<body>
    <form id="form1" runat="server">
    <div>

    <asp:Label
        id="lblSearch"
        Runat="server" />

    </div>
    </form>
</body>
</html>
```

ButtonSearchResultsTyped.aspx

Notice that the page in second listing includes a <%@ PreviousPageType %> directive. This directive casts the value returned by the PreviousPage property as an instance of the ButtonSearchTyped class. Without this directive, the PreviousPage property would return the previous page as an instance of the generic Page class. You can use either method when performing cross-page posts. The first method provides you with an untyped method of retrieving values from the previous page, and the second method provides you with a typed method.

Specifying a Default Button

You can specify a default button for a form by using the DefaultButton property of the server-side Form control. If you specify a default button, pressing the keyboard Enter key invokes the button. For example, the page in next listing contains a simple search form. The <form> tag sets the btnSearch Button control as the default button on the page.

```
Code View: Scroll / Show All
<%@ Page Language="C#" %>
<!DOCTYPE html PUBLIC "-//W3C//DTD XHTML 1.0 Transitional//EN"
"http://www.w3.org/TR/xhtml1/DTD/xhtml1-transitional.dtd">
<script runat="server">

    protected void btnSearch_Click(object sender, EventArgs e)
    {
        lblResult.Text = "Search for: " + txtSearch.Text;
    }
</script>
<html xmlns="http://www.w3.org/1999/xhtml" >
<head id="Head1" runat="server">
    <title>Button Default Button</title>
</head>
<body>
    <form id="form1" defaultbutton="btnSearch" runat="server">
    <div>

    <asp:Label
        id="lblSearch"
        Text="Search:"
        AssociatedControlID="txtSearch"
        Runat="server" />
    <asp:TextBox
        id="txtSearch"
```

```
        Runat="server" />
    <asp:Button
        id="btnSearch"
        Text="Search"
        OnClick="btnSearch_Click"
        Runat="server" />
    <asp:Button
        id="btnCancel"
        Text="Cancel"
        Runat="server" />

    <hr />

    <asp:Label
        id="lblResult"
        Runat="server" />

    </div>
    </form>
</body>
</html>
```

ButtonDefaultButton.aspx

If you open the page in above listing, type a search phrase, and press the keyboard Enter key, the form is submitted to the server. Pressing the Enter key causes the btnSearch_Click event handler to execute because the btnSearch button is the default button on the page.

Handling the Command Event

All three Button controls support both the Click event and the Command event. The difference between these events is that you can pass a command name and command argument to a Command event handler but not to a Click event handler.

For example, the page in next listing contains two Button controls and a BulletedList control. When you click the first button, the items displayed by the BulletedList control are sorted in ascending order, and when you click the second button, the items displayed by the BulletedList control are sorted in descending order.

```
Code View: Scroll / Show All
<%@ Page Language="C#" %>
<%@ Import Namespace="System.Collections.Generic" %>
<!DOCTYPE html PUBLIC "-//W3C//DTD XHTML 1.0 Transitional//EN"
"http://www.w3.org/TR/xhtml1/DTD/xhtml1-transitional.dtd">
<script runat="server">

    private List<String> groceries = new List<String>();

    void Page_Load()
    {
        groceries.Add("Milk");
        groceries.Add("Steak");
        groceries.Add("Fish");
    }

    protected void Sort_Command(object sender, CommandEventArgs e)
    {
        if (e.CommandName == "Sort")
```

```
        {
            switch (e.CommandArgument.ToString())
            {
                case "ASC":
                    groceries.Sort(SortASC);
                    break;
                case "DESC":
                    groceries.Sort(SortDESC);
                    break;
            }
        }
    }

    void Page_PreRender()
    {
        bltGroceries.DataSource = groceries;
        bltGroceries.DataBind();
    }

    int SortASC(string x, string y)
    {
        return String.Compare(x, y);
    }

    int SortDESC(string x, string y)
    {
        return String.Compare(x, y) * -1;
    }

</script>
<html xmlns="http://www.w3.org/1999/xhtml" >
<head id="Head1" runat="server">
    <title>Button Command</title>
</head>
<body>
    <form id="form1" runat="server">
    <div>

    <asp:Button
        id="btnSortAsc"
        Text="Sort ASC"
        CommandName="Sort"
        CommandArgument="ASC"
        OnCommand="Sort_Command"
        Runat="server" />

    <asp:Button
        id="btnSortDESC"
        Text="Sort DESC"
        CommandName="Sort"
        CommandArgument="DESC"
        OnCommand="Sort_Command"
        Runat="server" />

    <br /><br />

    <asp:BulletedList
        id="bltGroceries"
```

```
            Runat="server" />

        </div>
        </form>
    </body>
    </html>
```

ButtonCommand.aspx

Both Button controls include CommandName and CommandArgument properties. Furthermore, both Button controls are wired to the same Sort_Command() event handler. This event handler checks the CommandName and CommandArgument properties when determining how the elements in the BulletedList should be sorted.

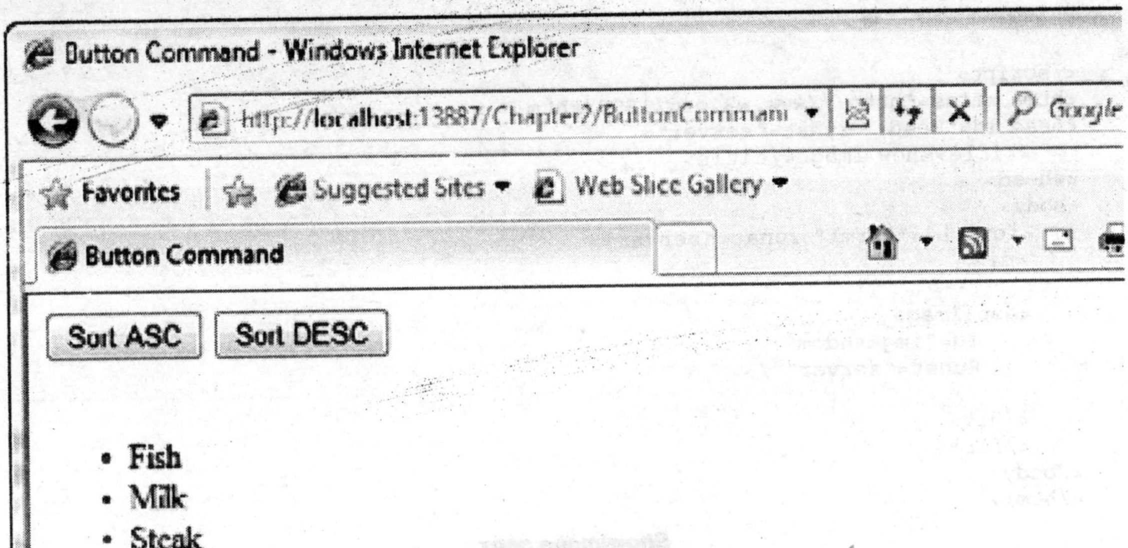

Handling the Command event.

Displaying Images

The ASP.NET Framework includes two controls for displaying images: Image and ImageMap. The Image control simply displays an image. The ImageMap control enables you to create a client-side, clickable, image map.

Using the Image Control

The page in next listing randomly displays one of three images. The image is displayed by setting the ImageUrl property of the Image control contained in the body of the page.

```
Code View: Scroll / Show All
<%@ Page Language="C#" %>
<!DOCTYPE html PUBLIC "-//W3C//DTD XHTML 1.0 Transitional//EN"
"http://www.w3.org/TR/xhtml1/DTD/xhtml1-transitional.dtd">
<script runat="server">

    void Page_Load()
    {
        Random rnd = new Random();
        switch (rnd.Next(3))
        {
```

```
            case 0:
                imgRandom.ImageUrl = "Picture1.gif";
                imgRandom.AlternateText = "Picture 1";
                break;
            case 1:
                imgRandom.ImageUrl = "Picture2.gif";
                imgRandom.AlternateText = "Picture 2";
                break;
            case 2:
                imgRandom.ImageUrl = "Picture3.gif";
                imgRandom.AlternateText = "Picture 3";
                break;
        }
    }
</script>
<html xmlns="http://www.w3.org/1999/xhtml" >
<head id="Head1" runat="server">
    <title>Show Image</title>
</head>
<body>
    <form id="form1" runat="server">
    <div>

    <asp:Image
        id="imgRandom"
        Runat="server" />

    </div>
    </form>
</body>
</html>
```

ShowImage.aspx

The Image control supports the following properties (this is not a complete list):

- **AlternateText**— Enables you to provide alternate text for the image (required for accessibility).
- **DescriptionUrl**— Enables you to provide a link to a page that contains a detailed description of the image (required to make a complex image accessible).
- **GenerateEmptyAlternateText**— Enables you to set the AlternateText property to an empty string.
- **ImageAlign**— Enables you to align the image relative to other HTML elements in the page. Possible values are AbsBottom, AbsMiddle, Baseline, Bottom, Left, Middle, NotSet, Right, TextTop, and Top.
- **ImageUrl**— Enables you to specify the URL to the image.

The Image control supports three methods for supplying alternate text. If an image represents page content, you should supply a value for the AlternateText property. For example, if you have an image for your company's logo, you should assign the text "My Company Logo" to the AlternateText property. If an Image control represents something complex—such as a bar chart, pie graph, or company organizational chart—you should supply a value for the DescriptionUrl property. The DescriptionUrl property links to a page that contains a long textual description of the image. Finally, if the image is used purely for decoration (it expresses no content), you should set the GenerateEmptyAlternateText property to the value True. When this property has the value True, an alt="" attribute is included in the rendered <img> tag. Screen readers know to ignore images with empty alt attributes.

Using the ImageMap Control

The ImageMap control enables you to create a client-side image map. An image map displays an image. When you click different areas of the image, things happen. For example, you can use an image map as a fancy navigation bar. In that case, clicking different areas of the image map navigates to different pages in your website.

You also can use an image map as an input mechanism. For example, you can click different product images to add a particular product to a shopping cart. An ImageMap control is composed out of instances of the HotSpot class. A HotSpot defines the clickable regions in an image map. The ASP.NET Framework ships with three HotSpot classes:

- **CircleHotSpot**— Enables you to define a circular region in an image map.
- **PolygonHotSpot**— Enables you to define an irregularly shaped region in an image map.
- **RectangleHotSpot**— Enables you to define a rectangular region in an image map.

The page in next listing contains a navigation bar created with an ImageMap control, which contains three RectangleHotSpots that delimit the three buttons displayed by the navigation bar.


```
Code View: Scroll / Show All
<%@ Page Language="C#" %>
<!DOCTYPE html PUBLIC "-//W3C//DTD XHTML 1.0 Transitional//EN"
"http://www.w3.org/TR/xhtml1/DTD/xhtml1-transitional.dtd">
<html xmlns="http://www.w3.org/1999/xhtml" >
<head id="Head1" runat="server">
    <title>ImageMap Navigate</title>
</head>
<body>
    <form id="form1" runat="server">
    <div>

    <asp:ImageMap
        id="mapNavigate"
        ImageUrl="ImageBar.jpg"
        Runat="server">
        <asp:RectangleHotSpot
            NavigateUrl="Home.aspx"
            Left="0"
            Top="0"
            Right="100"
            Bottom="50"
            AlternateText="Navigate to Home" />
        <asp:RectangleHotSpot
            NavigateUrl="Products.aspx"
            Left="100"
            Top="0"
            Right="200"
            Bottom="50"
            AlternateText="Navigate to Products" />
        <asp:RectangleHotSpot
            NavigateUrl="Services.aspx"
            Left="200"
            Top="0"
            Right="300"
            Bottom="50"
            AlternateText="Navigate to Services" />
```

```
    </asp:ImageMap>

    </div>
    </form>
</body>
</html>
```

ImageMapNavigate.aspx

Each RectangleHotSpot includes Left, Top, Right, and Bottom properties that describe the area of the rectangle. Each RectangleHotSpot also includes a NavigateUrl property that contains the URL to which the region of the image map links. Rather than use an image map to link to different pages, you can use it to post back to the same page. For example, the page in next listing uses an ImageMap control to display a menu. When you click different menu items represented by different regions of the image map, the text contained in the TextBox control is changed.

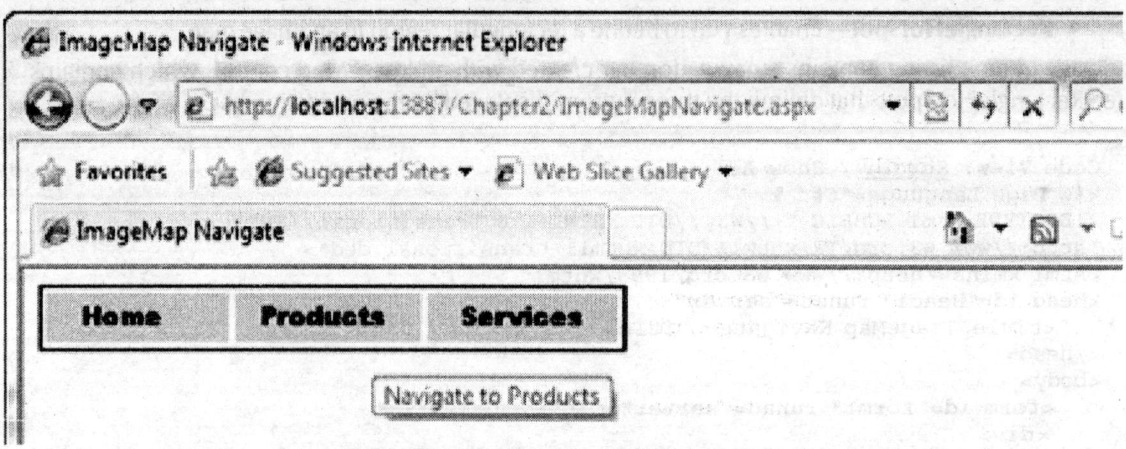

Navigating with an ImageMap control.

```
Code View: Scroll / Show All
<%@ Page Language="C#" %>
<!DOCTYPE html PUBLIC "-//W3C//DTD XHTML 1.0 Transitional//EN"
"http://www.w3.org/TR/xhtml1/DTD/xhtml1-transitional.dtd">
<script runat="server">

    protected void mapMenu_Click(object sender, ImageMapEventArgs e)
    {
        switch (e.PostBackValue)
        {
            case "ToUpper":
                txtText.Text = txtText.Text.ToUpper();
                break;
            case "ToLower":
                txtText.Text = txtText.Text.ToLower();
                break;
            case "Erase":
                txtText.Text = String.Empty;
                break;
        }
    }
</script>
<html xmlns="http://www.w3.org/1999/xhtml" >
```

```
<head id="Head1" runat="server">
    <title>ImageMap PostBack</title>
</head>
<body>
    <form id="form1" runat="server">
    <div>

    <asp:ImageMap
        id="mapMenu"
        ImageUrl="MenuBar.gif"
        HotSpotMode="PostBack"
        Runat="server" OnClick="mapMenu_Click">
        <asp:RectangleHotSpot
            PostBackValue="ToUpper"
            Left="0"
            Top="0"
            Right="100"
            Bottom="30"
            AlternateText="To Uppercase" />
        <asp:RectangleHotSpot
            PostBackValue="ToLower"
            Left="100"
            Top="0"
            Right="200"
            Bottom="30"
            AlternateText="To Lowercase" />
        <asp:RectangleHotSpot
            PostBackValue="Erase"
            Left="200"
            Top="0"
            Right="300"
            Bottom="30"
            AlternateText="Erase Text" />
    </asp:ImageMap>

    <br />

    <asp:TextBox
        id="txtText"
        TextMode="MultiLine"
        Columns="40"
        Rows="5"
        Runat="server" />

    </div>
    </form>
</body>
</html>
```

ImageMapPostBack.aspx

Notice that the ImageMap control has its HotSpotMode property set to the value PostBack. Also, the ImageMap is wired to a Click event handler named mapMenu_Click.

Each HotSpot contained in the ImageMap control has a PostBackValue property. The mapMenu_Click handler reads the PostBackValue from the region clicked and modifies the text displayed by the TextBox control.

The ImageMap control supports the following properties (this is not a complete list):

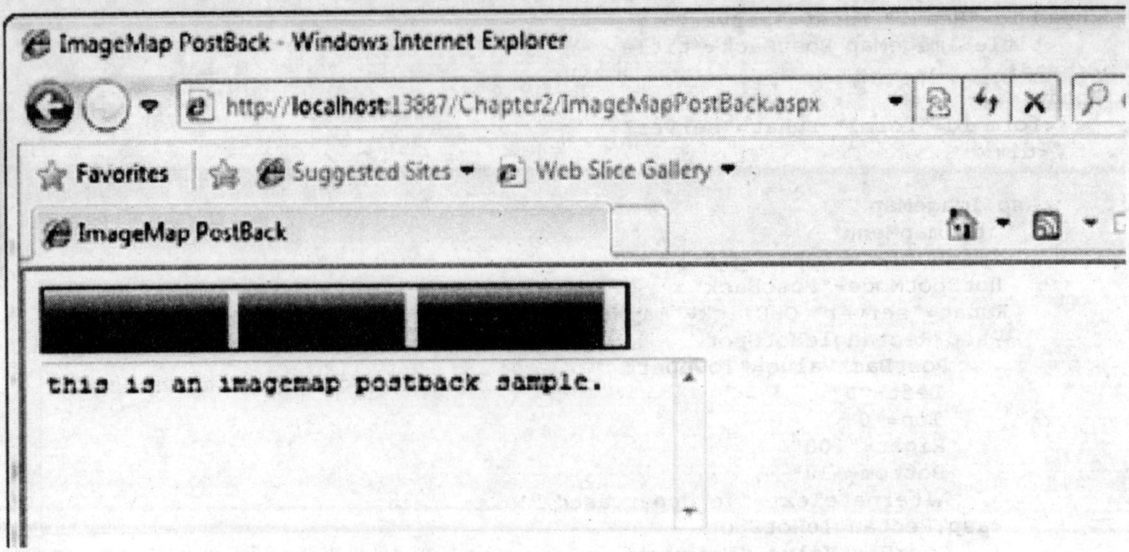

Figure Posting back to the server with an ImageMap control.

- **AccessKey**— Enables you to specify a key that navigates to the ImageMap control.
- **AlternateText**— Enables you to provide alternate text for the image (required for accessibility).
- **DescriptionUrl**— Enables you to provide a link to a page that contains a detailed description of the image (required to make a complex image accessible).
- **GenerateEmptyAlternateText**— Enables you to set the AlternateText property to an empty string.
- **HotSpotMode**— Enables you to specify the behavior of the image map when you click a region. Possible values are Inactive, Navigate, NotSet, and PostBack.
- **HotSpots**— Enables you to retrieve the collection of HotSpots contained in the ImageMap control.
- **ImageAlign**— Enables you to align the image map with other HTML elements in the page. Possible values are AbsBottom, AbsMiddle, Baseline, Bottom, Left, Middle, NotSet, Right, TextTop, and Top.
- **ImageUrl**— Enables you to specify the URL to the image.
- **TabIndex**— Enables you to specify the tab order of the ImageMap control.
- **Target**— Enables you to open a page in a new window.

The ImageMap control also supports the following method:

- **Focus**— Enables you to set the initial form focus to the ImageMap control.

Finally, the ImageMap control supports the following event:

- **Click**— Raised when you click a region of the ImageMap and the HotSpotMode property is set to the value PostBack.

Using the Panel Control

The Panel control enables you to work with a group of ASP.NET controls. For example, you can use a Panel control to hide or show a group of ASP.NET controls. The page in next listing contains a list of RadioButton controls which can be used to select your favorite programming language. The last RadioButton is labeled Other. If you select the Other radio button, the contents of a Panel control are revealed.

```
Code View: Scroll / Show All
<%@ Page Language="C#" %>
<!DOCTYPE html PUBLIC "-//W3C//DTD XHTML 1.0 Transitional//EN"
"http://www.w3.org/TR/xhtml1/DTD/xhtml1-transitional.dtd">
<script runat="server">

    protected void btnSubmit_Click(object sender, EventArgs e)
    {
        if (rdlOther.Checked)
            pnlOther.Visible = true;
        else
            pnlOther.Visible = false;
    }
</script>
<html xmlns="http://www.w3.org/1999/xhtml" >
<head id="Head1" runat="server">
    <title>Show Panel</title>
</head>
<body>
    <form id="form1" runat="server">
    <div>

    Select your favorite programming language:
    <br /><br />
    <asp:RadioButton
        id="rdlVisualBasic"
        GroupName="language"
        Text="Visual Basic"
        Runat="server" />
    <br /><br />
    <asp:RadioButton
        id="rdlCSharp"
        GroupName="language"
        Text="C#"
        Runat="server" />
    <br /><br />
    <asp:RadioButton
        id="rdlOther"
        GroupName="language"
        Text="Other Language"
        Runat="server" />
    <br />
    <asp:Panel
        id="pnlOther"
        Visible="false"
        Runat="server">

        <asp:Label
            id="lblOther"
            Text="Other Language:"
            AssociatedControlID="txtOther"
            Runat="server" />
        <asp:TextBox
            id="txtOther"
            Runat="server" />

    </asp:Panel>
```

```
        <br /><br />

        <asp:Button
            id="btnSubmit"
            Text="Submit"
           Runat="server" OnClick="btnSubmit_Click" />

        </div>
        </form>
</body>
</html>
```

ShowPanel.aspx

Notice that the Panel control is declared with a Visible property that has the value False. Because the Visible property is set to the value False, the Panel control and any controls contained in the Panel control are not rendered when the page is requested. If you select the RadioButton control labeled Other, the Visible property is set to the value True and the contents of the Panel control display.

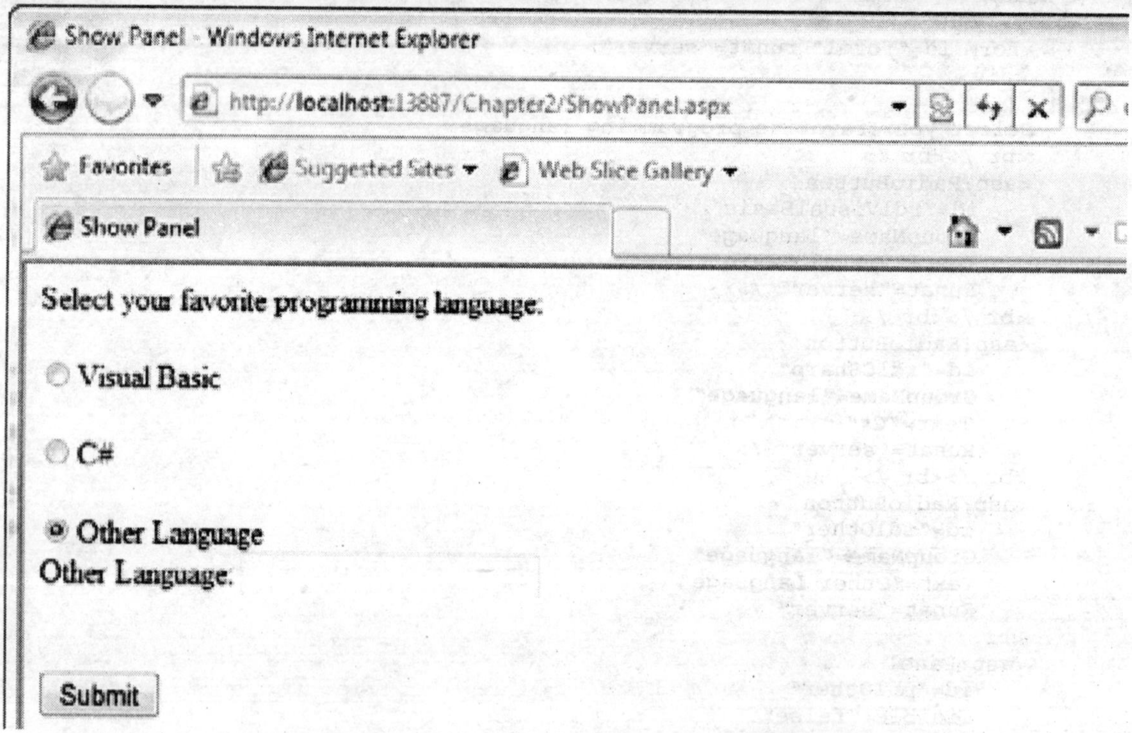

Hiding and displaying controls with the Panel control.

Every control in ASP.NET supports the Visible property. When Visible is set to the value False, the control does not render its contents.

The Panel control supports the following properties (this is not a complete list):

- **DefaultButton**— Enables you to specify the default button in a Panel. The default button is invoked when you press the Enter button.
- **Direction**— Enables you to get or set the direction in which controls that display text are rendered. Possible values are NotSet, LeftToRight, and RightToLeft.

- **GroupingText**— Enables you to render the Panel control as a fieldset with a particular legend.
- **HorizontalAlign**— Enables you to specify the horizontal alignment of the contents of the Panel. Possible values are Center, Justify, Left, NotSet, and Right.
- **ScrollBars**— Enables you to display scrollbars around the panel's contents. Possible values are Auto, Both, Horizontal, None, and Vertical.

By default, a Panel control renders a <div> tag around its contents. If you set the GroupingText property, however, the Panel control renders a <fieldset> tag. The value that you assign to the GroupingText property appears in the <fieldset> tag's <legend> tag. The next listing demonstrates how you can use the GroupingText property.

Code View: Scroll / Show All

```
<%@ Page Language="C#" %>
<!DOCTYPE html PUBLIC "-//W3C//DTD XHTML 1.0 Transitional//EN"
"http://www.w3.org/TR/xhtml1/DTD/xhtml1-transitional.dtd">
<html xmlns="http://www.w3.org/1999/xhtml" >
<head id="Head1" runat="server">
    <title>Panel Grouping Text</title>
</head>
<body>
    <form id="form1" runat="server">
    <div>

    <asp:Panel
        id="pnlContact"
        GroupingText="Contact Information"
        Runat="server">

    <asp:Label
        id="lblFirstName"
        Text="First Name:"
        AssociatedControlID="txtFirstName"
        Runat="server" />
    <br />
    <asp:TextBox
        id="txtFirstName"
        AutoCompleteType="FirstName"
        Runat="server" />
    <br /><br />
    <asp:Label
        id-"lblLastname"
        Text="Last Name:"
        AssociatedControlID="txtLastName"
        Runat="server" />
    <br />
    <asp:TextBox
        id="txtLastName"
        AutoCompleteType="LastName"
        Runat="server" />
    <br /><br />
    <asp:Button
        id="btnSubmit"
        Text="Submit"
        Runat="server" />

    </asp:Panel>
```

```
        </div>
        </form>
</body>
</html>
```

PanelGroupingText.aspx

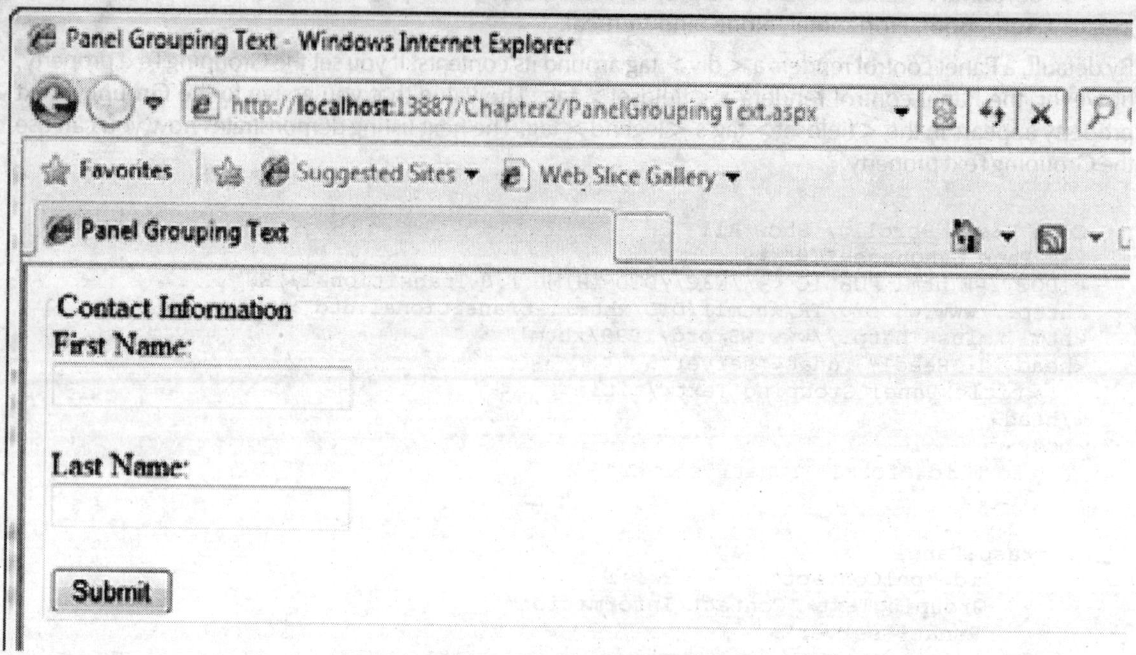

Setting the GroupingText property.

Web Standards Note

According to the accessibility guidelines, you should use <fieldset> tags when grouping related form fields in long forms.

The ScrollBars property enables you to display scrollbars around a panel's contents. For example, the page in next listing contains a Panel control that contains a BulletedList control that displays 100 items. The panel is configured to scroll when its contents overflow its width or height.

```
Code View: Scroll / Show All
<%@ Page Language="C#" %>
<!DOCTYPE html PUBLIC "-//W3C//DTD XHTML 1.0 Transitional//EN"
"http://www.w3.org/TR/xhtml1/DTD/xhtml1-transitional.dtd">
<script runat="server">

    void Page_Load()
    {
        for (int i = 0; i < 100; i++)
            bltList.Items.Add("Item " + i.ToString());
    }

</script>
<html xmlns="http://www.w3.org/1999/xhtml" >
<head id="Head1" runat="server">
    <style type="text/css">
```

```
        html
        {
            background-color:silver;
        }
        .contents
        {
            background-color:white;
            width:200px;
            height:200px;
        }
    </style>
    <title>Panel ScrollBars</title>
</head>
<body>
    <form id="form1" runat="server">
    <div>

    <asp:Panel
        id="pnlContent"
        ScrollBars="Auto"
        CssClass="contents"
        Runat="server">
        <asp:BulletedList
            id="bltList"
            Runat="server" />
    </asp:Panel>

    </div>
    </form>
</body>
</html>
```

PanelScrollBars.aspx

Web Standards Note

Don't use the values Horizontal or Vertical with the ScrollBars property when you want the scrollbars to appear in browsers other than Microsoft Internet Explorer. If you want the scrollbars to appear in FireFox and Opera, use either the value Auto or Both.

When enabling scrollbars with the Panel control, you must specify a particular width and height to display the scrollbars. In listing 2.31, the width and height are specified in a Cascading Style Sheet class. Alternatively, you can specify the width and height with the Panel control's Width and Height properties.

Using the HyperLink Control

The HyperLink control enables you to create a link to a page. Unlike the LinkButton control, the HyperLink control does not submit a form to a server. For example, the page in next listing displays a hyperlink that randomly links to a page in your application.

```
Code View: Scroll / Show All
<%@ Page Language="C#" %>
<%@ Import Namespace="System.IO" %>
<!DOCTYPE html PUBLIC "-//W3C//DTD XHTML 1.0 Transitional//EN"
"http://www.w3.org/TR/xhtml1/DTD/xhtml1-transitional.dtd">
<script runat="server">

    void Page_Load()
```

```
    {
        lnkRandom.NavigateUrl = GetRandomFile();
    }

    string GetRandomFile()
    {
        string[] files = Directory.GetFiles(MapPath(Request.ApplicationPath),
"*.aspx");
        Random rnd = new Random();
        string rndFile = files[rnd.Next(files.Length)];
        return Path.GetFileName(rndFile);
    }

</script>
<html xmlns="http://www.w3.org/1999/xhtml" >
<head id="Head1" runat="server">
    <title>Show HyperLink</title>
</head>
<body>
    <form id="form1" runat="server">
    <div>

    <asp:HyperLink
        id="lnkRandom"
        Text="Random Link"
        Runat="server" />

    </div>
    </form>
</body>
</html>
```

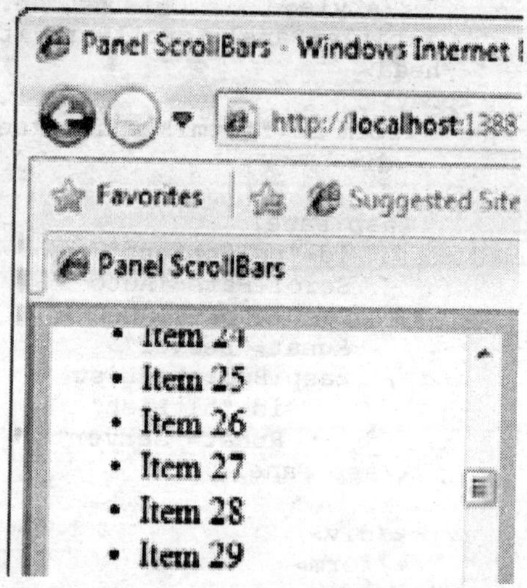

Displaying scrollbars with a Panel control.

ShowHyperLink.aspx

In the Page_Load event handler in above listing, a random filename from the current application is assigned to the NavigateUrl property of the HyperLink control. The HyperLink control supports the following properties (this is not a complete list):

- **Enabled**— Enables you to disable the hyperlink.
- **ImageUrl**— Enables you to specify an image for the hyperlink.
- **NavigateUrl**— Enables you to specify the URL represented by the hyperlink.
- **Target**— Enables you to open a new window.
- **Text**— Enables you to label the hyperlink.

Notice that you can specify an image for the HyperLink control by setting the ImageUrl property. If you set both the Text and ImageUrl properties, the ImageUrl property takes precedence.

CHAPTER 3

Using the Navigation Controls

In this chapter you will read about:

- Understanding Site Maps.
- Using the Menu Control.
- Using the TreeView Control.
- Building a SQL Hierarchical Data Source Control.

Introduction

Now, you will learn how to use the `SiteMapPath`, `Menu`, and `TreeView` controls. You can use all three of these controls to enable users to navigate your website. Furthermore, you can use the `Menu` and `TreeView` controls independently of website navigation. You can bind these two controls to other data sources such as XML documents or database data. This chapter explores different methods of binding the `Menu` and `TreeView` controls to different data sources and shows you how to format the rendered output of both of these controls. You also learn how to take advantage of Ajax when working with the `TreeView` control.Finally, we build a `SqlHierarchicalDataSource` control, which enables you to bind controls such as the `TreeView` and `Menu` controls to hierarchical database data.

Understanding Site Maps

Before you learn about the navigation controls, you first need to understand Site Maps. All three navigation controls use Site Maps to retrieve navigation information. A Site Map enables you to represent the navigational relationships between the pages in an application, independent of the actual physical relationship between pages as stored in the file system. Site Maps use the provider model. By default, the navigation controls assume the existence of an XML file named `Web.sitemap`, which is located in the root of your application.

For example, next listing contains a simple Site Map.

```
Code View: Scroll / Show All
<?xml version="1.0" encoding="utf-8" ?>
<siteMap xmlns="http://schemas.microsoft.com/AspNet/SiteMap-File-1.0" >

<siteMapNode
  url="~/Default.aspx"
  title="Home"
  description="The home page of the Website">

  <!— Product Nodes —>
  <siteMapNode
    title="Products"
    description="Website products">
    <siteMapNode
      url="~/Products/FirstProduct.aspx"
      title="First Product"
      description="The first product" />
    <siteMapNode
      url="~/Products/SecondProduct.aspx"
      title="Second Product"
      description="The second product" />
  </siteMapNode>

  <!— Services Nodes —>
  <siteMapNode
    title="Services"
    description="Website services">
    <siteMapNode
      url="~/Service/FirstService.aspx"
      title="First Service"
      description="The first service" />
    <siteMapNode
      url="~/Products/SecondService.aspx"
      title="Second Service"
```

```
      description="The second service" />
  </siteMapNode>

</siteMapNode>

</siteMap>
```

listing Web.sitemap

A Site Map file contains <siteMapNode> elements. There can be only one top-level node. In the case of above listing, the top-level node represents the website's home page.

A <siteMapNode> supports three main attributes:

- title— A brief title that you want to associate with a node.
- description— A longer description that you want to associate with a node.
- url— A URL that points to a page or other resource.

The url attribute is not required. Both the Products and Services nodes do not include a url attribute because these nodes do not represent pages to which you can navigate. Each <siteMapNode> can contain any number of child nodes. In above listing, both the Products and Services nodes include two child nodes.

The Site Map in above listing represents a website that has the following folder and page structure:

```
Default.aspx
Products
  FirstProduct.aspx
  SecondProduct.aspx
Services
  FirstService.aspx
  SecondService.aspx
```

The navigational structure of a website as represented by a Site Map is not required to have any relationship to the navigational structure of a website as stored in the file system. You can create any relationship between the nodes in a Site Map that you want.

Using the Menu Control

The Menu control enables you to create two types of menus. You can use the Menu control to create the left-column menu that appears in many websites. In other words, you can use the Menu control to display a vertical list of links. You also can use the Menu control to create a menu that more closely resembles the drop-down menus that appear in traditional desktop applications. In this case, the Menu control renders a horizontal list of links.

Unlike the SiteMapPath control, the Menu control can represent other types of data than Site Map data. Technically, you can bind a Menu control to any data source that implements the IHiearchicalDataSource or IHiearchicalEnumerable interface. Now, you learn how to create different types of menus with the Menu control. First, you learn how to add menu declaratively items to a Menu control. You also examine how you can bind the Menu control to different types of data sources. You learn how to use the Menu control with Site Map data, XML data, and database data.

Declaratively Adding Menu Items

You can display a menu with the Menu control by adding one or more MenuItem objects to its Items property. For example, the page in next listing uses a Menu control to create a simple vertical menu.

Displaying a menu with the Menu control.

Code View: Scroll / Show All

```
<%@ Page Language="C#" %>
<!DOCTYPE html PUBLIC "-//W3C//DTD XHTML 1.1//EN"
 "http://www.w3.org/TR/xhtml11/DTD/xhtml11.dtd">
<html xmlns="http://www.w3.org/1999/xhtml">
<head id="Head1" runat="server">
   <title>Menu HyperLink</title>
</head>
<body>
    <form id="form1" runat="server">
    <div>

    <asp:Menu
        id="Menu1"
        Runat="server">
        <Items>
            <asp:MenuItem
                Text="Products"
                NavigateUrl="Products.aspx" />
            <asp:MenuItem
                Text="Services"
                NavigateUrl="Services.aspx">
                <asp:MenuItem
                    Text="Training"
                    NavigateUrl="Training.aspx" />
                <asp:MenuItem
                    Text="Consulting"
                    NavigateUrl="Consulting.aspx" />
            </asp:MenuItem>
        </Items>
    </asp:Menu>

    </div>
    </form>
</body>
</html>
```

listing MenuHyperLink.aspx

The `Menu` in above listing is created from `MenuItem` objects. Each menu item in above listing contains a link to another page. `MenuItem` objects can be nested. The second `MenuItem` object—Services—includes two child `MenuItem` objects. When you hover your mouse over a parent menu item, the child menu items display.

Each `MenuItem` in above listing includes a `Text` and `NavigateUrl` property. Rather than use a `MenuItem` to link to a new page, you also can use a `MenuItem` to link back to the same page. In other words, each

MenuItem can act like a Linkbutton control instead of a HyperLink control. For example, each MenuItem object in next listing includes a Text and Value property. When you click a menu item, the same page is reloaded, and the value of the selected menu item displays.

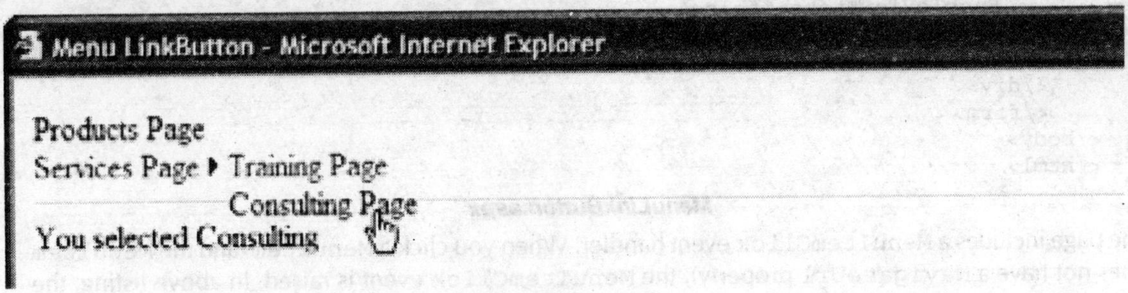

Selecting menu items.

Code View: Scroll / Show All

```
<%@ Page Language="C#" %>
<!DOCTYPE html PUBLIC "-//W3C//DTD XHTML 1.1//EN"
"http://www.w3.org/TR/xhtml11/DTD/xhtml11.dtd">
<script runat="server">

    protected void Menu1_MenuItemClick(object sender, MenuEventArgs e)
    {
        lblMessage.Text = "You selected " + Menu1.SelectedValue;
    }
</script>
<html xmlns="http://www.w3.org/1999/xhtml" >
<head id="Head1" runat="server">
    <title>Menu LinkButton</title>
</head>
<body>
    <form id="form1" runat="server">
    <div>

    <asp:Menu
        id="Menu1"
        OnMenuItemClick="Menu1_MenuItemClick"
        Runat="server">
        <Items>
            <asp:MenuItem
                Text="Products Page"
                Value-"Products" />
            <asp:MenuItem
                Text="Services Page"
                Value="Services">
                <asp:MenuItem
                    Text="Training Page"
                    Value="Training" />
                <asp:MenuItem
                    Text="Consulting Page"
                    Value="Consulting" />
            </asp:MenuItem>
        </Items>
    </asp:Menu>
```

```
    <hr />

    <asp:Label
        id="lblMessage"
        EnableViewState="false"
        Runat="server" />

    </div>
    </form>
</body>
</html>
```

MenuLinkButton.aspx

The page includes a `MenuItemClick` event handler. When you click a `MenuItem` (and the `MenuItem` does not have a `NavigateUrl` property), the `MenuItemClick` event is raised. In above listing, the `MenuItemClick` handler displays the value of the selected `MenuItem` in a `Label` control.

Using the Menu Control with the MultiView Control

When the `Menu` control is used with the `MultiView` control, you can create tabbed pages. You use the `Menu` control to display the tabs, and the `MultiView` control to display the content that corresponds to the selected tab. For example, the page in next listing displays three tabs.

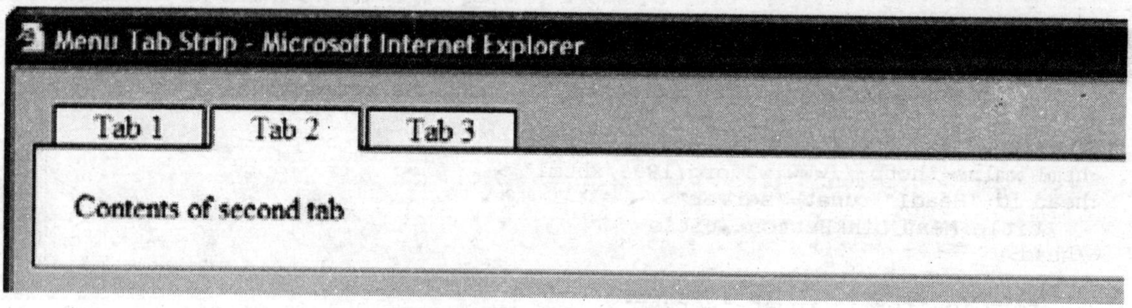

Displaying a tabbed page.

Code View: Scroll / Show All

```
<%@ Page Language="C#" %>
<!DOCTYPE html PUBLIC "-//W3C//DTD XHTML 1.1//EN"
"http://www.w3.org/TR/xhtml11/DTD/xhtml11.dtd">
<script runat="server">

    protected void menuTabs_MenuItemClick(object sender, MenuEventArgs e)
    {
        multiTabs.ActiveViewIndex = Int32.Parse(menuTabs.SelectedValue);
    }
</script>
<html xmlns="http://www.w3.org/1999/xhtml" >
<head id="Head1" runat="server">
    <style type="text/css">
        html
        {
            background-color:silver;
        }
        .menuTabs
        {
            position:relative;
```

```
            top:1px;
            left:10px;
        }
        .tab
        {
            border:Solid 1px black;
            border-bottom:none;
            padding:0px 10px;
            background-color:#eeeeee;
        }
        .selectedTab
        {
            border:Solid 1px black;
            border-bottom:Solid 1px white;
            padding:0px 10px;
            background-color:white;
        }
        .tabBody
        {
            border:Solid 1px black;
            padding:20px;
            background-color:white;
        }
    </style>
    <title>Menu Tab Strip</title>
</head>
<body>
    <form id="form1" runat="server">
    <div>

    <asp:Menu
        id="menuTabs"
        CssClass="menuTabs"
        StaticMenuItemStyle-CssClass="tab"
        StaticSelectedStyle-CssClass="selectedTab"
        Orientation="Horizontal"
        OnMenuItemClick="menuTabs_MenuItemClick"
        Runat="server">
        <Items>
        <asp:MenuItem
            Text="Tab 1"
            Value="0"
            Selected="true" />
        <asp:MenuItem
            Text="Tab 2"
            Value="1"/>
        <asp:MenuItem
            Text="Tab 3"
            Value="2" />

        </Items>
    </asp:Menu>

    <div class="tabBody">
    <asp:MultiView
        id="multiTabs"
        ActiveViewIndex="0"
        Runat="server">
```

CHAPTER 3

```
        <asp:View ID="view1" runat="server">

         Contents of first tab

         </asp:View>
        <asp:View ID="view2" runat="server">

         Contents of second tab

         </asp:View>
        <asp:View ID="view3" runat="server">

         Contents of third tab

         </asp:View>
    </asp:MultiView>
    </div>

    </div>
    </form>
</body>
</html>
```

MenuTabStrip.aspx

After you open the page in above listing and click a tab, the `MenuItemClick` event is raised. The `MenuItemClick` event handler changes the `ActiveViewIndex` property of the `MultiView` control to display the content of the selected tab.

Binding to a Site Map

Like the `SiteMapPath` control, you can use the `Menu` control with a Site Map. Users can click menu items to navigate to particular pages in your website. Unlike the `SiteMapPath` control, however, the `Menu` control does not automatically bind to a Site Map. You must explicitly bind the `Menu` control to a `SiteMapDataSource` control to display nodes from a Site Map.

For example, the page in next listing contains a menu that contains links to all the pages in a website.

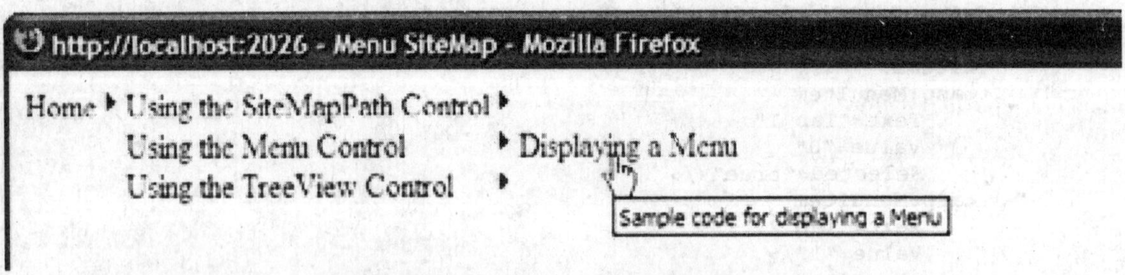

Displaying a Site Map with a Menu control.

```
<%@ Page Language="C#" %>
<!DOCTYPE html PUBLIC "-//W3C//DTD XHTML 1.1//EN"
  "http://www.w3.org/TR/xhtml11/DTD/xhtml11.dtd">
<html xmlns="http://www.w3.org/1999/xhtml" >
<head id="Head1" runat="server">
    <title>Menu SiteMap</title>
</head>
<body>
    <form id="form1" runat="server">
    <div>
```

```
    <asp:Menu
        id="Menu1"
        DataSourceID="srcSiteMap"
        Runat="server" />

    <asp:SiteMapDataSource
        id="srcSiteMap"
        Runat="server" />

    </div>
    </form>
</body>
</html>
```

listing UsingMenu/MenuSiteMap.aspx

When you initially open the page in above listing, the only menu item that appears is the link to the Home page. If you hover your mouse over this link, links to additional pages display. Normally, you do not want the Home link to display in a navigation menu. Instead, you want to display the second level of menu items. You can use the `ShowStartingNode` property of the `SiteMapDataSource` control to hide the topmost node in a Site Map.

For example, the page in next listing uses a `Menu` control that renders a standard left-column navigational menu.

Displaying a navigation menu.

```
Code View: Scroll / Show All
<%@ Page Language="C#" %>
<!DOCTYPE html PUBLIC "-//W3C//DTD XHTML 1.1//EN"
  "http://www.w3.org/TR/xhtml11/DTD/xhtml11.dtd">
<html xmlns="http://www.w3.org/1999/xhtml" >
<head id="Head1" runat="server">
    <style type="text/css">
        html
        {
            background-color:silver;
        }
        .navigation
        {
            float:left;
            width:280px;
            height:500px;
            padding:20px;
            background-color:#eeeeee;
        }
```

```
        .content
        {
            float:left;
            width:550px;
            height:500px;
            padding:20px;
            background-color:white;
        }
        .menuItem
        {
            border:Outset 1px black;
            background-color:Gray;
            font:14px Arial;
            color:White;
            padding:8px;
        }
    </style>
    <title>Menu Navigate</title>
</head>
<body>
    <form id="form1" runat="server">

    <div class="navigation">

    <asp:Menu
        id="Menu1"
        DataSourceID="srcSiteMap"
        StaticMenuItemStyle-CssClass="menuItem"
        DynamicMenuItemStyle-CssClass="menuItem"
        Runat="server" />

    <asp:SiteMapDataSource
        id="srcSiteMap"
        ShowStartingNode="false"
        Runat="server" />

    </div>

    <div class="content">

    <h1>Displaying a Website menu with the Menu control</h1>

    </div>

    </form>
</body>
</html>
```

UsingMenu/MenuNavigate.aspx

When you open the page in above listing, the second-level nodes from the Site Map initially display. Furthermore, the Menu control is styled to appear more like a traditional website navigation menu.

Binding to an XML File

As an alternative to binding a Menu control to a SiteMapDataSource control, you can bind the control to an XML document by using the XmlDataSource control. For example, suppose that you have the XML file in next listing.

```
<?xml version="1.0" encoding="utf-8" ?>
<menu>
  <appetizer>
    <soup />
    <cheese />
  </appetizer>
  <entree>
    <duck />
    <chicken />
  </entree>
  <dessert>
    <cake />
    <pie />
  </dessert>
</menu>
```

Menu.xml

The page in next listing displays the contents of above listing by using an `XmlDataSource` control to represent the XML document.

```
Code View: Scroll / Show All
<%@ Page Language="C#" %>
<!DOCTYPE html PUBLIC "-//W3C//DTD XHTML 1.1//EN"
  "http://www.w3.org/TR/xhtml11/DTD/xhtml11.dtd">
<html xmlns="http://www.w3.org/1999/xhtml" >
<head id="Head1" runat="server">
    <title>Menu XML</title>
</head>
<body>
    <form id="form1" runat="server">
    <div>

    <asp:Menu
         id="Menu1"
        DataSourceID="srcMenu"
        Runat="server" />

    <asp:XmlDataSource
         id="srcMenu"
        DataFile="Menu.xml"
        Runat="server" />

    </div>
    </form>
</body>
</html>
```

MenuXML.aspx

When using the `XmlDataSource` control, you can use the `XPath` property to supply an `xpath` query that restricts the nodes returned by the `XmlDataSource`. You also can use either the `Transform` or `TransformFile` property to apply an XSLT Style Sheet to the XML document and transform the nodes returned by the `XmlDataSource`.

The XML file in above listing is simple. The nodes do not contain any attributes. When you bind the `Menu` control to the XML file, the `ToString()` method is called on each XML file node.

You also can bind the Menu control to more complex XML documents. For example, the item nodes in the XML document in next listing include two attributes: text and price.

```
<?xml version="1.0" encoding="utf-8" ?>
<menu>
  <category text="appetizer">
    <item text="soup" price="12.56" />
    <item text="cheese" price="17.23" />
  </category>
  <category text="entree">
    <item text="duck" price="89.21" />
    <item text="chicken" price="34.56" />
  </category>
  <category text="dessert">
    <item text="cake" price="23.43" />
    <item text="pie" price="115.46" />
  </category>
</menu>
```

listing MenuComplex.xml

When you bind to the XML document in above listing, you must specify one or more menu item bindings. The menu item bindings specify the relationship between node attributes and the menu items displayed by the `Menu` control. The `Menu` control in next listing includes `MenuItemBinding` subtags.

Displaying an XML document with the Menu control.

```
Code View: Scroll / Show All
<%@ Page Language="C#" %>
<!DOCTYPE html PUBLIC "-//W3C//DTD XHTML 1.1//EN"
  "http://www.w3.org/TR/xhtml11/DTD/xhtml11.dtd">
<html xmlns="http://www.w3.org/1999/xhtml" >
<head id="Head1" runat="server">
    <title>Menu XML Complex</title>
</head>
<body>
    <form id="form1" runat="server">
     <div>

     <asp:Menu
          id="Menu1"
         DataSourceID="srcMenu"
         Runat="server">
         <DataBindings>
         <asp:MenuItemBinding
              DataMember="category"
              TextField="text" />
         <asp:MenuItemBinding
              DataMember="item"
              TextField="text"
```

```
            ValueField="price" />
        </DataBindings>
    </asp:Menu>

    <asp:XmlDataSource
        id="srcMenu"
        DataFile="MenuComplex.xml"
        Runat="server" />

    </div>
    </form>
</body>
</html>
```

MenuXMLComplex.aspx

The Menu control includes a `<DataBindings>` element. This element includes two `MenuItemBinding` subtags. The first subtag represents the relationship between the category nodes in the XML file and the menu items. The second subtag represents the relationship between the item nodes in the XML file and the menu items.

Binding to Database Data

You can't bind a `Menu` control directly to database data. Neither the `SqlDataSource` nor `ObjectDataSource` controls implement the `IHierachicalDataSource` interface. Therefore, if you want to represent database data with the `Menu` control, you need to perform some more work.

One option is to create your own `SqlHiearachicalDataSource` control. You can do this either by deriving from the base `HiearchicalDataSourceControl` class or implementing the `IHiearchicalDataSource` interface. You take this approach in the final section of this chapter, when a custom `SqlHierarchicalDataSource` control is built.

A second option is to build the menu items programmatically in the `Menu` control. This is the approach followed here. Imagine that you want to represent the contents of the following database table with a `Menu` control:

CategoryId	ParentId	Name
1	null	Beverages
2	null	Fruit
3	1	Milk
4	1	Juice
5	4	Apple Juice
6	4	Orange Juice
7	2	Apples
8	2	Pears

This database table represents product categories. The categories are nested with the help of the ParentId column. For example, the Orange Juice category is nested below the Juice category, and the Juice category is nested below the Beverages category. The page in next listing illustrates how you can display this database table with a `Menu` control.

```
Code View: Scroll / Show All
<%@ Page Language="C#" %>
<%@ Import Namespace="System.Web.Configuration" %>
<%@ Import Namespace="System.Data" %>
```

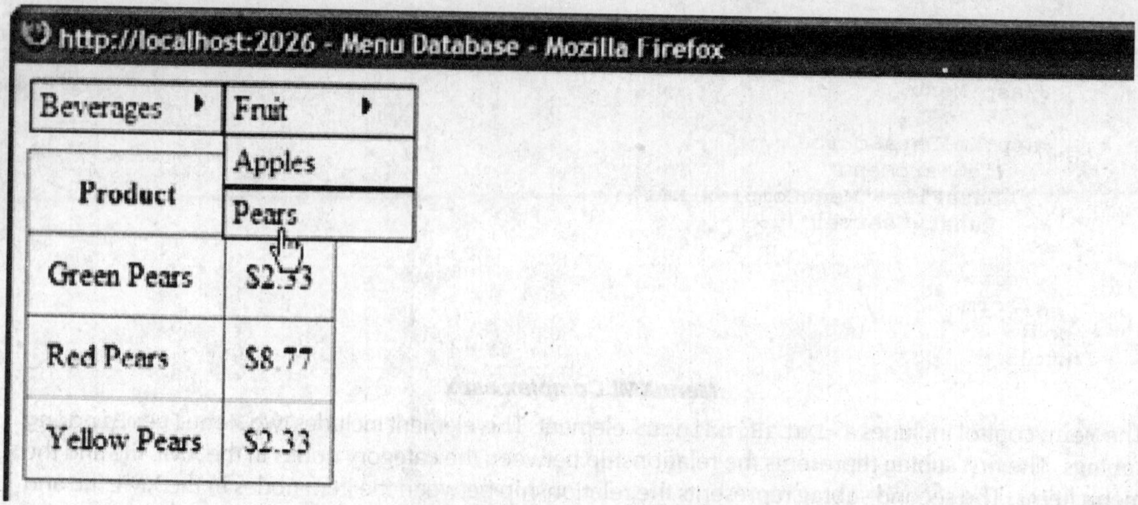

Displaying database data with the Menu control.

```
<%@ Import Namespace="System.Data.SqlClient" %>
<!DOCTYPE html PUBLIC "-//W3C//DTD XHTML 1.1//EN"
"http://www.w3.org/TR/xhtml11/DTD/xhtml11.dtd">
<script runat="server">
    /// <summary>
    /// Only populate the menu when the page first loads
    /// </summary>
    void Page_Load()
    {
        if (!Page.IsPostBack)
            PopulateMenu();
    }

    /// <summary>
    /// Get the data from the database and create the top-level
    /// menu items
    /// </summary>
    private void PopulateMenu()
    {
        DataTable menuData = GetMenuData();
        AddTopMenuItems(menuData);
    }

    /// <summary>
    /// Use a DataAdapter and DataTable to grab the database data
    /// </summary>
    /// <returns></returns>
    private DataTable GetMenuData()
    {
        // Get Categories table
        string selectCommand = "SELECT CategoryId,ParentId,Name FROM
Categories";
        string conString =
WebConfigurationManager.ConnectionStrings["Categories"].ConnectionString;
        SqlDataAdapter dad = new SqlDataAdapter(selectCommand, conString);
        DataTable dtblCategories = new DataTable();
```

```
        dad.Fill(dtblCategories);
        return dtblCategories;
    }

    /// <summary>
    /// Filter the data to get only the rows that have a
    /// null ParentID (these are the top-level menu items)
    /// </summary>
    private void AddTopMenuItems(DataTable menuData)
    {
        DataView view = new DataView(menuData);
        view.RowFilter = "ParentID IS NULL";
        foreach (DataRowView row in view)
        {
            MenuItem newMenuItem = new MenuItem(row["Name"].ToString(),
row["CategoryId"].ToString());
            Menu1.Items.Add(newMenuItem);
            AddChildMenuItems(menuData, newMenuItem);
        }

    }

    /// <summary>
    /// Recursively add child menu items by filtering by ParentID
    /// </summary>
    private void AddChildMenuItems(DataTable menuData, MenuItem
parentMenuItem)
    {
        DataView view = new DataView(menuData);
        view.RowFilter = "ParentID=" + parentMenuItem.Value;
        foreach (DataRowView row in view)
        {
            MenuItem newMenuItem = new MenuItem(row["Name"].ToString(),
row["CategoryId"].ToString());
            parentMenuItem.ChildItems.Add(newMenuItem);
            AddChildMenuItems(menuData, newMenuItem);
        }
    }

</script>
<html xmlns="http://www.w3.org/1999/xhtml" >
<head id="Head1" runat="server">
    <style type="text/css">
        .menuItem
        {
            border:Solid 1px black;
            width:100px;
            padding:2px;
            background-color:#eeeeee;
        }
        .menuItem a
        {
            color:blue;
        }
        .grid
        {
            margin-top:10px;
```

```
        }

        .grid td, .grid th
        {
            padding:10px;
        }
    </style>
    <title>Menu Database</title>
</head>
<body>
    <form id="form1" runat="server">
    <div>

    <asp:Menu
        id="Menu1"
        Orientation="horizontal"
        StaticMenuItemStyle-CssClass="menuItem"
        DynamicMenuItemStyle-CssClass="menuItem"
        Runat="server" />

    <asp:GridView
        id="grdProducts"
        DataSourceID="srcProducts"
        CssClass="grid"
        AutoGenerateColumns="false"
        Runat="server">
        <Columns>
        <asp:BoundField
            DataField="ProductName"
            HeaderText="Product" />
        <asp:BoundField
            DataField="Price"
            HeaderText="Price"
            DataFormatString="{0:c}" />
        </Columns>
    </asp:GridView>

    <asp:SqlDataSource
        id="srcProducts"
        ConnectionString="<%$ ConnectionStrings:Categories %>"
        SelectCommand="SELECT ProductName,Price FROM Products
            WHERE CategoryId=@CategoryId"
        Runat="server">
        <SelectParameters>
        <asp:ControlParameter
            Name="CategoryId"
            ControlID="Menu1" />
        </SelectParameters>
    </asp:SqlDataSource>


    </div>
    </form>
</body>
</html>
```

MenuDatabase.aspx

The menu items are added to the `Menu` control in the `PopulateMenu()` method. This method first grabs a DataTable that contains the contents of the Categories database table. Next, it creates a menu item for each row that does not have a parent row (each row where the ParentId column has the value `null`). The child menu items for each menu item are added recursively. The ParentId column is used to filter the contents of the Categories DataTable.

The page in above listing also includes a `GridView` control that displays a list of products that match the category selected in the menu. `GridView` is bound to a `SqlDataSource` control, which includes a `ControlParameter` that filters the products based on the selected menu item.

Formatting the Menu Control

The `Menu` control supports an abundance of properties that can be used to format the appearance of the control. Many of these properties have an effect on static menu items, and many of these properties have an effect on dynamic menu items. Static menu items are menu items that always appear. Dynamic menu items are menu items that appear only when you hover your mouse over another menu item.

First, the `Menu` control supports the following general properties related to formatting:

- `DisappearAfter`— Enables you to specify the amount of time, in milliseconds, that a dynamic menu item is displayed after a user moves the mouse away from the menu item.
- `DynamicBottomSeparatorImageUrl`— Enables you to specify the URL to an image that appears under each dynamic menu item.
- `DynamicEnableDefaultPopOutImage`— Enables you to disable the image (triangle) that indicates that a dynamic menu item has child menu items.
- `DynamicHorizontalOffset`— Enables you to specify the number of pixels that a dynamic menu item is shifted relative to its parent menu item.
- `DynamicItemFormatString`— Enables you to format the text displayed in a dynamic menu item.
- `DynamicPopOutImageTextFormatString`— Enables you to format the alt text displayed for the popout image.
- `DynamicPopOutImageUrl`— Enables you to specify the URL for the dynamic popout image. (By default, a triangle is displayed.)
- `DynamicTopSeparatorImageUrl`— Enables you to specify the URL to an image that appears above each dynamic menu item.
- `DynamicVerticalOffset`— Enables you to specify the number of pixels that a dynamic menu item is shifted relative to its parent menu item.
- `ItemWrap`— Enables you to specify whether the text in menu items should wrap.
- `MaximumDynamicDisplayLevels`— Enables you to specify the maximum number of levels of dynamic menu items to display.
- `Orientation`— Enables you to display a menu horizontally or vertically. (The default value is Vertical.)
- `ScollDownImageUrl`— Enables you to specify the URL to an image that is displayed and that enables you to scroll down through menu items.
- `ScrollDownText`— Enables you to specify alt text for the ScrollDown image.
- `ScrollUpImageUrl`— Enables you to specify the URL to an image that is displayed and that enables you to scroll up through menu items.

- `ScrollUpText`— Enables you to specify alt text for the ScrollUp image.
- `SkipLinkText`— Enables you to modify the text displayed by the skip link. (The skip link enables blind users to skip past the contents of a menu.)
- `StaticBottomSeparatorImageUrl`— Enables you to specify the URL to an image that appears below each static menu item.
- `StaticDisplayLevels`— Enables you to specify the number of static levels of menu items to display.
- `StaticEnableDefaultPopOutImage`— Enables you to disable the default popout image that indicates that a menu item has child menu items.
- `StaticItemFormatString`— Enables you to format the text displayed in each static menu item.
- `StaticImagePopOutFormatString`— Enables you to specify the alt text displayed by the popout image.
- `StaticPopOutImageUrl`— Enables you to specify the URL for the popout image.
- `StaticSubMenuIndent`— Enables you to specify the number of pixels that a static menu item is indented relative to its parent menu item.
- `StaticTopSeparatorImageUrl`— Enables you to specify the URL to an image that appears above each static menu item.
- `Target`— Enables you to specify the window in which a new page opens when you click a menu item.

This list includes several interesting properties. For example, you can specify images for scrolling up and down through a list of menu items. These images appear when you constrain the height of either the static or dynamic menu.

The `Menu` control also exposes several Style objects. You can use these Style objects as hooks to which you can attach Cascading Style Sheet (CSS) classes:

- `DynamicHoverStyle`— Style applied to a dynamic menu item when you hover your mouse over it.
- `DynamicMenuItemStyle`— Style applied to each dynamic menu item.
- `DynamicMenuStyle`— Style applied to the container tag for the dynamic menu.
- `DynamicSelectedStyle`— Style applied to the selected dynamic menu item.
- `StaticHoverStyle`— Style applied to a static menu item when you hover your mouse over it.
- `StaticMenuItemStyle`— Style applied to each static menu item.
- `StaticMenuStyle`— Style applied to the container tag for the static menu.
- `StaticSelectedStyle`— Style applied to the selected static menu item.

Furthermore, you can apply styles to menu items based on their level in the menu. For example, you might want the font size to get progressively smaller depending on how deeply nested a menu item is within a menu. You can use three properties of the `Menu` control to format menu items, depending on their level:

- `LevelMenuItemStyles`— Contains a çollection of `MenuItemStyle` controls, which correspond to different menu levels

Applying styles to different menu levels.

- `LevelSelectedStyles`— Contains a collection of `MenuItemStyle` controls, which correspond to different menu levels of selected menu items
- `LevelSubMenuStyles`— Contains a collection of `MenuItemStyle` controls, which correspond to different menu levels of static menu items

For example, the page in next listing illustrates how you can apply different formatting to menu items that appear at different menu levels.

Code View: Scroll / Show All

```
<%@ Page Language="C#" %>
<!DOCTYPE html PUBLIC "-//W3C//DTD XHTML 1.1//EN"
 "http://www.w3.org/TR/xhtml11/DTD/xhtml11.dtd">
<html xmlns="http://www.w3.org/1999/xhtml" >
<head id="Head1" runat="server">
    <style type="text/css">
        .menuLevel1
        {
            font:40px Arial,Sans-Serif;
        }
        .menuLevel2
        {
            font:20px Arial,Sans-Serif;
        }
        .menuLevel3
        {
            font:10px Arial,Sans-Serif;
        }
    </style>
    <title>Menu Level Styles</title>
</head>
<body>
    <form id="form1" runat="server">
    <div>

    <asp:Menu
        id="Menu1"
        Runat="server">
        <LevelMenuItemStyles>
            <asp:MenuItemStyle CssClass="menuLevel1" />
            <asp:MenuItemStyle CssClass="menuLevel2" />
            <asp:MenuItemStyle CssClass="menuLevel3" />
        </LevelMenuItemStyles>
        <Items>
```

```
        <asp:MenuItem Text="Produce">
            <asp:MenuItem Text="Apples" />
            <asp:MenuItem Text="Oranges" />
        </asp:MenuItem>
        <asp:MenuItem Text="Beverages">
            <asp:MenuItem Text="Soda">
                <asp:MenuItem Text="Coke" />
                <asp:MenuItem Text="Pepsi" />
            </asp:MenuItem>
        </asp:MenuItem>
        </Items>
    </asp:Menu>

    </div>
    </form>
</body>
</html>
```

MenuLevelStyles.aspx

The `MenuItemStyle` controls are applied to the menu level that corresponds to their order of declaration. The first `MenuItemStyle` is applied to the first menu level, the second `MenuItemStyle` is applied to the second menu level, and so on. Finally, the `MenuItem` class itself includes several useful formatting properties:

- `ImageUrl`— Enables you to specify the URL for an image that is displayed next to a menu item.
- `PopOutImageUrl`— Enables you to specify the URL for an image that is displayed when a menu item contains child menu items.
- `SeparatorImageUrl`— Enables you to specify the URL for an image that appears below a menu item.
- `Selectable`— Enables you to prevent users from selecting (clicking) a menu item.
- `Selected`— Enables you to specify whether a menu item is selected.
- `Target`— Enables you to specify the name of the window that opens when you click a menu item.

For example, the page in next listing displays a menu that resembles a traditional desktop application menu.

Displaying a desktop application menu.

Code View: Scroll / Show All

```
<%@ Page Language="C#" %>
<!DOCTYPE html PUBLIC "-//W3C//DTD XHTML 1.1//EN"
  "http://www.w3.org/TR/xhtml11/DTD/xhtml11.dtd">
<html xmlns="http://www.w3.org/1999/xhtml" >
<head id="Head1" runat="server">
    <style type="text/css">
        .staticMenuItem
        {
            color:black;
            border:solid 1px black;
            padding:2px 4px;
        }
        .menuHover
        {
            color:white;
            background-color:blue;
        }
        .dynamicMenuItem
        {
            color:black;
            padding:2px 4px;
        }
        .dynamicMenu
        {
            border:Solid 1px black;
           filter:progid:DXImageTransform.Microsoft.dropshadow(OffX=5,
OffY=5,
 Color='gray', Positive='true')"
        }
    </style>
    <title>Menu Desktop</title>
</head>
<body>
    <form id="form1" runat="server">
    <div>

    <asp:Menu
        id="Menu1"
        Orientation="Horizontal"
        StaticMenuItemStyle-CssClass="staticMenuItem"
        StaticHoverStyle-CssClass="menuHover"
        DynamicHoverStyle-CssClass="menuHover"
        DynamicMenuItemStyle-CssClass="dynamicMenuItem"
        DynamicMenuStyle-CssClass="dynamicMenu"
        Runat="server">
        <Items>
        <asp:MenuItem
            Text="File"
            Selectable="false">
            <asp:MenuItem
                Text="Save" />
            <asp:MenuItem
                Text="Open" />
        </asp:MenuItem>
        <asp:MenuItem
            Text="Format"
            Selectable="false">
```

```
            <asp:MenuItem
                Text="Bold"
                ImageUrl="Images/Bold.gif" />
            <asp:MenuItem
                Text="Italic"
                ImageUrl="Images/Italic.gif" />
            <asp:MenuItem
                Text="Underline"
                ImageUrl="Images/Underline.gif"
                SeparatorImageUrl="Images/Divider.gif" />
            <asp:MenuItem
                Text="Left Align"
                ImageUrl="Images/JustifyLeft.gif" />
            <asp:MenuItem
                Text="Center Align"
                ImageUrl="Images/JustifyCenter.gif" />
            <asp:MenuItem
                Text="Right Align"
                ImageUrl="Images/JustifyRight.gif" />
        </asp:MenuItem>
        </Items>
    </asp:Menu>

    </div>
    </form>
</body>
</html>
```

MenuDesktop.aspx

Using Templates with the Menu Control

The Menu control supports templates. You can use templates to completely customize the appearance of the Menu control.

The Menu control supports the following two templates:

- DynamicItemTemplate— Applied to dynamic menu items.
- StaticItemTemplate— Applied to static menu items.

The page in next listing uses both templates to display menu items. The templates display a count of child items for each menu item.

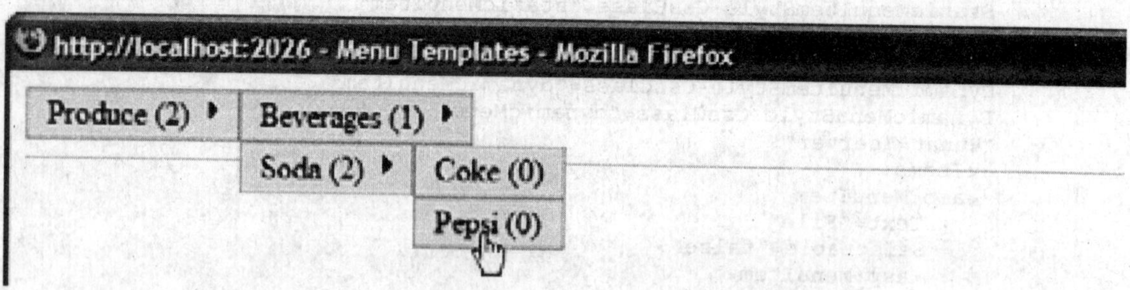

Using templates with the Menu control.

```
Code View: Scroll / Show All
<%@ Page Language="C#" %>
<!DOCTYPE html PUBLIC "-//W3C//DTD XHTML 1.1//EN"
"http://www.w3.org/TR/xhtml11/DTD/xhtml11.dtd">
```

```
<script runat="server">

    protected void Menu1_MenuItemClick(object sender, MenuEventArgs e)
    {
        lblMessage.Text = Menu1.SelectedValue;
    }
</script>
<html xmlns="http://www.w3.org/1999/xhtml" >
<head id="Head1" runat="server">
    <style type="text/css">
        .menuItem
        {
            color:black;
            border:Solid 1px Gray;
            background-color:#c9c9c9;
            padding:2px 5px;
        }
    </style>
    <title>Menu Templates</title>
</head>
<body>
    <form id="form1" runat="server">
    <div>

    <asp:Menu
        id="Menu1"
        OnMenuItemClick="Menu1_MenuItemClick"
        Orientation="Horizontal"
        StaticMenuItemStyle-CssClass="menuItem"
        DynamicMenuItemStyle-CssClass="menuItem"
        Runat="server">
        <StaticItemTemplate>
        <%# Eval("Text") %>
        (<%# Eval("ChildItems.Count") %>)
        </StaticItemTemplate>
        <DynamicItemTemplate>
        <%# Eval("Text") %>
        (<%# Eval("ChildItems.Count") %>)
        </DynamicItemTemplate>
        <Items>
        <asp:MenuItem Text="Produce">
            <asp:MenuItem Text="Apples" />
            <asp:MenuItem Text="Oranges" />
        </asp:MenuItem>
        <asp:MenuItem Text="Beverages">
            <asp:MenuItem Text="Soda">
                <asp:MenuItem Text="Coke" />
                <asp:MenuItem Text="Pepsi" />
            </asp:MenuItem>
        </asp:MenuItem>
        </Items>
    </asp:Menu>

    <hr />

    <asp:Label
        id="lblMessage"
        EnableViewState="false"
```

```
        Runat="server" />

      </div>
      </form>
  </body>
  </html>
```

MenuTemplates.aspx

You do not need to create `LinkButton` controls in the templates. The content of the template is wrapped in a link automatically when it is appropriate.

Using the TreeView Control

The `TreeView` control is similar to the `Menu` control. Like the `Menu` control, you can use the `TreeView` control to display hierarchical data. The `TreeView` control binds to any data source that implements the `IHierarchicalDataSource` or `IHiearchicalEnumerable` interface.

In this section, you learn how to add items declaratively to the `TreeView` control. You also learn how to bind a `TreeView` control to hierarchical data sources such as the `SiteMapDataSource` and `XmlDataSource` controls. You also see how you can use the `TreeView` control with database data. A `TreeView` is built programmatically from database data.

Finally, you learn how you can use AJAX with the `TreeView` control to display large sets of data efficiently. By taking advantage of AJAX, you can update a `TreeView` without posting a page back to the server.

Declaratively Adding Tree Nodes

A `TreeView` control is made up of `TreeNode` objects. You can build a `TreeView` control by declaring `TreeNode` objects in the `TreeView` control's Items collection. For example, next listing contains a `TreeView` which renders a nested set of links to pages.

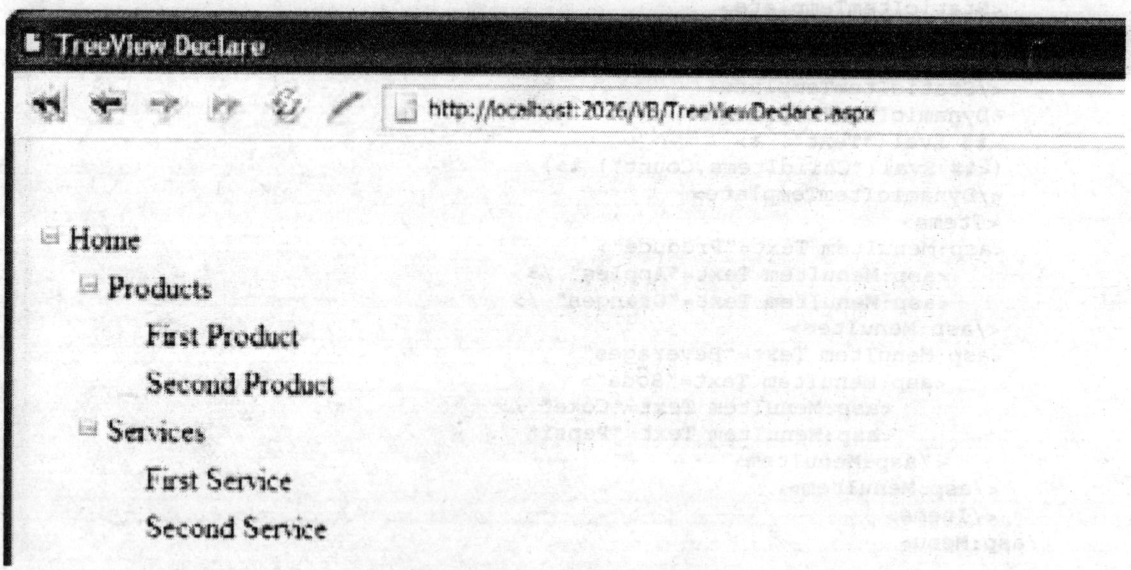

Displaying a TreeView control.

```
Code View: Scroll / Show All
<%@ Page Language="C#" %>
<!DOCTYPE html PUBLIC "-//W3C//DTD XHTML 1.1//EN"
```

```
"http://www.w3.org/TR/xhtml11/DTD/xhtml11.dtd">
<html xmlns="http://www.w3.org/1999/xhtml" >
<head id="Head1" runat="server">
   <title>TreeView Declare</title>
</head>
<body>
   <form id="form1" runat="server">
   <div>

   <asp:TreeView
       id="TreeView1"
       Runat="server">
       <Nodes>
       <asp:TreeNode
           Text="Home"
          NavigateUrl="~/Default.aspx">
           <asp:TreeNode
               Text="Products">
               <asp:TreeNode
                   Text="First Product"
                  NavigateUrl="~/Products/FirstProduct.aspx" />
               <asp:TreeNode
                   Text="Second Product"
                  NavigateUrl="~/Products/SecondProduct.aspx" />
           </asp:TreeNode>
           <asp:TreeNode
               Text="Services">
               <asp:TreeNode
                   Text="First Service"
                  NavigateUrl="~/Services/FirstService.aspx" />
               <asp:TreeNode
                   Text="Second Service"
                  NavigateUrl="~/Services/SecondService.aspx" />
           </asp:TreeNode>
       </asp:TreeNode>
       </Nodes>
   </asp:TreeView>


   </div>
   </form>
</body>
</html>
```

listing TreeViewDeclare.aspx

Some of the `TreeNodes` in above listing include a `Text` property, and some of the `TreeNodes` include both a `Text` and `NavigateUrl` property. You can click the `TreeNodes` that include a `NavigateUrl` property to link to a new page.

You also can associate a `Value` property with a `TreeNode`. This is useful when you want to post back to the same page. For example, the page in next listing enables you to display the value of the selected `TreeNode` in a Label control.

```
Code View: Scroll / Show All
<%@ Page Language="C#" %>
<!DOCTYPE html PUBLIC "-//W3C//DTD XHTML 1.1//EN"
"http://www.w3.org/TR/xhtml11/DTD/xhtml11.dtd">
```

```
<script runat="server">

   protected void TreeView1_SelectedNodeChanged(object sender, EventArgs e)
   {
      lblMessage.Text = TreeView1.SelectedValue;
   }
</script>
<html xmlns="http://www.w3.org/1999/xhtml" >
<head id="Head1" runat="server">
   <style type="text/css">
       html
       {
          background-color:silver;
       }
       .content
       {
          float:left;
          width:350px;
          height:500px;
          padding:20px;
          margin:10px;
          background-color:white;
       }
   </style>
   <title>TreeView Value</title>
</head>
<body>
   <form id="form1" runat="server">

   <div class="content">
   <asp:TreeView
       id="TreeView1"
     OnSelectedNodeChanged="TreeView1_SelectedNodeChanged"
       Runat="server" >
       <Nodes>
       <asp:TreeNode
          Text="Home"
          Value="Home">
          <asp:TreeNode
              Text="Products">
              <asp:TreeNode
                 Text="First Product"
                 Value="FirstProduct" />
              <asp:TreeNode
                 Text="Second Product"
                 Value="SecondProduct" />
          </asp:TreeNode>
          <asp:TreeNode
              Text="Services">
              <asp:TreeNode
                 Text="First Service"
                 Value="FirstService" />
              <asp:TreeNode
                 Text="Second Service"
                 Value="SecondService" />
          </asp:TreeNode>
       </asp:TreeNode>
       </Nodes>
```

```
        </asp:TreeView>
        </div>

        <div class="content">
        You selected:
        <asp:Label
            id="lblMessage"
            EnableViewState="false"
            Runat="server" />
        </div>

        </form>
    </body>
    </html>
```

TreeViewValue.aspx

The page in above listing includes a `SelectedNodeChanged` event handler. When you select a new node, the `SelectedNodeChanged` event handler displays the value of the selected `TreeNode` in a Label control.

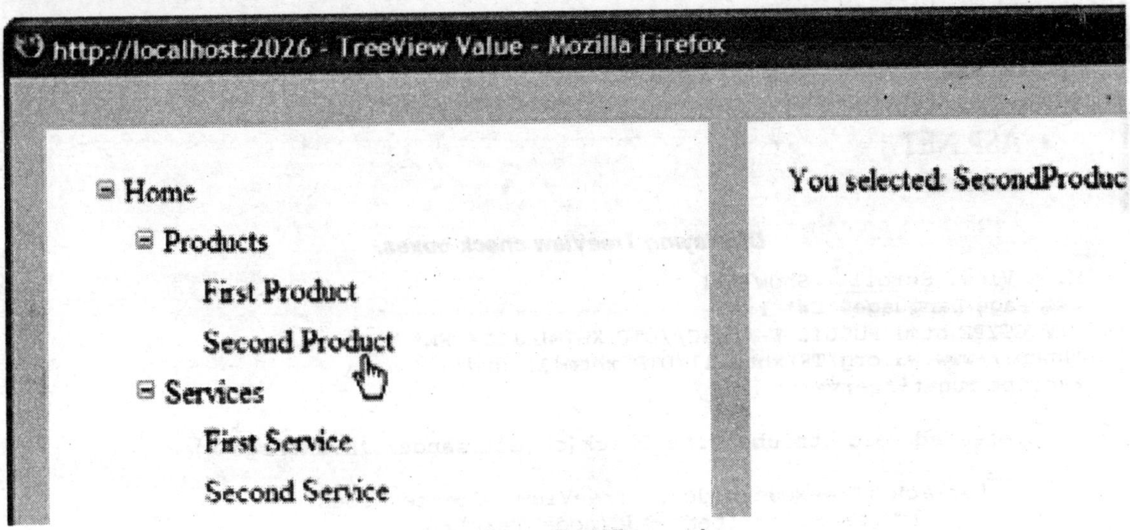

Selecting a TreeView node.

Displaying Check Boxes with the TreeView Control

You can display check boxes next to each node in a `TreeView` control by assigning a value to the `ShowCheckBoxes` property. This property accepts the following values:

- `All`
- `Leaf`
- `None`
- `Parent`
- `Root`

You can use a bitwise combination of these values when specifying the nodes to display with check boxes.

The page in next listing illustrates the `ShowCheckBoxes` property.

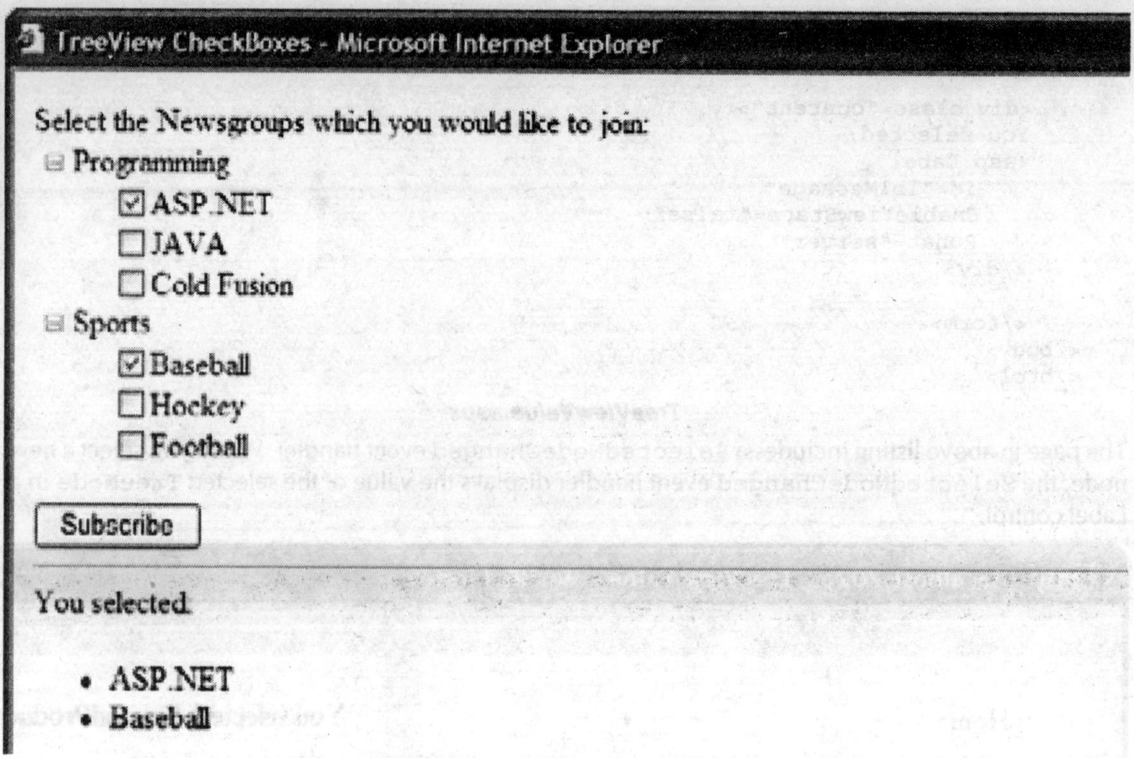

Displaying TreeView check boxes.

Code View: Scroll / Show All

```
<%@ Page Language="C#" %>
<!DOCTYPE html PUBLIC "-//W3C//DTD XHTML 1.1//EN"
"http://www.w3.org/TR/xhtml11/DTD/xhtml11.dtd">
<script runat="server">

    protected void btnSubscribe_Click(object sender, EventArgs e)
     {
        foreach (TreeNode node in TreeView1.CheckedNodes)
            bltSubscribed.Items.Add(node.Text);
     }
</script>
<html xmlns="http://www.w3.org/1999/xhtml" >
<head id="Head1" runat="server">
    <title>TreeView CheckBoxes</title>
</head>
<body>
    <form id="form1" runat="server">
     <div>

    Select the Newsgroups which you
    would like to join:

     <br />

     <asp:TreeView
         id="TreeView1"
         ShowCheckBoxes="Leaf"
```

```
        Runat="server">
        <Nodes>
        <asp:TreeNode
            Text="Programming">
            <asp:TreeNode Text="ASP.NET" />
            <asp:TreeNode Text="JAVA" />
            <asp:TreeNode Text="Cold Fusion" />
        </asp:TreeNode>
        <asp:TreeNode
            Text="Sports">
            <asp:TreeNode Text="Baseball" />
            <asp:TreeNode Text="Hockey" />
            <asp:TreeNode Text="Football" />
        </asp:TreeNode>
        </Nodes>
    </asp:TreeView>

    <br />

    <asp:Button
        id="btnSubscribe"
        Text="Subscribe"
        OnClick="btnSubscribe_Click"
        Runat="server" />

    <hr />

    You selected:

    <asp:BulletedList
        id="bltSubscribed"
        EnableViewState="false"
        Runat="server" />

    </div>
    </form>
</body>
</html>
```

TreeViewCheckBoxes.aspx

The page in above listing displays nested newsgroups. You can subscribe to the newsgroups by clicking the Subscribe button. When you click the Subscribe button, the `CheckedNodes` property returns a list of all the checked `TreeNodes`. This list displays in a `BulletedList` control.

Binding to a Site Map

You can use a `TreeView` control as a navigation element in your pages by binding the `TreeView` to a Site Map. The page in next listing demonstrates how you can bind a `TreeView` to a `SiteMapDataSource` control.

```
<%@ Page Language="C#" %>
<!DOCTYPE html PUBLIC "-//W3C//DTD XHTML 1.1//EN"
 "http://www.w3.org/TR/xhtml11/DTD/xhtml11.dtd">
<html xmlns="http://www.w3.org/1999/xhtml" >
<head id="Head1" runat="server">
    <title>TreeView Site Map</title>
</head>
<body>
```

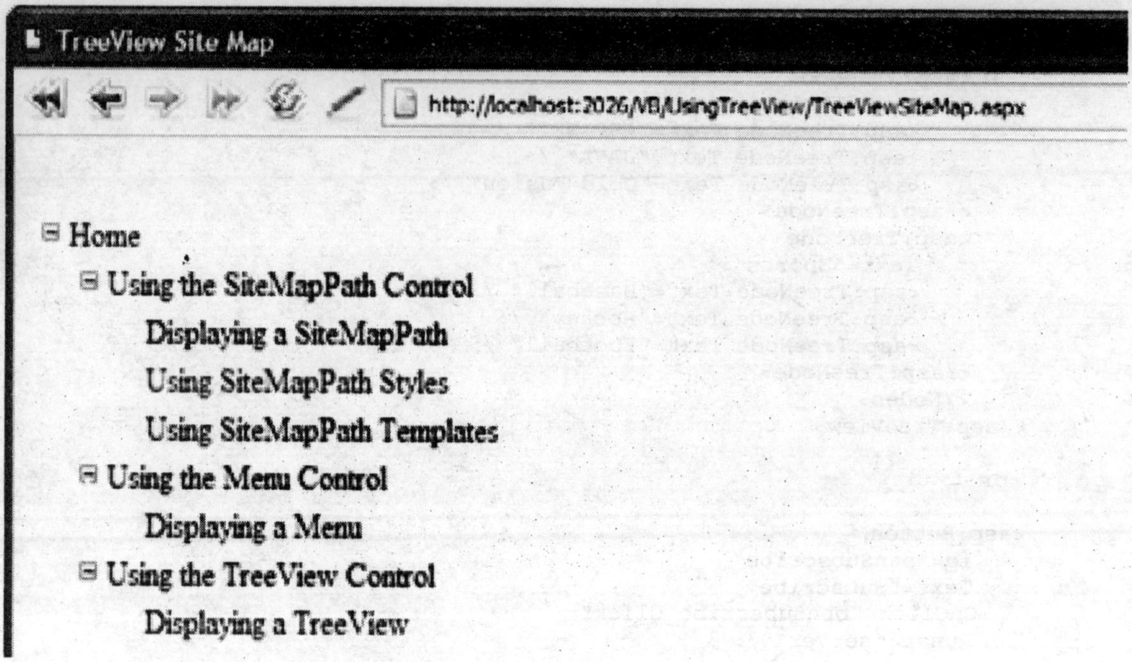

Displaying a Site Map with a TreeView control.

```
      <form id="form1" runat="server">
      <div>

      <asp:TreeView
          id="TreeView1"
          DataSourceID="srcSiteMap"
          Runat="server" />

      <asp:SiteMapDataSource
          id="srcSiteMap"
          Runat="server" />

      </div>
      </form>
  </body>
  </html>
```

UsingTreeView/TreeViewSiteMap.aspx

When you open the page in above listing, all the nodes from the Site Map display automatically in the `TreeView` control. By default, the `SiteMapDataSource` uses the `XmlSiteMapProvider`, which represents a file named `Web.sitemap` located at the root of an application.

Binding to an XML File

Because an `XmlDataSource` control returns hierarchical data, you can bind a `TreeView` directly to an `XmlDataSource`. For example, imagine that you need to display the XML document contained in next listing.

```
<?xml version="1.0" encoding="utf-8" ?>
<movies>
  <action>
```

```
      <StarWars />
      <IndependenceDay />
    </action>
    <horror>
      <Jaws />
      <NightmareBeforeChristmas />
    </horror>
  </movies>
```

Movies.xml

The page in next listing illustrates how you can display the contents of this XML document with a `TreeView` control.

```
Code View: Scroll / Show All
<%@ Page Language="C#" %>
<!DOCTYPE html PUBLIC "-//W3C//DTD XHTML 1.1//EN"
 "http://www.w3.org/TR/xhtml11/DTD/xhtml11.dtd">
<html xmlns="http://www.w3.org/1999/xhtml" >
<head id="Head1" runat="server">
    <title>TreeView XML</title>
</head>
<body>
    <form id="form1" runat="server">
     <div>

     <asp:TreeView
          id="TreeView1"
          DataSourceID="srcMovies"
          Runat="server" />

      <asp:XmlDataSource
          id="srcMovies"
          DataFile="~/Movies.xml"
          Runat="server" />

     </div>
     </form>
</body>
</html>
```

TreeViewXml.aspx

The `Movies.xml` document in above listing is extremely simple. The elements do not include any attributes. You can display more complicated XML documents with the `TreeView` control by declaring one or more `TreeNodeBinding` elements.

For example, the nodes in the XML document in next listing include `id` and `text` attributes.

```
<?xml version="1.0" encoding="utf-8" ?>
<movies>
  <category id="category1" text="Action">
    <movie id="movie1" text="Star Wars" />
    <movie id="movie2" text="Independence Day" />
  </category>
  <category id="category2" text="Horror">
    <movie id="movie3" text="Jaws" />
    <movie id="movie4" text="Nightmare Before Christmas" />
  </category>
</movies>
```

MoviesComplex.xml

The page in next listing displays the contents of the XML document in above listing.

```
Code View: Scroll / Show All
<%@ Page Language="C#" %>
<!DOCTYPE html PUBLIC "-//W3C//DTD XHTML 1.1//EN"
  "http://www.w3.org/TR/xhtml11/DTD/xhtml11.dtd">
<html xmlns="http://www.w3.org/1999/xhtml" >
<head id="Head1" runat="server">
    <title>TreeView XML Complex</title>
</head>
<body>
    <form id="form1" runat="server">
    <div>

    <asp:TreeView
        id="TreeView1"
        DataSourceID="srcMovies"
        Runat="server">
        <DataBindings>
        <asp:TreeNodeBinding
            DataMember="category"
            TextField="text"
            ValueField="id" />
        <asp:TreeNodeBinding
            DataMember="movie"
            TextField="text"
            ValueField="id" />
        </DataBindings>
    </asp:TreeView>

    <asp:XmlDataSource
        id="srcMovies"
        DataFile="~/MoviesComplex.xml"
        Runat="server" />

    </div>
    </form>
</body>
</html>
```

TreeViewXMLComplex.aspx

The `TreeView` in above listing includes a `DataBindings` subtag. This tag includes two `TreeNodeBinding` elements. The first `TreeNodeBinding` specifies the relationship between `<category>` nodes in the XML document and `TreeView` nodes. The second `TreeNodeBinding` specifies the relationship between `<movie>` nodes and `TreeView` nodes.

Binding to Database Data

You cannot bind a `TreeView` control directly to a `SqlDataSource` or `ObjectDataSource` control because neither of these two controls exposes hierarchical data. If you want to display database data with the `TreeView` control, you have a choice: create a custom `SqlHierarchicalDataSource` control or programmatically bind the `TreeView` to the database data.

The hard option is to build a SQL hierarchical `DataSource` control. You can do this by deriving a new control from the base `HierarchicalDataSourceControl` class or by implementing the `IHierarchicalDataSource` interface. We explore this option in the final section.

The second option is to build the `TreeView` control programmatically from a set of database records. This is the approach that we follow in this section.

Imagine that you have a database table that looks like this:

MessageId	**ParentId**	**Subject**
1	null	How do you use the `Menu` control?
2	null	What is the `TreeView` control?
3	1	RE:How do you use the `Menu` control?
4	1	RE:How do you use the `Menu` control?
5	2	RE:What is the `TreeView` control?
6	5	RE:RE:What is the `TreeView` control?

This database table represents a discussion forum. The relationship between the messages is determined by the `ParentId` column. The messages that have a null `ParentID` represent the threads, and the other messages represent replies to the threads.

The page in next listing uses a `TreeView` control to display the contents of the Discuss database table.

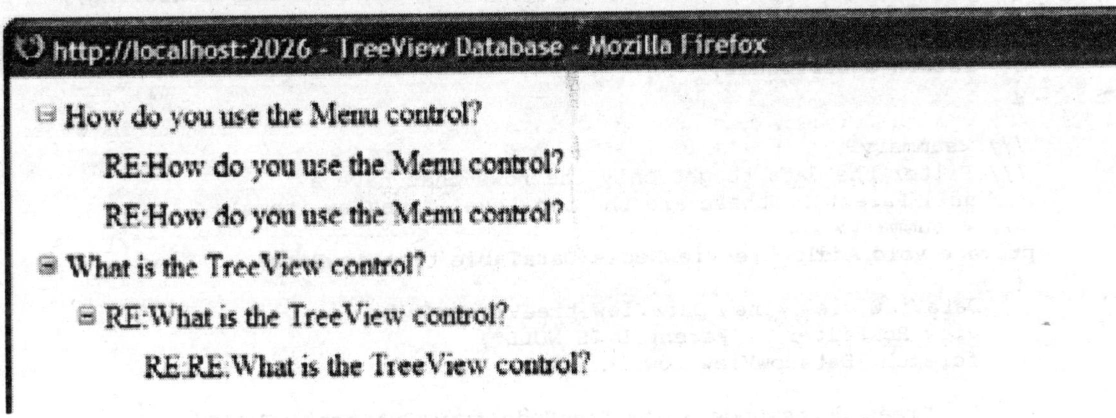

Displaying database data with a TreeView control.

Code View: Scroll / Show All

```
<%@ Page Language="C#" %>
<%@ Import Namespace="System.Web.Configuration" %>
<%@ Import Namespace="System.Data" %>
<%@ Import Namespace="System.Data.SqlClient" %>
<!DOCTYPE html PUBLIC "-//W3C//DTD XHTML 1.1//EN"
"http://www.w3.org/TR/xhtml11/DTD/xhtml11.dtd">
<script runat="server">

    /// <summary>
    /// Only populate the TreeView when the page first loads
    /// </summary>
    void Page_Load()
    {
        if (!Page.IsPostBack)
            PopulateTreeView();
    }

    /// <summary>
    /// Get the data from the database and create the top-level
```

```
    /// TreeView items
    /// </summary>
    private void PopulateTreeView()
    {
        DataTable treeViewData = GetTreeViewData();
        AddTopTreeViewNodes(treeViewData);
    }

    /// <summary>
    /// Use a DataAdapter and DataTable to grab the database data
    /// </summary>
    /// <returns></returns>
    private DataTable GetTreeViewData()
    {
        // Get Discuss table
        string selectCommand = "SELECT MessageId,ParentId,Subject FROM
Discuss";
        string conString =
WebConfigurationManager.ConnectionStrings["Discuss"].ConnectionString;
        SqlDataAdapter dad = new SqlDataAdapter(selectCommand, conString);
        DataTable dtblDiscuss = new DataTable();
        dad.Fill(dtblDiscuss);
        return dtblDiscuss;
    }

    /// <summary>
    /// Filter the data to get only the rows that have a
    /// null ParentID (these are the top-level TreeView items)
    /// </summary>
    private void AddTopTreeViewNodes(DataTable treeViewData)
    {
        DataView view = new DataView(treeViewData);
        view.RowFilter = "ParentID IS NULL";
        foreach (DataRowView row in view)
        {
            TreeNode newNode = new TreeNode(row["Subject"].ToString(),
row["MessageId"].ToString());
            TreeView1.Nodes.Add(newNode);
            AddChildTreeViewNodes(treeViewData, newNode);
        }

    }

    /// <summary>
    /// Recursively add child TreeView items by filtering by ParentID
    /// </summary>
    private void AddChildTreeViewNodes(DataTable treeViewData,
TreeNode parentTreeViewNode)
    {
        DataView view = new DataView(treeViewData);
        view.RowFilter = "ParentID=" + parentTreeViewNode.Value;
        foreach (DataRowView row in view)
        {
            TreeNode newNode = new TreeNode(row["Subject"].ToString(),
row["MessageId"].ToString());
            parentTreeViewNode.ChildNodes.Add(newNode);
            AddChildTreeViewNodes(treeViewData, newNode);
```

```
        }
    }

</script>
<html xmlns="http://www.w3.org/1999/xhtml" >
<head id="Head1" runat="server">
    <style type="text/css">
    </style>
    <title>TreeView Database</title>
</head>
<body>
    <form id="form1" runat="server">
    <div>

    <asp:TreeView
        id="TreeView1"
        Runat="server" />

    </div>
    </form>
</body>
</html>
```

TreeViewDatabase.aspx

The page in above listing filters the contents of the Discuss database table by its ParentID column. First, the top-level nodes are added to the `TreeView`. Next, the child nodes are recursively added to the `TreeView` with the help of the `AddChildTreeViewNodes()` method.

Using Populate On Demand and AJAX

You can use the `TreeView` control even when working with a large set of data. For example, the Microsoft MSDN website (msdn.Microsoft.com) has links to thousands of articles. This website uses a tree view to display the nested links to the articles.

Because thousands of articles are hosted at the MSDN website, not all the tree nodes are downloaded to the browser when you open a page. Instead, additional nodes are downloaded to your browser only when you expand a particular node. You can use a feature named Populate On Demand with the `TreeView` control. When you enable the `PopulateOnDemand` property for a Tree node, child nodes are not added to the parent node until the parent node is expanded.

For example, the page in next listing contains an infinitely expanding `TreeView`. Each time you expand a Tree node, five new child nodes display. Each time you expand a child node, five more child nodes display, and so on.

```
Code View: Scroll / Show All
<%@ Page Language="C#" %>
<!DOCTYPE html PUBLIC "-//W3C//DTD XHTML 1.1//EN"
"http://www.w3.org/TR/xhtml11/DTD/xhtml11.dtd">
<script runat="server">

        void TreeView1_TreeNodePopulate(object s, TreeNodeEventArgs e)
        {
            for (int i=0;i<5;i++)
            {
                TreeNode newNode = new TreeNode();
                newNode.Text = String.Format("{0}.{1}", e.Node.Text, i);
                newNode.PopulateOnDemand = true;
```

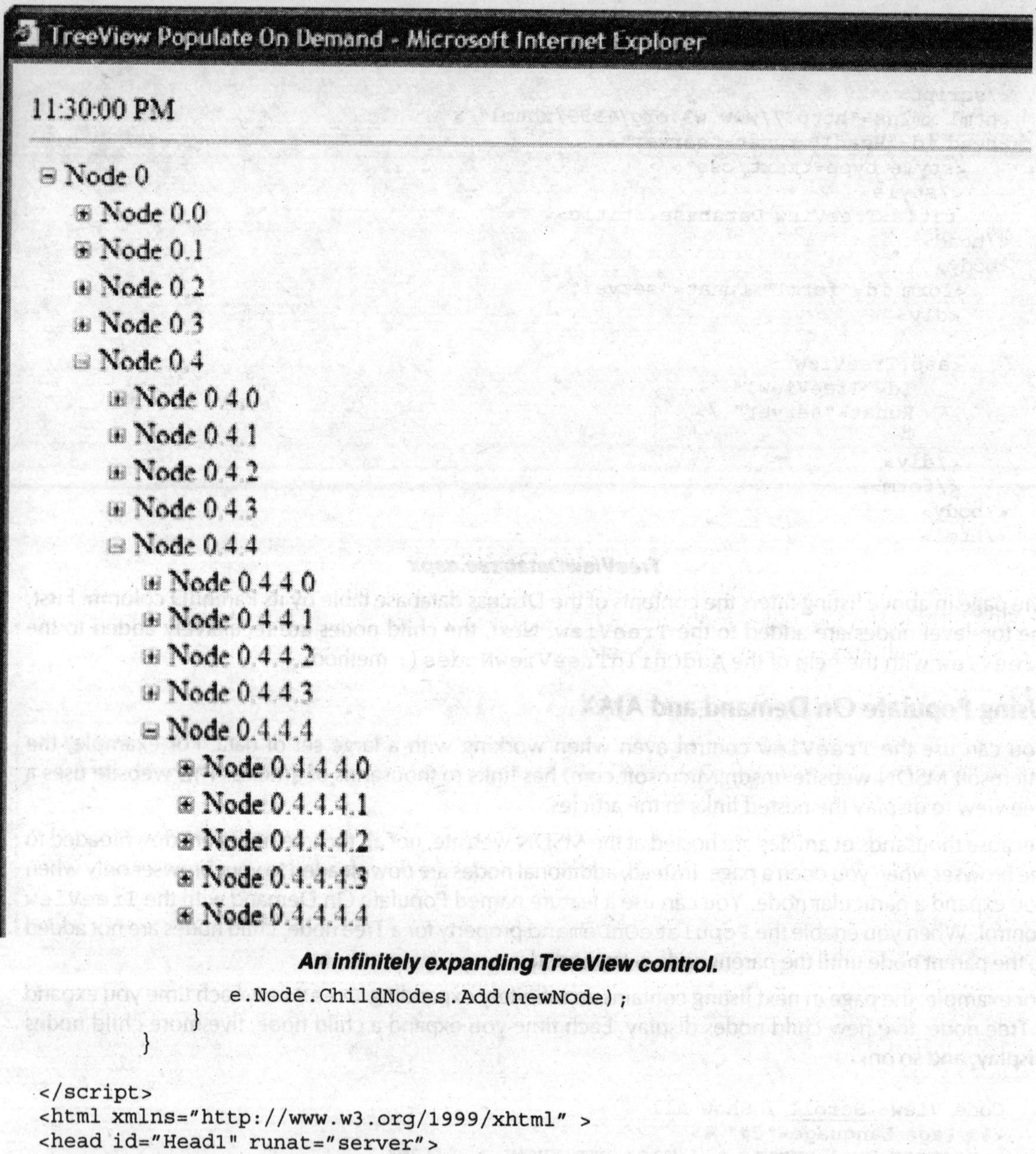

An infinitely expanding TreeView control.

```
                e.Node.ChildNodes.Add(newNode);
            }
        }

</script>
<html xmlns="http://www.w3.org/1999/xhtml" >
<head id="Head1" runat="server">
    <title>TreeView Populate On Demand</title>
</head>
<body>
    <form id="form1" runat="server">
    <div>

    <%=DateTime.Now.ToString("T") %>

    <hr />

    <asp:TreeView
```

```
ID="TreeView1"
ExpandDepth="0"
OnTreeNodePopulate="TreeView1_TreeNodePopulate"
Runat="server">
<Nodes>
<asp:TreeNode
    PopulateOnDemand="true"
    Text="Node 0" />
</Nodes>
</asp:TreeView>

</div>
</form>
</body>
</html>
```

TreeViewPopulateOnDemand.aspx

The TreeView in above listing includes a single statically declared TreeNode. This TreeNode includes a PopulateOnDemand property set to the value True.

Additionally, the TreeView control itself includes a TreeNodePopulate event handler. When you expand a TreeNode that has its PopulateOnDemand property enabled, the TreeNodePopulate event handler executes. In the case of above listing, the event handler adds five new TreeNodes to the TreeNode that was expanded.

When you use the Populate On Demand feature, the page containing the TreeView is not posted back to the server when you expand a TreeNode. Instead, the browser uses AJAX (Asynchronous JavaScript and XML) to communicate with the web server. The additional TreeNodes are retrieved from the server, without performing a postback.

The page in above listing displays the current time when you open the page. The time is not updated when you expand a particular TreeNode. The time is not updated because the only content in the page that is updated when you expand a node is the TreeView content. AJAX can have a dramatic impact on performance because it does not require the entire page to be re-rendered each time you expand a TreeNode.

The page in next listing contains a more realistic sample of using Populate On Demand and AJAX. This page uses a TreeView control to display the contents of the Discuss database table.

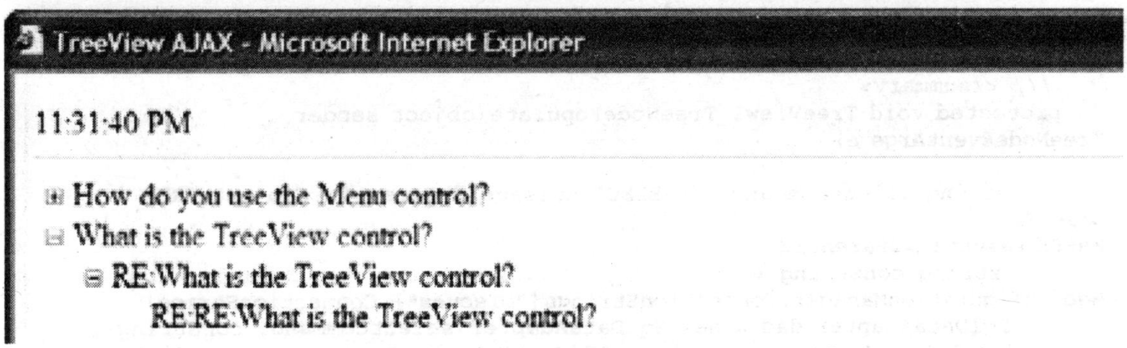

Displaying database data with AJAX.

```
Code View: Scroll / Show All
<%@ Page Language="C#" %>
<%@ Import Namespace="System.Web.Configuration" %>
<%@ Import Namespace="System.Data" %>
```

```
<%@ Import Namespace="System.Data.SqlClient" %>
<!DOCTYPE html PUBLIC "-//W3C//DTD XHTML 1.1//EN"
"http://www.w3.org/TR/xhtml11/DTD/xhtml11.dtd">
<script runat="server">

    /// <summary>
    /// Only populate the TreeView when the page first loads
    /// </summary>
    void Page_Load()
    {
        if (!Page.IsPostBack)
            PopulateTopNodes();
    }

    /// <summary>
    /// Get the top level nodes (nodes with a null ParentId)
    /// </summary>
    private void PopulateTopNodes()
    {
        string selectCommand = "SELECT MessageId,ParentId,Subject FROM
Discuss
 WHERE ParentId IS NULL";
        string conString =
WebConfigurationManager.ConnectionStrings["Discuss"].ConnectionString;
        SqlDataAdapter dad = new SqlDataAdapter(selectCommand, conString);
        DataTable dtblMessages = new DataTable();
        dad.Fill(dtblMessages);

        foreach (DataRow row in dtblMessages.Rows)
        {
            TreeNode newNode = new TreeNode(row["Subject"].ToString(),
row["MessageId"].ToString());
            newNode.PopulateOnDemand = true;
            TreeView1.Nodes.Add(newNode);
        }
    }

    /// <summary>
    /// Get the child nodes of the expanded node
    /// </summary>
    protected void TreeView1_TreeNodePopulate(object sender,
TreeNodeEventArgs e)
    {
        string selectCommand = "SELECT MessageId,ParentId,Subject FROM
Discuss
WHERE ParentId=@ParentId";
        string conString =
WebConfigurationManager.ConnectionStrings["Discuss"].ConnectionString;
        SqlDataAdapter dad = new SqlDataAdapter(selectCommand, conString);
        dad.SelectCommand.Parameters.AddWithValue("@ParentId", e.Node.Value);
        DataTable dtblMessages = new DataTable();
        dad.Fill(dtblMessages);

        foreach (DataRow row in dtblMessages.Rows)
        {
            TreeNode newNode = new TreeNode(row["Subject"].ToString(),
row["MessageId"].ToString());
```

```
            newNode.PopulateOnDemand = true;
            e.Node.ChildNodes.Add(newNode);
        }
    }

</script>
<html xmlns="http://www.w3.org/1999/xhtml" >
<head id="Head1" runat="server">
    <style type="text/css">
    </style>
    <title>TreeView AJAX</title>
</head>
<body>
    <form id="form1" runat="server">
    <div>

    <%= DateTime.Now.ToString("T") %>

    <hr />

    <asp:TreeView
        id="TreeView1"
        ExpandDepth="0"
       OnTreeNodePopulate="TreeView1_TreeNodePopulate"
        Runat="server" />

    </div>
    </form>
</body>
</html>
```

TreeViewAJAX.aspx

When the page in above listing first opens, only the first-level message subjects display. These messages are retrieved by the `PopulateTopNodes()` method. When you expand a thread, the matching replies are retrieved for the thread. These replies are retrieved in the `TreeView1_TreeNodePopulate()` event handler.

The `TreeView` in above listing performs well even when working with a large set of data. At any time, only the child messages of a message are retrieved from the database. At no time are all the messages retrieved from the database. When the page is used with a modern browser, AJAX retrieves the messages from the web server. The page does not need to be posted back to the web server when you expand a particular message thread.

Formatting the TreeView Control

The `TreeView` control supports an abundance of properties that have an effect on how the `TreeView` is formatted.

Following are some of the more useful properties of a `TreeView` control, which modify its appearance (this is not a complete list):

- `CollapseImageToolTip`— Enables you to specify the title attribute for the collapse image.
- `CollapseImageUrl`— Enables you to specify a URL to an image for the collapse image.
- `ExpandDepth`— Enables you to specify the number of `TreeNode` levels to display initially.
- `ExpandImageToolTip`— Enables you to specify the title attribute for the expand image.
- `ExpandImageUrl`— Enables you to specify the URL to an image for the expand image.

- `ImageSet`— Enables you to specify a set of images to use with the `TreeView` control.
- `LineImagesFolder`— Enables you to specify a folder that contains line images.
- `MaxDataBindDepth`— Enables you to specify the maximum levels of `TreeView` levels to display when binding to a data source.
- `NodeIndent`— Enables you to specify the number of pixels to indent a child Tree node.
- `NodeWrap`— Enables you to specify whether or not text is wrapped in a Tree node.
- `NoExpandImageUrl`— Enables you to specify the URL to an image for the `NoExpand` image (typically, an invisible spacer image).
- `ShowCheckBoxes`— Enables you to display check boxes next to each Tree node. Possible values are `All`, `Leaf`, `None`, `Parent`, and `Root`.
- `ShowExpandCollapse`— Enables you to disable the expand and collapse icons that appear next to each expandable node.
- `ShowLines`— Enables you to show connecting lines between Tree nodes.
- `SkipLinkText`— Enables you to specify the text used for skipping the contents of the `TreeView` control. (The Skip Link contains hidden text that is accessible only to users of assistive devices.)
- `Target`— Enables you to specify the name of the window that opens when you navigate to a URL with the `TreeView` control.

The two most interesting properties in this list are the `ImageSet` and the `ShowLines` properties. You can set the `ImageSet` property to any of the following values to modify the images displayed by the `TreeView` control:

- `Arrows`
- `BulletedList`
- `BulletedList2`
- `BulletedList3`
- `BulletedList4`
- `Contacts`
- `Custom`
- `Events`
- `Faq`
- `Inbox`
- `Msdn`
- `News`
- `Simple`
- `Simple2`
- `WindowsHelp`
- `XPFileExplorer`

The `ShowLines` property causes connecting line images to be rendered between `TreeView` nodes. Displaying lines between Tree nodes can make it easier to visually discern the nested relationships between nodes. If you want to create custom lines, you can specify a value for the `LinesImagesFolder` property.

The page in next listing illustrates how to use both the `ImageSet` and `ShowLines` properties.

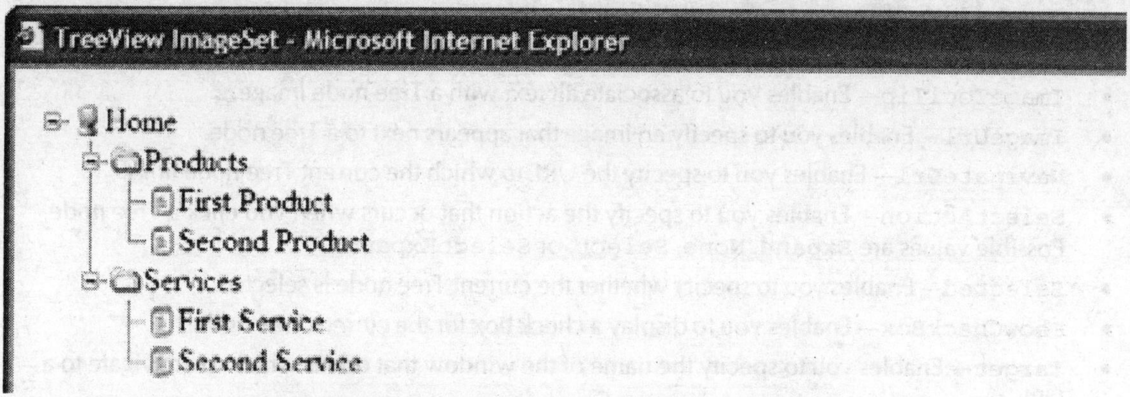

Formatting a TreeView with an image set and lines.

```
Code View: Scroll / Show All
<%@ Page Language="C#" %>
<!DOCTYPE html PUBLIC "-//W3C//DTD XHTML 1.1//EN"
  "http://www.w3.org/TR/xhtml11/DTD/xhtml11.dtd">
<html xmlns="http://www.w3.org/1999/xhtml" >
<head id="Head1" runat="server">
    <title>TreeView ImageSet</title>
</head>
<body>
    <form id="form1" runat="server">
     <div>

    <asp:TreeView
        id="TreeView1"
        ImageSet="XPFileExplorer"
        ShowLines="true"
        Runat="server">
        <Nodes>
        <asp:TreeNode
            Text="Home">
            <asp:TreeNode Text="Products">
                <asp:TreeNode Text="First Product" />
                <asp:TreeNode Text="Second Product" />
            </asp:TreeNode>
            <asp:TreeNode Text="Services">
                <asp:TreeNode Text="First Service" />
                <asp:TreeNode Text="Second Service" />
            </asp:TreeNode>
        </asp:TreeNode>
        </Nodes>
    </asp:TreeView>


    </div>
    </form>
</body>
</html>
```

TreeViewImageSet.aspx

The `TreeNode` object itself also supports several properties that have an effect on the appearance of its containing `TreeView`. Following is a list of the most useful properties of the `TreeNode` object:

- `Checked`— Enables you to check the check box that appears next to the Tree node.
- `Expanded`— Enables you to initially expand a node.
- `ImageToolTip`— Enables you to associate alt text with a Tree node image.
- `ImageUrl`— Enables you to specify an image that appears next to a Tree node.
- `NavigateUrl`— Enables you to specify the URL to which the current Tree node links.
- `SelectAction`— Enables you to specify the action that occurs when you click a Tree node. Possible values are `Expand`, `None`, `Select`, or `SelectExpand`.
- `Selected`— Enables you to specify whether the current Tree node is selected.
- `ShowCheckBox`— Enables you to display a check box for the current Tree node.
- `Target`— Enables you to specify the name of the window that opens when you navigate to a URL.
- `ToolTip`— Enables you to specify a title attribute for the current Tree node.

You can style the `TreeView` control by attaching Cascading Style Sheet classes to the `Style` object exposed by the `TreeView` control. The `TreeView` control supports the following `Style` objects:

- `HoverNodeStyle`— Applied to a Tree node when you hover your mouse over a node.
- `LeafNodeStyle`— Applied to leaf Tree nodes (Tree nodes without child nodes).
- `NodeStyle`— Applied to Tree nodes by default.
- `ParentNodeStyle`— Applied to parent nodes (Tree nodes with child nodes).
- `RootNodeStyle`— Applied to root nodes (Tree nodes with no parent nodes).
- `SelectedNodeStyle`— Applied to the selected node.

For example, the page in next listing uses several of these Style objects to format a `TreeView` control.

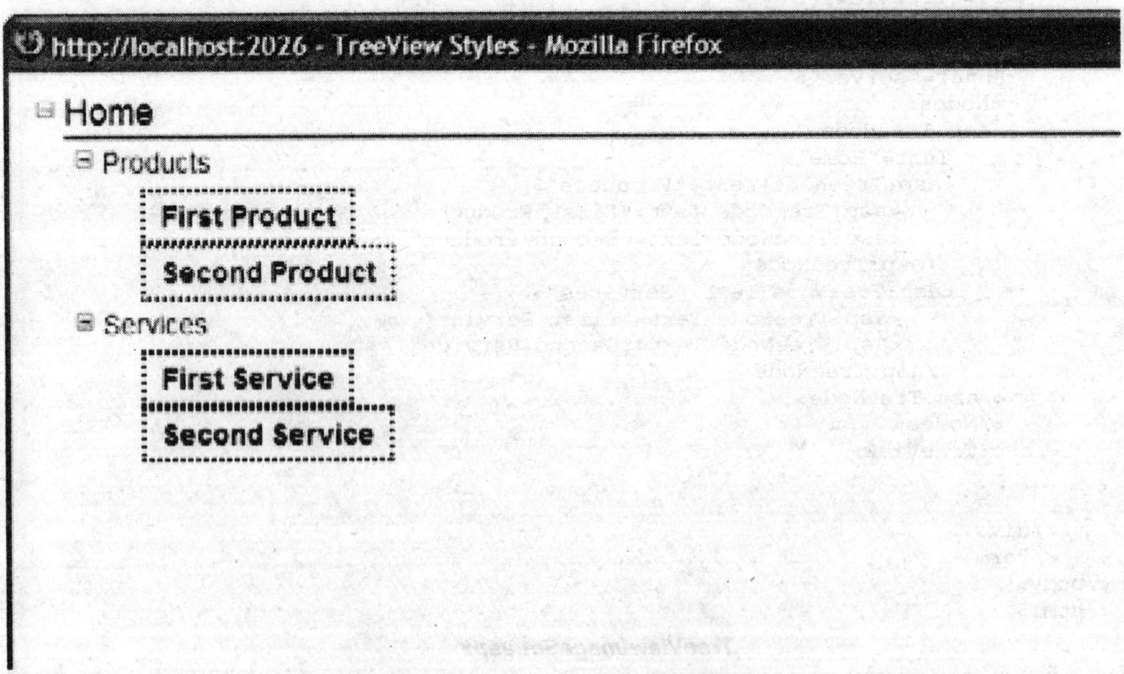

Using Styles with the TreeView control.

Code View: Scroll / Show All

```
<%@ Page Language="C#" %>
<!DOCTYPE html PUBLIC "-//W3C//DTD XHTML 1.1//EN"
 "http://www.w3.org/TR/xhtml11/DTD/xhtml11.dtd">
<html xmlns="http://www.w3.org/1999/xhtml" >
<head id="Head1" runat="server">
    <style type="text/css">
        .treeNode
        {
            color:blue;
            font:14px Arial, Sans-Serif;
        }
        .rootNode
        {
            font-size:18px;
            width:100%;
            border-bottom:Solid 1px black;
        }
        .leafNode
        {
            border:Dotted 2px black;
            padding:4px;
            background-color:#eeeeee;
            font-weight:bold;
        }
    </style>
    <title>TreeView Styles</title>
</head>
<body>
    <form id="form1" runat="server">
    <div>

    <asp:TreeView
        id="TreeView1"
        NodeStyle-CssClass="treeNode"
        RootNodeStyle-CssClass="rootNode"
        LeafNodeStyle-CssClass="leafNode"
        Runat="server">
        <Nodes>
        <asp:TreeNode
            Text="Home">
            <asp:TreeNode Text="Products">
                <asp:TreeNode Text="First Product" />
                <asp:TreeNode Text="Second Product" />
            </asp:TreeNode>
            <asp:TreeNode Text="Services">
                <asp:TreeNode Text="First Service" />
                <asp:TreeNode Text="Second Service" />
            </asp:TreeNode>
        </asp:TreeNode>
        </Nodes>
    </asp:TreeView>

    </div>
    </form>
</body>
</html>
```

TreeViewStyles.aspx

Furthermore, you can apply styles to particular Tree node levels by taking advantage of the `TreeView` control's `LevelStyles` property. The page in above listing uses the `LevelStyles` property to format first level nodes differently than second level nodes and third level nodes.

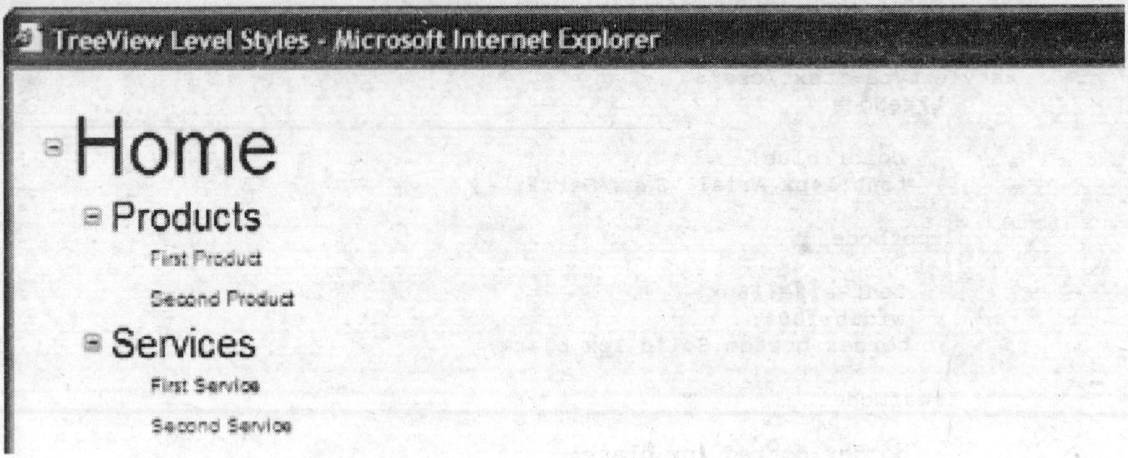

Applying styles to different TreeView node levels.

Code View: Scroll / Show All

```
<%@ Page Language="C#" %>
<!DOCTYPE html PUBLIC "-//W3C//DTD XHTML 1.1//EN"
  "http://www.w3.org/TR/xhtml11/DTD/xhtml11.dtd">
<html xmlns="http://www.w3.org/1999/xhtml" >
<head id="Head1" runat="server">
    <style type="text/css">
        .nodeLevel1
        {
            font:40px Arial,Sans-Serif;
        }
        .nodeLevel2
        {
            font:20px Arial,Sans-Serif;
        }
        .nodeLevel3
        {
            font:10px Arial,Sans-Serif;
        }
    </style>
    <title>TreeView Level Styles</title>
</head>
<body>
    <form id="form1" runat="server">
    <div>

    <asp:TreeView
        id="TreeView1"
        Runat="server">
        <LevelStyles>
        <asp:TreeNodeStyle CssClass="nodeLevel1" />
        <asp:TreeNodeStyle CssClass="nodeLevel2" />
        <asp:TreeNodeStyle CssClass="nodeLevel3" />
        </LevelStyles>
```

```
            <Nodes>
            <asp:TreeNode
                Text="Home">
                <asp:TreeNode Text="Products">
                    <asp:TreeNode Text="First Product" />
                    <asp:TreeNode Text="Second Product" />
                </asp:TreeNode>
                <asp:TreeNode Text="Services">
                    <asp:TreeNode Text="First Service" />
                    <asp:TreeNode Text="Second Service" />
                </asp:TreeNode>
            </asp:TreeNode>
            </Nodes>
        </asp:TreeView>

        </div>
        </form>
</body>
</html>
```

TreeViewLevelStyles.aspx

Building a SQL Hierarchical Data Source Control

In this final section of this chapter, we build a `SqlHierarchicalDataSource` control. This custom control enables you to declaratively and (thus) easily bind controls such as the `Menu` and `TreeView` controls to data retrieved from a database.

The page in next listing illustrates how you can use the `SqlHierarchicalDataSource` control to bind a `Menu` control to a database table that contains nested categories.

```
Code View: Scroll / Show All
<%@ Page Language="C#" %>
<%@ Register TagPrefix="custom" Namespace="AspNetUnleashed" %>
<!DOCTYPE html PUBLIC "-//W3C//DTD XHTML 1.1//EN"
"http://www.w3.org/TR/xhtml11/DTD/xhtml11.dtd">
<script runat="server">

    protected void Menu1_MenuItemClick(object sender, MenuEventArgs e)
    {
        lblSelected.Text = Menu1.SelectedValue;
    }
</script>
<html xmlns="http://www.w3.org/1999/xhtml" >
<head id="Head1" runat="server">
    <style type="text/css">
        .menu
        {
            border:solid 1px black;
            padding:4px;
        }
    </style>
    <title>Show Menu</title>
</head>
<body>
    <form id="form1" runat="server">
    <div>
```

```
<asp:Menu
    id="Menu1"
    DataSourceId="srcCategories"
    OnMenuItemClick="Menu1_MenuItemClick"
    Orientation="Horizontal"
    DynamicMenuStyle-CssClass="menu"
    Runat="server">
    <DataBindings>
        <asp:MenuItemBinding TextField="Name" ValueField="Name" />
    </DataBindings>
</asp:Menu>

<custom:SqlHierarchicalDataSource
    id="srcCategories"
    ConnectionString='<%$ ConnectionStrings:Categories %>'
    DataKeyName="CategoryId"
    DataParentKeyName="ParentId"
    SelectCommand="SELECT CategoryId, ParentId, Name FROM Categories"
    Runat="server" />

<hr />

<asp:Label
    id="lblSelected"
    Runat="server" />

</div>
</form>
</body>
</html>
```

ShowMenu.aspx

When you open the page in above listing, all the rows from the Categories table display in the `Menu` control. The `SqlHierarchicalDataSource` control includes two properties: `DataKeyName` and `DataParentKeyName`.

The `DataKeyName` property represents the name of a database column that contains a unique value for each database table row. The `DataParentKeyName` column represents the name of a database column that relates each row to its parent row.

Furthermore, the `Menu` control includes a `MenuItemBinding`, which associates the database Name column with the `Menu` item `Text` property and the Name column with the `Menu` item `Value` property.

You also can use the `SqlHierarchicalDataSource` control when working with the `TreeView` control.

The page in next listing displays all the rows from the Discuss database table in a `TreeView` control.

```
Code View: Scroll / Show All
<%@ Page Language="C#" %>
<%@ Register TagPrefix="custom" Namespace="AspNetUnleashed" %>
<!DOCTYPE html PUBLIC "-//W3C//DTD XHTML 1.1//EN"
"http://www.w3.org/TR/xhtml11/DTD/xhtml11.dtd">
<script runat="server">

    protected void TreeView1_SelectedNodeChanged(object sender, EventArgs e)
    {
        lblSelected.Text = TreeView1.SelectedValue;
```

```
    }
</script>
<html xmlns="http://www.w3.org/1999/xhtml" >
<head id="Head1" runat="server">
    <title>Show TreeView</title>
</head>
<body>
    <form id="form1" runat="server">
    <div>

    <asp:TreeView
        id="TreeView1"
        DataSourceID="srcDiscuss"
       OnSelectedNodeChanged="TreeView1_SelectedNodeChanged"
        ImageSet="News"
        Runat="server">
        <DataBindings>
            <asp:TreeNodeBinding
                TextField="Subject"
                ValueField="MessageId" />
        </DataBindings>
    </asp:TreeView>

    <custom:SqlHierarchicalDataSource
        id="srcDiscuss"
        ConnectionString='<%$ ConnectionStrings:Discuss %>'
        DataKeyName="MessageId"
        DataParentKeyName="ParentId"
        SelectCommand="SELECT MessageId,ParentId,Subject FROM Discuss"
        Runat="server" />

    <hr />

    You selected message number:
    <asp:Label
        id="lblSelected"
        Runat="server" />

    </div>
    </form>
</body>
</html>
```

ShowTreeView.aspx

When you open the page in above listing, the contents of the Discuss database table display in the `TreeView` control.

All the code for the `SqlHierarchicalDataSource` control is included on the book's website. The control is composed out of five separate classes:

- `SqlHierarchicalDataSource`— Represents the actual control. It inherits from the base `SqlDataSource` control and implements the `IHierarchicalDataSource` interface.
- `SqlHierarchicalDataSourceView`— Represents the hierarchical data returned by the control. It inherits from the base `HierarchicalDataSourceView` class.
- `SqlHierarchicalEnumerable`— Represents a collection of `SqlNodes`.

- `SqlNode`— Represents a particular database row from the data source. It includes methods for retrieving child and parent rows.
- `SqlNodePropertyDescriptor`— Inherits from the base `PropertyDescriptor` class. It converts the database columns represented by a `SqlNode` into class properties so that you can bind to the columns using `TreeView` and `Menu` control `DataBindings`.

CHAPTER 4

Using Validation Controls

In this chapter you will read about:

- Using the Validation Controls.
- Using the RequiredFieldValidator Control.
- Using the RangeValidator Control.
- Using the CompareValidator Control.
- Using RegularExpressionValidator Contol.
- Using CustomValidator Control
- Using the ValidationSummary Control.
- Creating Custom Validation Controls.

Using the Validation Controls

Now, you learn how to control how validation errors display, how to highlight validation error messages, and how to use validation groups. You are provided with sample code for using each of the standard validation controls. Next, we extend the basic validation controls with our own custom validation controls. For example, you learn how to create an `AjaxValidator` control that enables you to call a server-side validation function from the client.

Overview of the Validation Controls

ASP.NET 4 includes six validation controls:

- `RequiredFieldValidator`— Enables you to require a user to enter a value in a form field.
- `RangeValidator`— Enables you to check whether a value falls between a certain minimum and maximum value.
- `CompareValidator`— Enables you to compare a value against another value or perform a data type check.
- `RegularExpressionValidator`— Enables you to compare a value against a regular expression.
- `CustomValidator`— Enables you to perform custom validation.
- `ValidationSummary`— Enables you to display a summary of all validation errors in a page.

You can associate the validation controls with any form controls included in ASP.NET Framework. For example, if you want to require a user to enter a value into a `TextBox` control, you can associate a `RequiredFieldValidator` control with the `TextBox` control.

Note: Technically, you can use the validation controls with any control decorated with the `ValidationProperty` attribute.

The next listing contains a simple order entry form. It contains three `TextBox` controls that enable you to enter a product name, product price, and product quantity. The validation controls validate each of the form fields.

```
Code View: Scroll / Show All
<%@ Page Language="C#" %>
<!DOCTYPE html PUBLIC "-//W3C//DTD XHTML 1.0 Transitional//EN"
"http://www.w3.org/TR/xhtml1/DTD/xhtml1-transitional.dtd">
<script runat="server">

   void btnSubmit_Click(Object sender, EventArgs e)
   {
        if (Page.IsValid)
        {
            lblResult.Text = @"<br />Product: " + txtProductName.Text
                 + "<br />Price: " + txtProductPrice.Text
                 + "<br />Quantity: " + txtProductQuantity.Text;
        }
   }
</script>
<html xmlns="http://www.w3.org/1999/xhtml" >
<head id="Head1" runat="server">
   <title>Order Form</title>
</head>
<body>
   <form id="form1" runat="server">
```

```
<div>

<fieldset>
<legend>Product Order Form</legend>

<asp:Label
    id="lblProductName"
    Text="Product Name:"
    AssociatedControlID="txtProductName"
    Runat="server" />
<br />
<asp:TextBox
    id="txtProductName"
    Runat="server" />
<asp:RequiredFieldValidator
    id="reqProductName"
    ControlToValidate="txtProductName"
    Text="(Required)"
    Runat="server" />

<br /><br />

<asp:Label
    id="lblProductPrice"
    Text="Product Price:"
    AssociatedControlID="txtProductPrice"
    Runat="server" />
<br />
<asp:TextBox
    id="txtProductPrice"
    Columns="5"
    Runat="server" />
<asp:RequiredFieldValidator
    id="reqProductPrice"
    ControlToValidate="txtProductPrice"
    Text="(Required)"
    Display="Dynamic"
    Runat="server" />
<asp:CompareValidator
    id="cmpProductPrice"
    ControlToValidate="txtProductPrice"
    Text="(Invalid Price)"
    Operator="DataTypeCheck"
    Type="Currency"
    Runat="server" />

<br /><br />

<asp:Label
    id="lblProductQuantity"
    Text="Product Quantity:"
    AssociatedControlID="txtProductQuantity"
    Runat="server" />
<br />
<asp:TextBox
    id="txtProductQuantity"
    Columns="5"
    Runat="server" />
```

```
        <asp:RequiredFieldValidator
            id="reqProductQuantity"
            ControlToValidate="txtProductQuantity"
            Text="(Required)"
            Display="Dynamic"
            Runat="server" />
        <asp:CompareValidator
            id="CompareValidator1"
            ControlToValidate="txtProductQuantity"
            Text="(Invalid Quantity)"
            Operator="DataTypeCheck"
            Type="Integer"
            Runat="server" />

        <br /><br />

        <asp:Button
            id="btnSubmit"
            Text="Submit Product Order"
            OnClick="btnSubmit_Click"
            Runat="server" />

        </fieldset>

        <asp:Label
            id="lblResult"
            Runat="server" />

        </div>
        </form>
    </body>
    </html>
```

OrderForm.aspx

A separate `RequiredFieldValidator` control is associated with each of the three form fields. If you attempt to submit the form in the above listing without entering a value for a field, a validation error message display.

Each `RequiredFieldValidator` associates with a particular control through its `ControlToValidate` property. This property accepts the name of the control to validate on the page.

`CompareValidator` controls associate with the `txtProductPrice` and `txtProductQuantity` `TextBox` controls. The first `CompareValidator` checks whether the `txtProductPrice` text field contains a currency value, and the second `CompareValidator` checks whether the `txtProductQuantity` text field contains an integer value.

There is nothing wrong with associating more than one validation control with a form field. If you need to make a form field required and check the data type entered into the form field, you need to associate both a `RequiredFieldValidator` and `CompareValidator` control with the form field.

Finally, the `Page.IsValid` property is checked in the `Page_Load()` handler before the form data displays. When using the validation controls, you should always check the `Page.IsValid` property before doing anything with the data submitted to a page. This property returns the value `true` when, and only when, no validation errors are on the page.

Validation Controls and JavaScript

By default, the validation controls perform validation on both the client (the browser) and the server. The

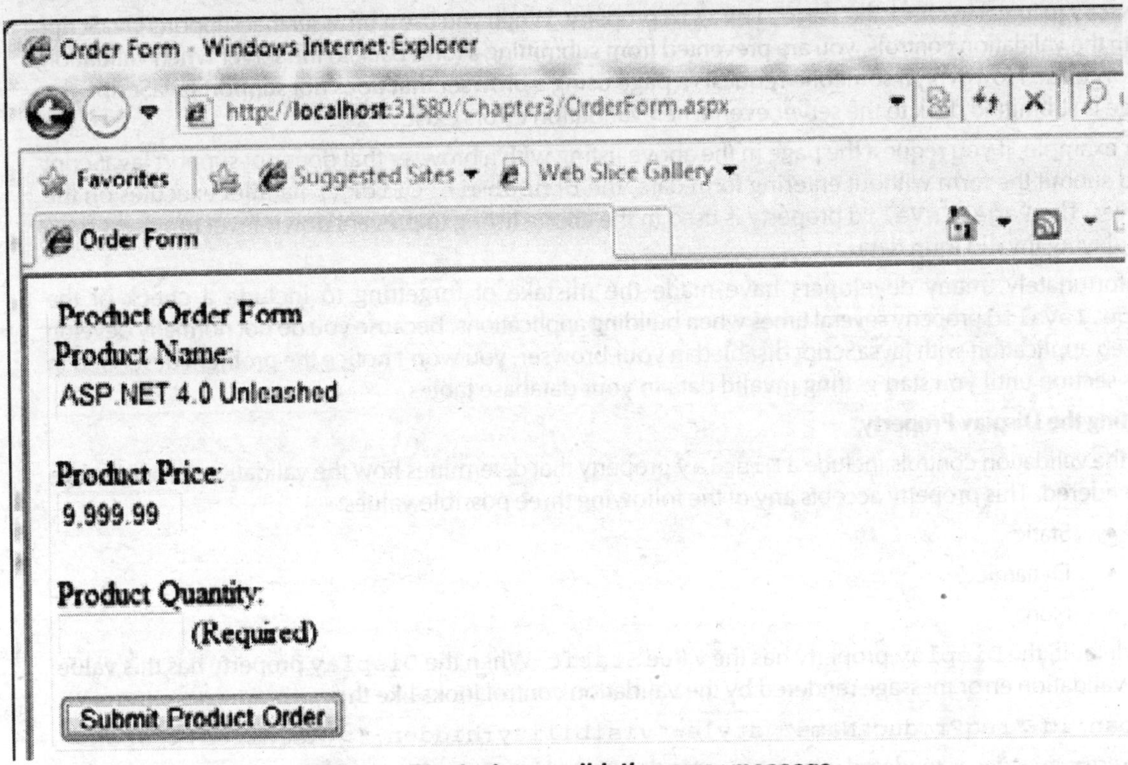

Figure Displaying a validation error message.

validation controls use client-side JavaScript. This is great from a user experience perspective because you get immediate feedback whenever you enter an invalid value into a form field.

Note: The `RequiredFieldValidator` does not perform client-side validation until after you attempt to submit a form at least once or you enter and remove data in a form field.

Almost all desktop browsers support client-side JavaScript. Supported browsers include Internet Explorer, Firefox, Chrome, Safari, and Opera. It is becoming more common to browse the web on mobile devices such as cell phones. Many of these mobile browsers do not yet support JavaScript.

You can use the validation controls with browsers that do not support JavaScript (or do not have JavaScript enabled). If a browser does not support JavaScript, the form must be posted back to the server before a validation error message displays.

Even when validation happens on the client, validation is still performed on the server. This is done for security reasons. If someone creates a fake form and submits the form data to your web server, the person still can't to submit invalid data.

If you prefer, you can disable client-side validation for any of the validation controls by assigning the value `False` to the validation control's `EnableClientScript` property.

Using Page.Is Valid

As previously mentioned, you should always check the `Page.IsValid` property when working with data submitted with a form that contains validation controls. Each of the validation controls includes an `IsValid` property that returns the value `True` when a validation error doesn't exist. The `Page.IsValid` property returns the value `True` when the `IsValid` property for of the validation controls in a page returns the value `True`.

It is easy to forget to check the `Page.IsValid` property. When you use a browser that supports JavaScript with the validation controls, you are prevented from submitting a form back to the server when validation errors exist. However, if someone requests a page using a browser that does not support JavaScript, the page is submitted back to the server even when validation errors exist.

For example, if you request the page in the above listing with a browser that does not support JavaScript and submit the form without entering form data, the `btnSubmit_Click()` handler executes on the server. The `Page.IsValid` property is used in the above listing to prevent down-level browsers from displaying invalid form data.

Unfortunately, many developers have made the mistake of forgetting to include a check of the `Page.IsValid` property several times when building applications. Because you do not normally develop a web application with JavsaScript disabled in your browser, you won't notice the problem described in this section until you start getting invalid data in your database tables.

Setting the Display Property

All the validation controls include a `Display` property that determines how the validation error message is rendered. This property accepts any of the following three possible values:

- Static
- Dynamic
- None

By default, the `Display` property has the value `Static`. When the `Display` property has this value, the validation error message rendered by the validation control looks like this:

```
<span id="reqProductName" style="visibility:hidden;">(Required)</span>
```

The error message is rendered in a `<span>` tag that includes a Cascading Style Sheet (CSS) style attribute that sets the visibility of the `<span>` tag to `hidden`. If, on the other hand, you set the `Display` property to the value `Dynamic`, the error message is rendered like this:

```
<span id="reqProductName" style="display:none;">(Required)</span>
```

In this case, a CSS `display` attribute hides the contents of the `<span>` tag.

You can use both the visibility and display attributes to hide text in a browser. However, text hidden with the `visibility` attribute still occupies screen real estate. Text hidden with the `display` attribute, on the other hand, does not occupy screen real estate. In general, you should set a validation control's `Display` property to the value `Dynamic`. That way, if other content displays next to the validation control, the content is not pushed to the right. All modern browsers (Internet Explorer, Firefox, Chrome, Safari, and Opera) support the CSS `display` attribute.

The third possible value of the `Display` property is `None`. If you prefer, you can prevent the individual validation controls from displaying an error message and display the error messages with a `ValidationSummary` control. You learn how to use the `ValidationSummary` control later in this chapter.

Highlighting Validation Errors

When a validation control displays a validation error, the control displays the value of its `Text` property. Normally, you assign a simple text string, such as "`(Required)`" to the `Text` property; however, the `Text` property accepts any HTML string.

For example, the page in next listing displays an image when you submit the form without entering a value for the First Name text field.

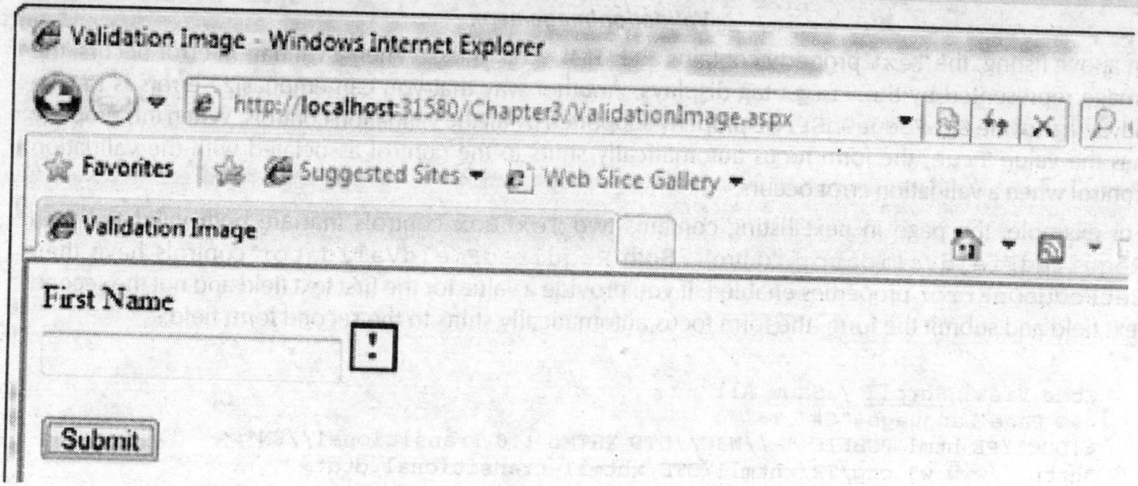

Displaying an image for a validation error.

Code View: Scroll / Show All

```
<%@ Page Language="C#" %>
<!DOCTYPE html PUBLIC "-//W3C//DTD XHTML 1.0 Transitional//EN"
"http://www.w3.org/TR/xhtml1/DTD/xhtml1-transitional.dtd">
<html xmlns="http://www.w3.org/1999/xhtml" >
<head id="Head1" runat="server">
    <title>Validation Image</title>
</head>
<body>
    <form id="form1" runat="server">
    <div>

    <asp:Label
        id="lblFirstName"
        Text="First Name"
        AssociatedControlID="txtFirstName"
        Runat="server" />
    <br />
    <asp:TextBox
        id="txtFirstName"
        Runat="server" />
    <asp:RequiredFieldValidator
        id="reqFirstName"
        ControlToValidate="txtFirstName"
        Text="<img src='Error.gif' alt='First name is required.' />"
        Runat="server" />

    <br /><br />

    <asp:Button
        id="btnSubmit"
        Text="Submit"
        Runat="server" />

    </div>
    </form>
</body>
```

```
</html>
```

ValidationImage.aspx

In above listing, the `Text` property contains an HTML `<img>` tag. When a validation error occurs, the image represented by the `<img>` tag displays. Another way that you can emphasize errors is to take advantage of the `SetFocusOnError` property supported by all the validation controls. When this property has the value `True`, the form focus automatically shifts to the control associated with the validation control when a validation error occurs.

For example, the page in next listing contains two `TextBox` controls that are both validated with `RequiredFieldValidator` controls. Both `RequiredFieldValidator` controls have their `SetFocusOnError` properties enabled. If you provide a value for the first text field and not the second text field and submit the form, the form focus automatically shifts to the second form field.

```
Code View: Scroll / Show All
<%@ Page Language="C#" %>
<!DOCTYPE html PUBLIC "-//W3C//DTD XHTML 1.0 Transitional//EN"
"http://www.w3.org/TR/xhtml1/DTD/xhtml1-transitional.dtd">
<html xmlns="http://www.w3.org/1999/xhtml" >
<head id="Head1" runat="server">
    <title>Show SetFocusOnError</title>
</head>
<body>
    <form id="form1" runat="server">
    <div>

    <asp:Label
        id="lblFirstName"
        Text="First Name"
       AssociatedControlID="txtFirstName"
        Runat="server" />
    <br />
    <asp:TextBox
        id="txtFirstName"
        Runat="server" />
   <asp:RequiredFieldValidator
        id="reqFirstName"
       ControlToValidate="txtFirstName"
        Text="(Required)"
        SetFocusOnError="true"
        Runat="server" />

    <br /><br />

    <asp:Label
        id="lblLastName"
        Text="Last Name"
       AssociatedControlID="txtLastName"
        Runat="server" />
    <br />
    <asp:TextBox
        id="txtLastname"
        Runat="server" />
   <asp:RequiredFieldValidator
        id="reqLastName"
       ControlToValidate="txtLastName"
```

```
        Text="(Required)"
        SetFocusOnError="true"
        Runat="server" />

     <br /><br />

     <asp:Button
        id="btnSubmit"
        Text="Submit"
        Runat="server" />

    </div>
    </form>
</body>
</html>
```


ShowSetFocusOnError.aspx

Finally, if you want to really emphasize the controls associated with a validation error, you can take advantage of the `Page.Validators` property. This property exposes the collection of all the validation controls in a page. In next listing, the `Page.Validators` property highlights each control that has a validation error.

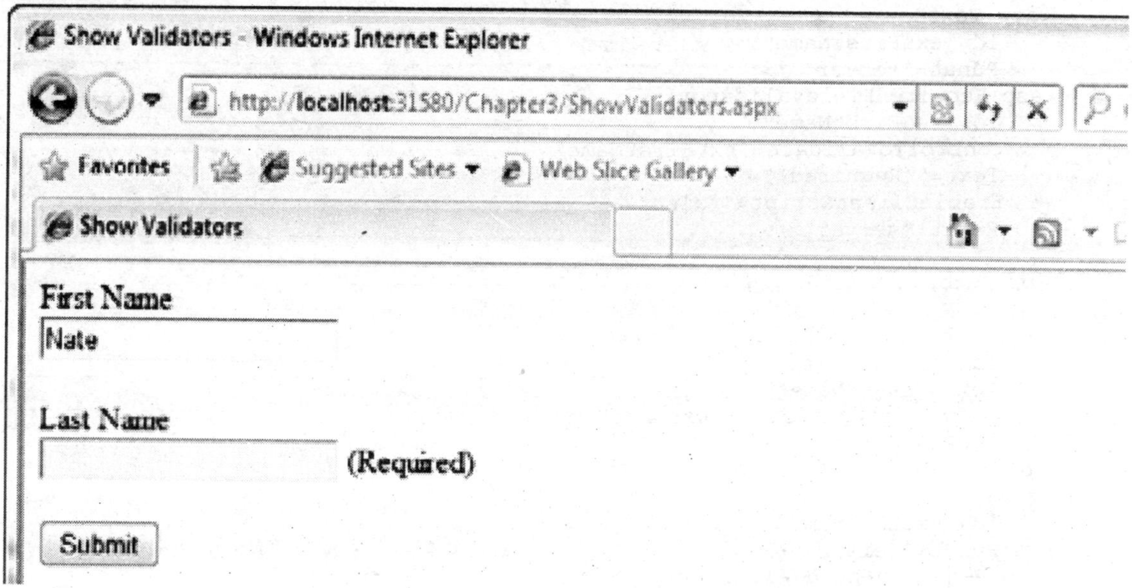

Changing the background color of form fields.

```
Code View: Scroll / Show All
<%@ Page Language="C#" %>
<!DOCTYPE html PUBLIC "-//W3C//DTD XHTML 1.0 Transitional//EN"
"http://www.w3.org/TR/xhtml1/DTD/xhtml1-transitional.dtd">
<script runat="server">

    void Page_PreRender()
    {
        foreach (BaseValidator valControl in Page.Validators)
        {
            WebControl assControl =
```

```
(WebControl)Page.FindControl(valControl.ControlToValidate);
            if (!valControl.IsValid)
                assControl.BackColor = System.Drawing.Color.Yellow;
            else
                assControl.BackColor = System.Drawing.Color.White;
        }
    }
</script>
<html xmlns="http://www.w3.org/1999/xhtml" >
<head id="Head1" runat="server">
    <title>Show Validators</title>
</head>
<body>
    <form id="form1" runat="server">
    <div>

    <asp:Label
        id="lblFirstName"
        Text="First Name"
        AssociatedControlID="txtFirstName"
        Runat="server" />
    <br />
    <asp:TextBox
        id="txtFirstName"
        Runat="server" />
    <asp:RequiredFieldValidator
        id="reqFirstName"
        ControlToValidate="txtFirstName"
        Text="(Required)"
        EnableClientScript="false"
        Runat="server" />

    <br /><br />

    <asp:Label
        id="lblLastName"
        Text="Last Name"
        AssociatedControlID="txtLastName"
        Runat="server" />
    <br />
    <asp:TextBox
        id="txtLastname"
        Runat="server" />
    <asp:RequiredFieldValidator
        id="reqLastName"
        ControlToValidate="txtLastName"
        Text="(Required)"
        EnableClientScript="false"
        Runat="server" />

    <br /><br />

    <asp:Button
        id="btnSubmit"
        Text="Submit"
        Runat="server" />

    </div>
```

```
    </form>
</body>
</html>
```

ShowValidators.aspx

The `Page.Validators` property is used in the `Page_PreRender()` handler. The `IsValid` property is checked for each control in the `Page.Validators` collection. If `IsValid` returns `False`, the control validated by the validation control is highlighted with a yellow background color.

Using Validation Groups

In the first version of the ASP.NET Framework, there was no easy way to add two forms to the same page. If you added more than one form to a page, and both forms contained validation controls, the validation controls in both forms were evaluated regardless of which form you submitted.

For example, imagine that you wanted to create a page that contained both a login and registration form. The login form appeared in the left column and the registration form appeared in the right column. If both forms included validation controls, submitting the login form caused any validation controls contained in the registration form to be evaluated.

Since the release of ASP.NET 2.0, you no longer face this limitation. The ASP.NET 2.0 Framework introduced the idea of validation groups. A validation group enables you to group related form fields together. For example, the page in next listing contains both a login and registration form, and both forms contain independent sets of validation controls.

```
Code View: Scroll / Show All
<%@ Page Language="C#" %>
<!DOCTYPE html PUBLIC "-//W3C//DTD XHTML 1.0 Transitional//EN"
"http://www.w3.org/TR/xhtml1/DTD/xhtml1-transitional.dtd">
<script runat="server">

    void btnLogin_Click(Object sender, EventArgs e)
    {
        if (Page.IsValid)
            lblLoginResult.Text = "Log in successful!";
    }

    void btnRegister_Click(Object sender, EventArgs e)
    {
        if (Page.IsValid)
            lblRegisterResult.Text = "Registration successful!";
    }
</script>
<html xmlns="http://www.w3.org/1999/xhtml" >
<head id="Head1" runat="server">
    <style type="text/css">
        html
        {
            background-color:silver;
        }
        .column
        {
            float:left;
            width:300px;
            margin-left:10px;
            background-color:white;
            border:solid 1px black;
```

```
            padding:10px;
        }

    </style>
    <title>Show Validation Groups</title>
</head>
<body>
    <form id="form1" runat="server">

    <div class="column">
    <fieldset>
    <legend>Login</legend>
    <p>
    Please log in to our Website.
    </p>
    <asp:Label
        id="lblUserName"
        Text="User Name:"
        AssociatedControlID="txtUserName"
        Runat="server" />
    <br />
    <asp:TextBox
        id="txtUserName"
        Runat="server" />
    <asp:RequiredFieldValidator
        id="reqUserName"
        ControlToValidate="txtUserName"
        Text="(Required)"
        ValidationGroup="LoginGroup"
        Runat="server" />
    <br /><br />
    <asp:Label
        id="lblPassword"
        Text="Password:"
        AssociatedControlID="txtPassword"
        Runat="server" />
    <br />
    <asp:TextBox
        id="txtPassword"
        TextMode="Password"
        Runat="server" />
    <asp:RequiredFieldValidator
        id="reqPassword"
        ControlToValidate="txtPassword"
        Text="(Required)"
        ValidationGroup="LoginGroup"
        Runat="server" />
    <br /><br />
    <asp:Button
        id="btnLogin"
        Text="Login"
        ValidationGroup="LoginGroup"
        Runat="server" OnClick="btnLogin_Click" />
    </fieldset>

    <asp:Label
        id="lblLoginResult"
        Runat="server" />
```

```
</div>

<div class="column">
<fieldset>
<legend>Register</legend>
<p>
If you do not have a User Name, please
register at our Website.
</p>
<asp:Label
    id="lblFirstName"
    Text="First Name:"
    AssociatedControlID="txtFirstName"
    Runat="server" />
<br />
<asp:TextBox
    id="txtFirstName"
    Runat="server" />
<asp:RequiredFieldValidator
    id="reqFirstName"
    ControlToValidate="txtFirstName"
    Text="(Required)"
    ValidationGroup="RegisterGroup"
    Runat="server" />
<br /><br />
<asp:Label
    id="lblLastName"
    Text="Last Name:"
    AssociatedControlID="txtLastName"
    Runat="server" />
<br />
<asp:TextBox
    id="txtLastName"
    Runat="server" />
<asp:RequiredFieldValidator
    id="reqLastName"
    ControlToValidate="txtLastName"
    Text="(Required)"
    ValidationGroup="RegisterGroup"
    Runat="server" />
<br /><br />
<asp:Button
    id="btnRegister"
    Text="Register"
    ValidationGroup="RegisterGroup"
    Runat="server" OnClick="btnRegister_Click" />
</fieldset>

<asp:Label
    id="lblRegisterResult"
    Runat="server" />

</div>

</form>
</body>
</html>
```

ShowValidationGroups.aspx

The validation controls and the button controls all include `ValidationGroup` properties. The controls associated with the login form all have the value `"LoginGroup"` assigned to their `ValidationGroup` properties. The controls associated with the register form all have the value `"RegisterGroup"` assigned to their `ValidationGroup` properties.

Because the form fields are grouped into different validation groups, you can submit the two forms independently. Submitting the Login form does not trigger the validation controls in the Register form.

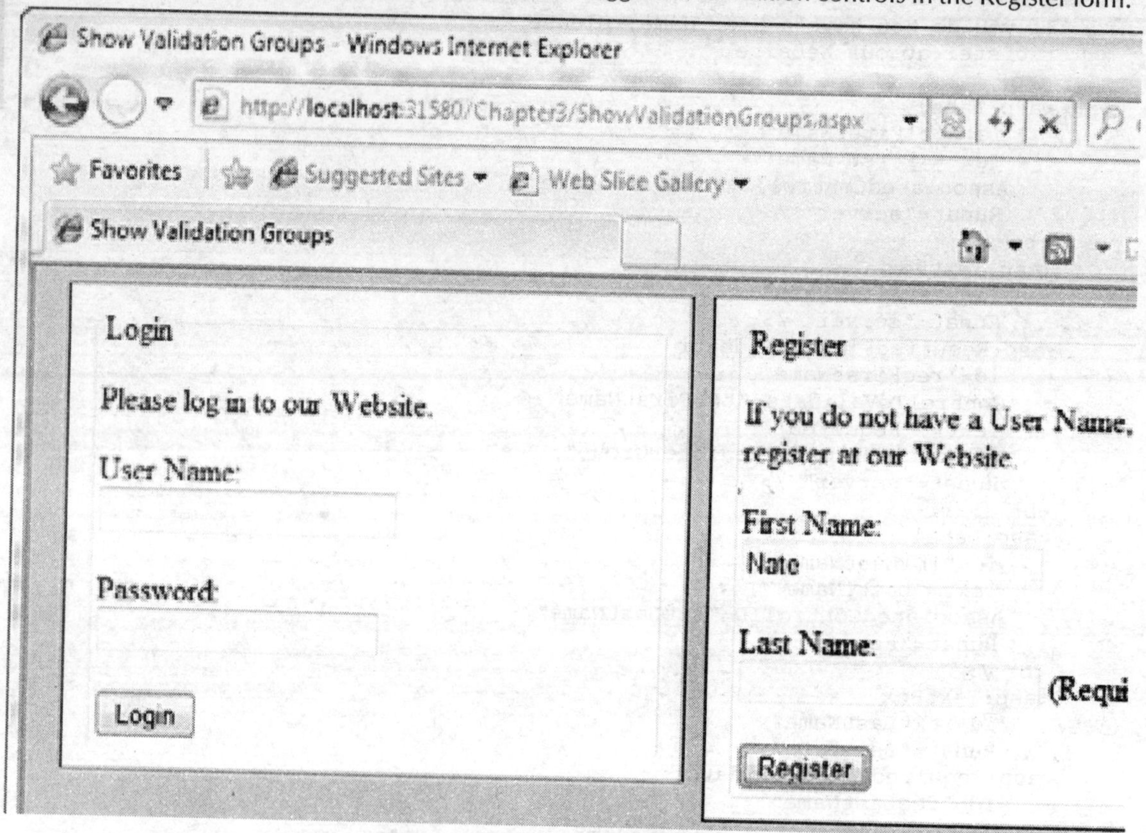

Figure Using validation groups.

You can assign any string to the `ValidationGroup` property. The only purpose of the string is to associate different controls in a form together into different groups.

Using validation groups is particularly important when working with Web Parts because multiple Web Parts with different forms might be added to the same page.

Disabling Validation

All the button controls—`Button`, `LinkButton`, and `ImageButton`—include a `CausesValidation` property. If you assign the value `False` to this property, clicking the button bypasses any validation in the page. Bypassing validation is useful when creating a Cancel button. For example, the page in next listing includes a Cancel button that redirects the user back to the `Default.aspx` page.

Code View: Scroll / Show All

```
<%@ Page Language="C#" %>
<!DOCTYPE html PUBLIC "-//W3C//DTD XHTML 1.0 Transitional//EN"
"http://www.w3.org/TR/xhtml1/DTD/xhtml1-transitional.dtd">
```

```
<script runat="server">

    void btnCancel_Click(Object sender, EventArgs e)
    {
        Response.Redirect("~/Default.aspx");
    }
</script>
<html xmlns="http://www.w3.org/1999/xhtml" >
<head id="Head1" runat="server">
    <title>Show Disable Validation</title>
</head>
<body>
    <form id="form1" runat="server">
    <div>

    <asp:Label
        id="lblFirstName"
        Text="First Name:"
        AssociatedControlID="txtFirstName"
        Runat="server" />
    <asp:TextBox
        id="txtFirstName"
        Runat="server" />
    <asp:RequiredFieldValidator
        id="reqFirstName"
        ControlToValidate="txtFirstName"
        Text="(Required)"
        Runat="server" />
    <br /><br />
    <asp:Button
        id="btnSubmit"
        Text="Submit"
        Runat="server" />
    <asp:Button
        id="btnCancel"
        Text="Cancel"
        OnClick="btnCancel_Click"
        CausesValidation="false"
        Runat="server" />

    </div>
    </form>
</body>
</html>
```

ShowDisableValidation.aspx

The Cancel button in above listing includes the `CausesValidation` property with the value `False`. If the button did not include this property, the `RequiredFieldValidator` control would prevent you from submitting the form when you click the Cancel button.

Using the RequiredFieldValidator Control

The `RequiredFieldValidator` control enables you to require a user to enter a value into a form field before submitting the form. You must set two important properties when using the `RequiredFieldValidator` control:

- `ControlToValidate`— The ID of the form field validated.

- `Text`— The error message displayed when validation fails.

The page in next listing illustrates how you can use the `RequiredFieldValidator` control to require a user to enter both a first and last name.

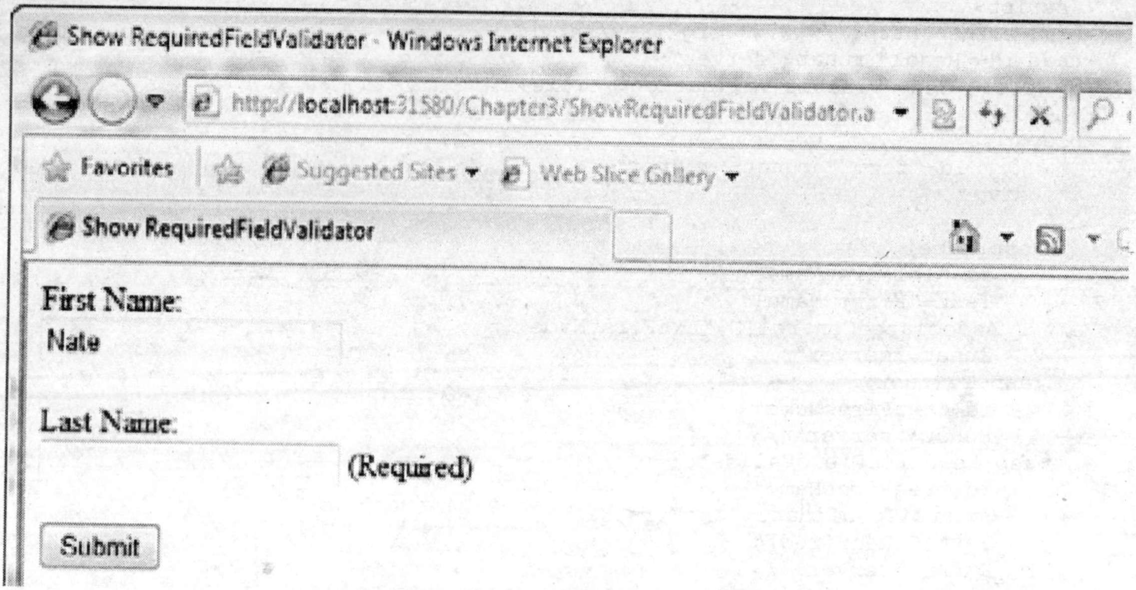

Requiring a user to enter form field values.

```
Code View: Scroll / Show All
<%@ Page Language="C#" %>
<!DOCTYPE html PUBLIC "-//W3C//DTD XHTML 1.0 Transitional//EN"
"http://www.w3.org/TR/xhtml1/DTD/xhtml1-transitional.dtd">
<html xmlns="http://www.w3.org/1999/xhtml" >
<head id="Head1" runat="server">
    <title>Show RequiredFieldValidator</title>
</head>
<body>
    <form id="form1" runat="server">
    <div>

    <asp:Label
        id="lblFirstName"
        Text="First Name:"
        AssociatedControlID="txtFirstName"
        Runat="server" />
    <br />
    <asp:TextBox
        id="txtFirstName"
        Runat="server" />
    <asp:RequiredFieldValidator
        id="reqFirstName"
        ControlToValidate="txtFirstName"
        Text="(Required)"
        Runat="server" />

    <br /><br />
```

```
    <asp:Label
        id="lblLastName"
        Text="Last Name:"
        AssociatedControlID="txtLastName"
        Runat="server" />
    <br />
    <asp:TextBox
        id="txtLastName"
        Runat="server" />
    <asp:RequiredFieldValidator
        id="reqLastName"
        ControlToValidate="txtLastName"
        Text="(Required)"
        Runat="server" />

    <br /><br />

    <asp:Button
        id="btnSubmit"
        Text="Submit"
        Runat="server" />

    </div>
    </form>
</body>
</html>
```

ShowRequiredFieldValidator.aspx

By default, the `RequiredFieldValidator` checks for a nonempty string (spaces don't count). If you enter anything into the form field associated with the `RequiredFieldValidator`, the `RequiredFieldValidator` does not display its validation error message.

You can use the `RequiredFieldValidator` control's `InitialValue` property to specify a default value other than an empty string. For example, the page in next listing uses a `RequiredFieldValidator` to validate a `DropDownList` control.

```
Code View: Scroll / Show All
<%@ Page Language="C#" %>
<!DOCTYPE html PUBLIC "-//W3C//DTD XHTML 1.0 Transitional//EN"
"http://www.w3.org/TR/xhtml1/DTD/xhtml1-transitional.dtd">
<script runat="server">

    void btnSubmit_Click(Object sender, EventArgs e)
    {
        if (Page.IsValid)
            lblResult.Text = dropFavoriteColor.SelectedValue;
    }
</script>
<html xmlns="http://www.w3.org/1999/xhtml" >
<head id="Head1" runat="server">
    <title>Show Initial Value</title>
</head>
<body>
    <form id="form1" runat="server">
    <div>

    <asp:Label
```

```
        id="lblFavoriteColor"
        Text="Favorite Color:"
       AssociatedControlID="dropFavoriteColor"
        Runat="server" />
    <br />
    <asp:DropDownList
        id="dropFavoriteColor"
        Runat="server">
       <asp:ListItem Text="Select Color" Value="none" />
       <asp:ListItem Text="Red" Value="Red" />
       <asp:ListItem Text="Blue" Value="Blue" />
       <asp:ListItem Text="Green" Value="Green" />
    </asp:DropDownList>
    <asp:RequiredFieldValidator
        id="reqFavoriteColor"
        Text="(Required)"
        InitialValue="none"
       ControlToValidate="dropFavoriteColor"
        Runat="server" />

    <br /><br />

    <asp:Button
        id="btnSubmit"
        Text="Submit"
       Runat="server" OnClick="btnSubmit_Click" />

    <hr />

    <asp:Label
        id="lblResult"
        Runat="server" />

    </div>
    </form>
</body>
</html>
```

ShowInitialValue.aspx

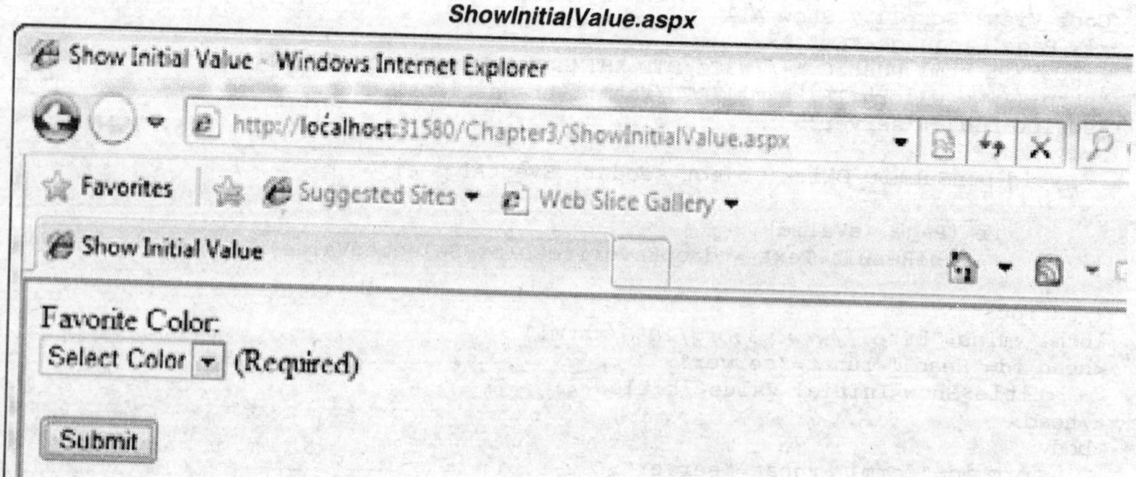

Using a RequiredFieldValidator with a DropDownList control.

The first list item displayed by the `DropDownList` control displays the text `"Select Color"`. If you submit the form without selecting a color from the `DropDownList` control, a validation error message displays. The `RequiredFieldValidator` control includes an `InitialValue` property. The value of the first list from the `DropDownList` control is assigned to this property.

Using the RangeValidator Control

The `RangeValidator` control enables you to check whether the value of a form field falls between a certain minimum and maximum value. You must set five properties when using this control:

- `ControlToValidate`— The ID of the form field validated.
- `Text`— The error message displayed when validation fails.
- `MinimumValue`— The minimum value of the validation range.
- `MaximumValue`— The maximum value of the validation range.
- `Type`— The type of comparison to perform. Possible values are `String`, `Integer`, `Double`, `Date`, and `Currency`.

For example, the page in next listing includes a `RangeValidator` that validates an age form field. If you do not enter an age between 5 and 100, a validation error displays.

Code View: Scroll / Show All

```
<%@ Page Language="C#" %>
<!DOCTYPE html PUBLIC "-//W3C//DTD XHTML 1.0 Transitional//EN"
"http://www.w3.org/TR/xhtml1/DTD/xhtml1-transitional.dtd">
<html xmlns="http://www.w3.org/1999/xhtml" >
<head id="Head1" runat="server">
    <title>Show RangeValidator</title>
</head>
<body>
    <form id="form1" runat="server">
    <div>

    <asp:Label
        id="lblAge"
        Text="Age:"
       AssociatedControlID="txtAge"
        Runat="server" />
    <asp:TextBox
        id="txtAge"
        Runat="server" />
    <asp:RangeValidator
        id="reqAge"
        ControlToValidate="txtAge"
        Text="(Invalid Age)"
        MinimumValue="5"
        MaximumValue="100"
        Type="Integer"
        Runat="server" />

    <br /><br />

    <asp:Button
        id="btnSubmit"
        Text="Submit"
        Runat="server" />
```

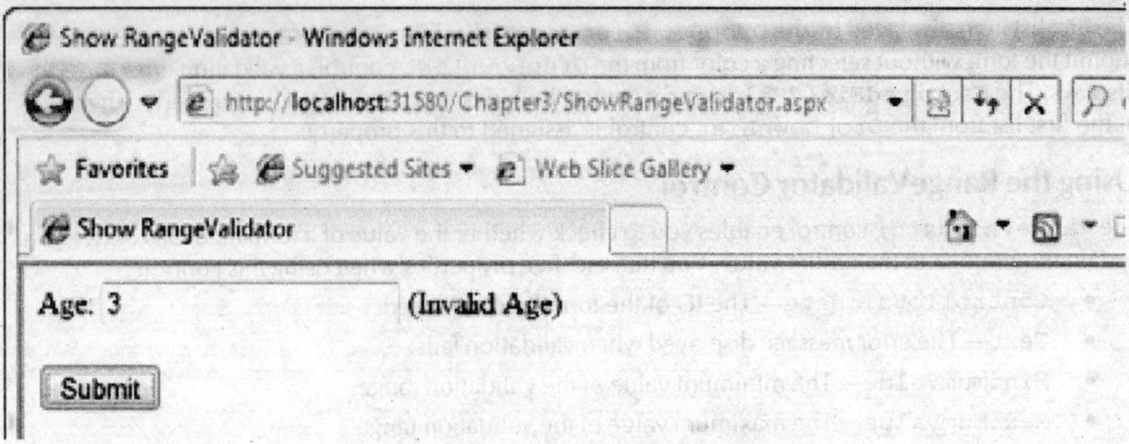

Validating a form field against a range of values.

```
        </div>
        </form>
    </body>
    </html>
```

ShowRangeValidator.aspx

If you submit the form in next listing with an age less than 5 or greater than 100, the validation error message displays. The validation message also displays if you enter a value that is not a number. If the value entered into the form field cannot be converted into the data type represented by the `RangeValidator` control's `Type` property, the error message displays.

If you don't enter any value into the age field and submit the form, no error message displays. If you want to require a user to enter a value, you must associate a `RequiredFieldValidator` with the form field. Don't forget to set the `Type` property when using the `RangeValidator` control. By default, the `Type` property has the value `String`, and the `RangeValidator` performs a string comparison to determine whether a value falls between the minimum and maximum value.

Using the CompareValidator Control

The `CompareValidator` control enables you to perform three different types of validation tasks. You can use the `CompareValidator` to perform a data type check. In other words, you can use the control to determine whether a user has entered the proper type of value into a form field, such as a date in a birth date field. You also can use the `CompareValidator` to compare the value entered into a form field against a fixed value. For example, if you build an auction website, you can use the `CompareValidator` to check whether a new minimum bid is greater than the previous minimum bid.

Finally, you can use the `CompareValidator` to compare the value of one form field against another. For example, you use the `CompareValidator` to check whether the value entered into the meeting start date is less than the value entered into the meeting end date.

The `CompareValidator` has six important properties:

- `ControlToValidate`— The ID of the form field validated.
- `Text`— The error message displayed when validation fails.
- `Type`— The type of value compared. Possible values are `String`, `Integer`, `Double`, `Date`, and `Currency`.

- `Operator`— The type of comparison to perform. Possible values are `DataTypeCheck`, `Equal`, `GreaterThan`, `GreaterThanEqual`, `LessThan`, `LessThanEqual`, and `NotEqual`.
- `ValueToCompare`— The fixed value against which to compare.
- `ControlToCompare`— The ID of a control against which to compare.

The page in next listing illustrates how you can use the `CompareValidator` to perform a data type check. The page contains a birth date field. If you enter a value that is not a date, the validation error message displays.

```
Code View: Scroll / Show All
<%@ Page Language="C#" %>
<!DOCTYPE html PUBLIC "-//W3C//DTD XHTML 1.0 Transitional//EN"
"http://www.w3.org/TR/xhtml1/DTD/xhtml1-transitional.dtd">
<html xmlns="http://www.w3.org/1999/xhtml" >
<head id="Head1" runat="server">
    <title>Show Data Type Check</title>
</head>
<body>
    <form id="form1" runat="server">
     <div>

     <asp:Label
         id="lblBirthDate"
         Text="Birth Date:"
        AssociatedControlID="txtBirthDate"
         Runat="server" />
     <asp:TextBox
         id="txtBirthDate"
         Runat="server" />
    <asp:CompareValidator
         id="cmpBirthDate"
         Text="(Invalid Date)"
        ControlToValidate="txtBirthDate"
         Type="Date"
        Operator="DataTypeCheck"
         Runat="server" />

     <br /><br />

     <asp:Button
         id="btnSubmit"
         Text="Submit"
         Runat="server" />

     </div>
     </form>
</body>
</html>
```

ShowDataTypeCheck.aspx

The page in above listing contains a `CompareValidator` control. Its `Type` property has the value `Date`, and its `Operator` property has the value `DataTypeCheck`. If you enter a value other than a date into the birth date field, the validation error message displays.

An important limitation of the `CompareValidator` concerns how it performs a data type check. You cannot enter a long date into the form in above listing (for example, December 25, 1966). You must enter

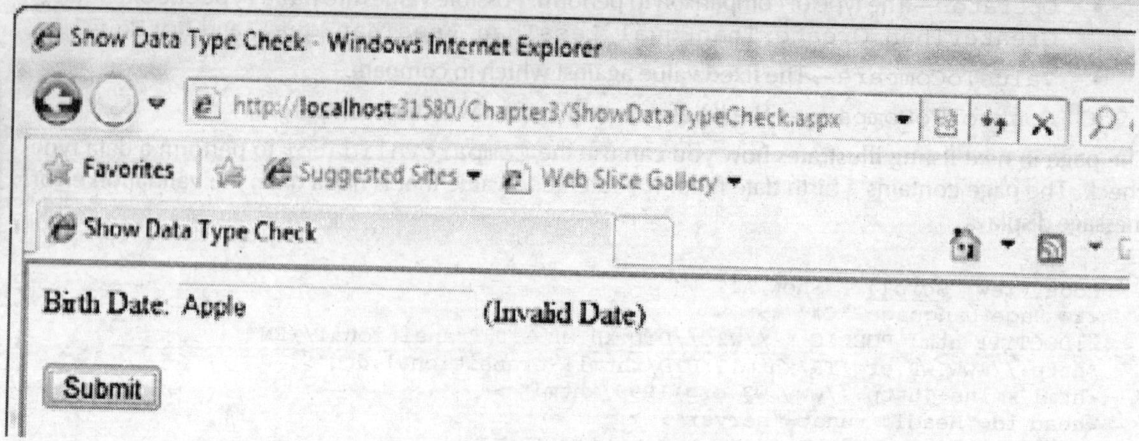

Performing a data type check.

a short date (for example, 12/25/1966). When validating currency amounts, you cannot enter the currency symbol. If these limitations concern you, you can use either the `RegularExpression` or `CustomValidator` controls to perform a more flexible data type check.

You can also use the `CompareValidator` to perform a comparison against a fixed value. For example, the page in next listing uses a `CompareValidator` to check whether a date entered into a form field is greater than the current date.

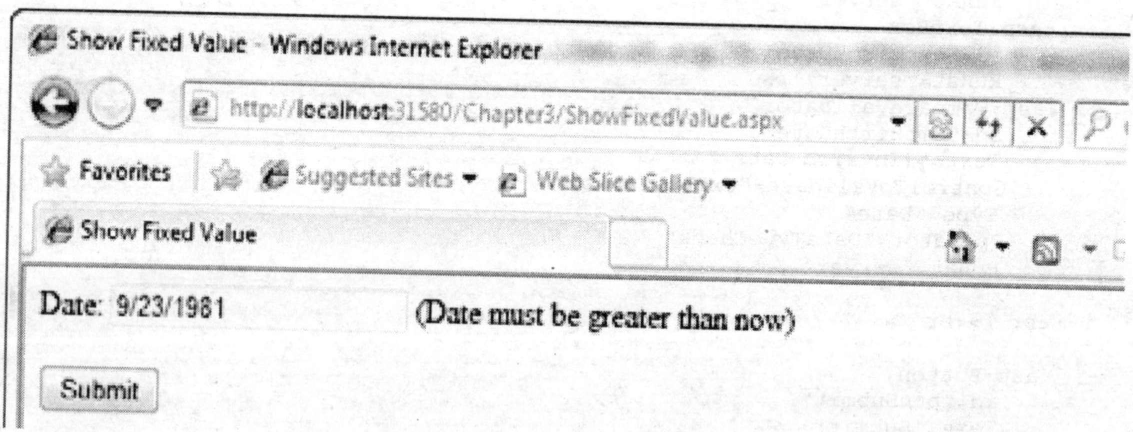

Figure Comparing a form field against a fixed value.

```
Code View: Scroll / Show All
<%@ Page Language="C#" %>
<!DOCTYPE html PUBLIC "-//W3C//DTD XHTML 1.0 Transitional//EN"
"http://www.w3.org/TR/xhtml1/DTD/xhtml1-transitional.dtd">
<script runat="server">

  void Page_Load()
  {
     cmpDate.ValueToCompare = DateTime.Now.ToString("d");
  }
</script>
<html xmlns="http://www.w3.org/1999/xhtml" >
```

```
<head id="Head1" runat="server">
    <title>Show Fixed Value</title>
</head>
<body>
    <form id="form1" runat="server">
    <div>

    <asp:Label
        id="lblDate"
        Text="Date:"
        AssociatedControlID="txtDate"
        Runat="server" />
    <asp:TextBox
        id="txtDate"
        Runat="server" />
    <asp:CompareValidator
        id="cmpDate"
        Text="(Date must be greater than now)"
        ControlToValidate="txtDate"
        Type="Date"
        Operator="GreaterThan"
        Runat="server" />

    <br /><br />

    <asp:Button
        id="btnSubmit"
        Text="Submit"
        Runat="server" />

    </div>
    </form>
</body>
</html>
```

ShowFixedValue.aspx

Finally, you can use a `CompareValidator` to compare the value of one form field against another form field. The page in next listing contains a meeting start date and meeting end date field. If you enter a value into the first field that is greater than the second field, a validation error displays.

Code View: Scroll / Show All

```
<%@ Page Language="C#" %>
<!DOCTYPE html PUBLIC "-//W3C//DTD XHTML 1.0 Transitional//EN"
"http://www.w3.org/TR/xhtml1/DTD/xhtml1-transitional.dtd">
<html xmlns="http://www.w3.org/1999/xhtml" >
<head id="Head1" runat="server">
    <title>Show Compare Values</title>
</head>
<body>
    <form id="form1" runat="server">
    <div>

    <asp:Label
        id="lblStartDate"
        Text="Start Date:"
        Runat="server" />
    <asp:TextBox
```

CHAPTER 4

```
        id="txtStartDate"
        Runat="server" />

    <br /><br />

    <asp:Label
        id="lblEndDate"
        Text="End Date:"
        Runat="server" />
    <asp:TextBox
        id="txtEndDate"
        Runat="server" />
    <asp:CompareValidator
        id="cmpDate"
        Text="(End date must be greater than start date)"
        ControlToValidate="txtEndDate"
        ControlToCompare="txtStartDate"
        Type="Date"
        Operator="GreaterThan"
        Runat="server" />

    <br /><br />

    <asp:Button
        id="btnSubmit"
        Text="Submit"
        Runat="server" />

    </div>
    </form>
</body>
</html>
```

ShowCompareValues.aspx

Just like the RangeValidator, the CompareValidator does not display an error if you don't enter a value into the form field being validated. If you want to require that a user enter a value, you must associate a RequiredFieldValidator control with the field.

Using the RegularExpressionValidator Control

The RegularExpressionValidator control enables you to compare the value of a form field against a regular expression. You can use a regular expression to represent string patterns such as email addresses, Social Security numbers, phone numbers, dates, currency amounts, and product codes.

For example, the page in next listing enables you to validate an email address.

```
Code View: Scroll / Show All
<%@ Page Language="C#" %>
<!DOCTYPE html PUBLIC "-//W3C//DTD XHTML 1.0 Transitional//EN"
"http://www.w3.org/TR/xhtml1/DTD/xhtml1-transitional.dtd">
<html xmlns="http://www.w3.org/1999/xhtml" >
<head id="Head1" runat="server">
   <title>Show RegularExpressionValidator</title>
</head>
<body>
   <form id="form1" runat="server">
   <div>
```

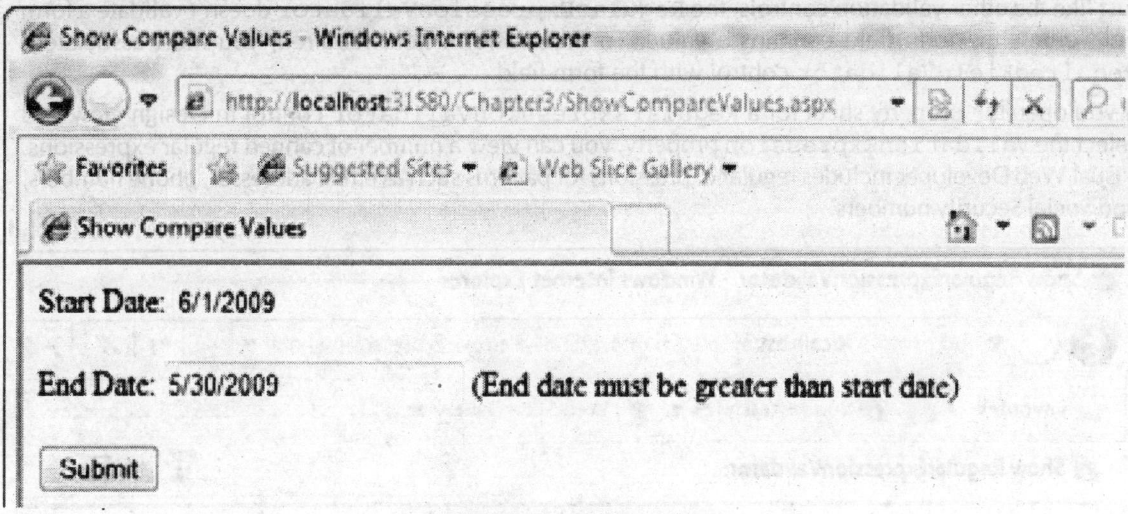

Comparing two form fields.

```
<asp:Label
    id="lblEmail"
    Text="Email Address:"
   AssociatedControlID="txtEmail"
    Runat="server" />
<asp:TextBox
    id="txtEmail"
    Runat="server" />
<asp:RegularExpressionValidator
    id="regEmail"
   ControlToValidate="txtEmail"
    Text="(Invalid email)"
  ValidationExpression="\w+([-+.']\w+)*@\w+([-.]\w+)*\.\w+([-.]\w+)*"
    Runat="server" />

<br /><br />

<asp:Button
    id="btnSubmit"
    Text="Submit"
    Runat="server" />

</div>
</form>
</body>
</html>
```

ShowRegularExpressionValidator.aspx

The regular expression is assigned to the `RegularExpressionValidator` control's `ValidationExpression` property. It looks like this:

```
\w+([-+.']\w+)*@\w+([-.]\w+)*\.\w+([-.]\w+)*
```

Regular expressions are not fun to read. This pattern matches a simple email address. The `\w` expression represents any nonwhitespace character. Therefore, roughly, this regular expression matches an email address that contains nonwhitespace characters, followed by an @ sign, followed by nonwhitespace characters, followed by a period, followed by more nonwhitespace characters.

Just like the other validation controls, the `RegularExpressionValidator` doesn't validate a form field unless the form field contains a value. To make a form field required, you must associate a `RequiredFieldValidator` control with the form field.

If you open the property sheet for a `RegularExpressionValidator` control in Design view and select the `ValidationExpression` property, you can view a number of canned regular expressions. Visual Web Developer includes regular expressions for patterns such as email addresses, phone numbers, and Social Security numbers.

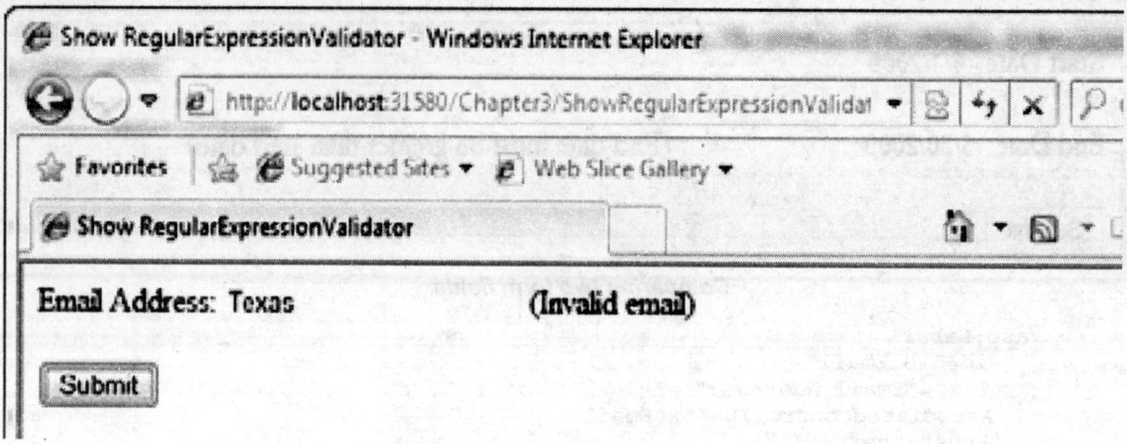

Validating an email address.

Using the CustomValidator Control

If none of the other validation controls perform the type of validation that you need, you can always use the `CustomValidator` control. You can associate a custom validation function with the `CustomValidator` control.

The `CustomValidator` control has three important properties:

- `ControlToValidate`— The ID of the form field being validated.
- `Text`— The error message displayed when validation fails.
- `ClientValidationFunction`— The name of a client-side function used to perform client-side validation.

The `CustomValidator` also supports one event:

- `ServerValidate`— This event is raised when the `CustomValidator` performs validation.

You associate your custom validation function with the `CustomValidator` control by handling the `ServerValidate` event. For example, imagine that you want to validate the length of a string entered into a form field. You want to ensure that a user does not enter more than 10 characters into a multiline `TextBox` control. The page in next listing contains an event handler for a `CustomValidator` control's `ServerValidate` event, which checks the string's length.

```
Code View: Scroll / Show All
<%@ Page Language="C#" %>
<!DOCTYPE html PUBLIC "-//W3C//DTD XHTML 1.0 Transitional//EN"
"http://www.w3.org/TR/xhtml1/DTD/xhtml1-transitional.dtd">
<script runat="server">
```

```
    void valComments_ServerValidate(Object source, ServerValidateEventArgs
args)
    {
        if (args.Value.Length > 10)
            args.IsValid = false;
        else
            args.IsValid = true;
    }
</script>
<html xmlns="http://www.w3.org/1999/xhtml" >
<head id="Head1" runat="server">
    <title>Show CustomValidator</title>
</head>
<body>
    <form id="form1" runat="server">
    <div>

    <asp:Label
        id="lblComments"
        Text="Comments:"
        AssociatedControlID="txtComments"
        Runat="server" />
    <br />
    <asp:TextBox
        id="txtComments"
        TextMode="MultiLine"
        Columns="30"
        Rows="5"
        Runat="server" />
    <asp:CustomValidator
        id="valComments"
        ControlToValidate="txtComments"
        Text="(Comments must be less than 10 characters)"
        OnServerValidate="valComments_ServerValidate"
        Runat="server" />

    <br /><br />

    <asp:Button
        id="btnSubmit"
        Text="Submit"
        Runat="server" />

    </div>
    </form>
</body>
</html>
```

ShowCustomValidator.aspx

The second parameter passed to the `ServerValidate` event handler is an instance of the `ServerValidateEventArgs` class. This class has three properties:

- `Value`— Represents the value of the form field being validated.
- `IsValid`— Represents whether validation fails or succeeds.
- `ValidateEmptyText`— Represents whether validation is performed when the form field being validated does not contain a value.

In above listing, if the string represented by the `Value` property is longer than 10 characters, the value `False` is assigned to the `IsValid` property and validation fails. Otherwise, the value `True` is assigned to the `IsValid` property and the input field passes the validation check.

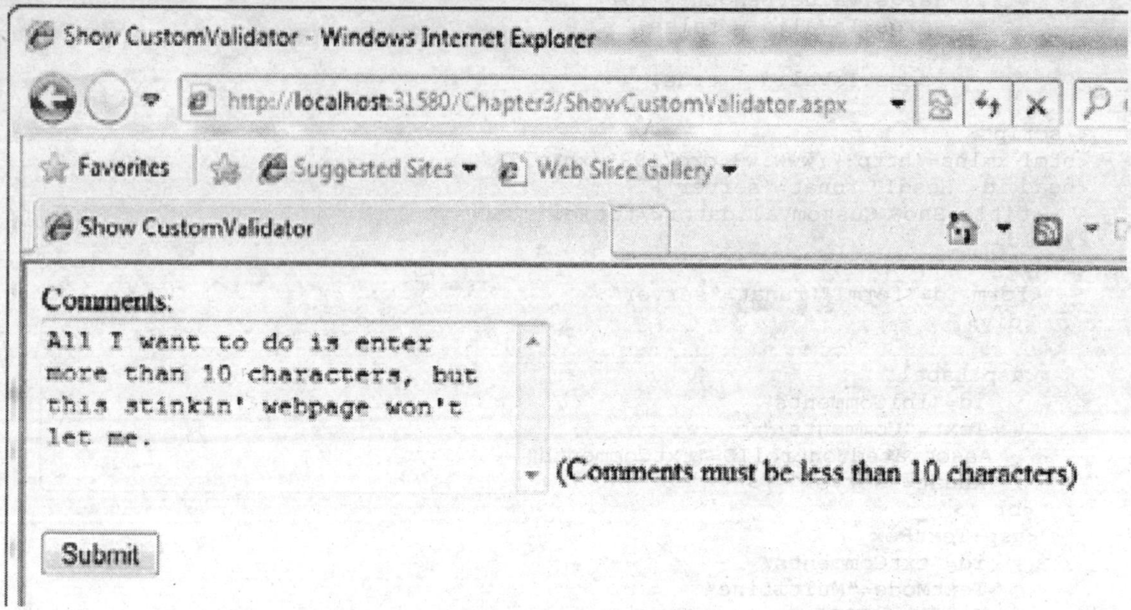

Figure Validating field length with the CustomValidator control.

The `ServerValidate` event handler in the last listing is a server-side function. Therefore, validation does not occur until the page is posted back to the web server. If you want to perform validation on both the client (browser) and server, you need to supply a client-side validation function.

If you don't associate a client validation function with a `CustomValidator` control, the `CustomValidator` doesn't render an error message until you post the page back to the server. Because the other validation controls prevent a page from posting if the page contains any validation errors, you won't see the error message rendered by the `CustomValidator` control until you pass every other validation check in a page.

The page in next listing illustrates how you can associate a client-side validation function with the `CustomValidator` control. This page also checks the length of the string entered into a `TextBox` control. However, it checks the length on both the browser and server.

```
Code View: Scroll / Show All
<%@ Page Language="C#" %>
<!DOCTYPE html PUBLIC "-//W3C//DTD XHTML 1.0 Transitional//EN"
"http://www.w3.org/TR/xhtml1/DTD/xhtml1-transitional.dtd">
<script runat="server">

  void valComments_ServerValidate(Object source, ServerValidateEventArgs
args)
     {
        if (args.Value.Length > 10)
            args.IsValid = false;
        else
            args.IsValid = true;
     }
```

```
</script>
<html xmlns="http://www.w3.org/1999/xhtml" >
<head id="Head1" runat="server">
   <script type="text/javascript">
   function valComments_ClientValidate(source, args)
   {
       if (args.Value.length > 10)
           args.IsValid = false;
       else
           args.IsValid = true;
   }

   </script>
   <title>Show CustomValidator with JavaScript</title>
</head>
<body>
   <form id="form1" runat="server">
   <div>

   <asp:Label
       id="lblComments"
       Text="Comments:"
       AssociatedControlID="txtComments"
       Runat="server" />
   <br />
   <asp:TextBox
       id="txtComments"
       TextMode="MultiLine"
       Columns="30"
       Rows="5"
       Runat="server" />
   <asp:CustomValidator
       id="valComments"
       ControlToValidate="txtComments"
       Text="(Comments must be less than 10 characters)"
       OnServerValidate="valComments_ServerValidate"
       ClientValidationFunction="valComments_ClientValidate"
       Runat="server" />

   <br /><br />

   <asp:Button
       id="btnSubmit"
       Text="Submit"
       Runat="server" />

   </div>
   </form>
</body>
</html>
```

ShowCustomValidatorJS.aspx

The `CustomValidator` control in above listing includes a `ClientValidationFunction` property. This property contains the name of a JavaScript function defined in the page's `<head>` tag.

The JavaScript validation function accepts the same two parameters as the server-side validation function. The first parameter represents the `CustomValidator` control, and the second parameter represents an object that includes both a `Value` and an `IsValid` property. The client-side function is nearly identical to the server-side function (with the important difference that it is written in JavaScript).

Unlike the `RangeValidator`, `CompareValidator`, and `RegularExpressionValidator` controls, you can validate a form field with the `CustomValidator` control even when the form field is left blank. The `CustomValidator` control includes a property named the `ValidateEmptyText` property. You can use this property to cause the `CustomValidator` control to validate a form field even when the user hasn't entered a value into the form field. For example, the page in next listing contains a `TextBox` that requires a product code that contains exactly four characters.

```
Code View: Scroll / Show All
<%@ Page Language="C#" %>
<!DOCTYPE html PUBLIC "-//W3C//DTD XHTML 1.0 Transitional//EN"
"http://www.w3.org/TR/xhtml1/DTD/xhtml1-transitional.dtd">
<script runat="server">

    void valProductCode_ServerValidate(Object source, ServerValidateEventArgs
args)
    {
        if (args.Value.Length == 4)
            args.IsValid = true;
        else
            args.IsValid = false;
    }
</script>
<html xmlns="http://www.w3.org/1999/xhtml" >
<head id="Head1" runat="server">
    <title>Show Validate Empty Text</title>
</head>
<body>
    <form id="form1" runat="server">
    <div>

    <asp:Label
        id="lblProductCode"
        Text="Product Code:"
        AssociatedControlID="txtProductCode"
        Runat="server" />
    <br />
    <asp:TextBox
        id="txtProductCode"
        Runat="server" />
    <asp:CustomValidator
        id="valProductCode"
        ControlToValidate="txtProductCode"
        Text="(Invalid product code)"
        ValidateEmptyText="true"
        OnServerValidate="valProductCode_ServerValidate"
        Runat="server" />

    <br /><br />

    <asp:Button
        id="btnSubmit"
        Text="Submit"
        Runat="server" />
```

```
        </div>
        </form>
    </body>
    </html>
```

ShowValidateEmptyText.aspx

The `CustomValidator` control in above listing includes a `ValidateEmptyText` property that has the value `True`. If the `ValidateEmptyText` property was not included, and you submitted the form without entering any data, no validation error would display. Finally, unlike the other validation controls, you are not required to associate the `CustomValidator` control with any form field. In other words, you don't need to include a `ControlToValidate` property.

For example, the page in next listing contains a timed test. If you don't answer the question within 5 seconds, the `CustomValidator` control displays a validation error message.

```
Code View: Scroll / Show All
<%@ Page Language="C#" %>
<!DOCTYPE html PUBLIC "-//W3C//DTD XHTML 1.0 Transitional//EN"
"http://www.w3.org/TR/xhtml1/DTD/xhtml1-transitional.dtd">
<script runat="server">

    void Page_Load()
    {
        if (!Page.IsPostBack)
            ResetStartTime();
    }

    void btnAgain_Click(Object sender, EventArgs e)
    {
        ResetStartTime();
    }

    void ResetStartTime()
    {
        Session["StartTime"] = DateTime.Now;
    }


    void valAnswer_ServerValidate(Object source, ServerValidateEventArgs
args)
    {
        DateTime startTime = (DateTime)Session["StartTime"];
        if (startTime.AddSeconds(5) > DateTime.Now)
            args.IsValid = true;
        else
            args.IsValid = false;
    }
</script>
<html xmlns="http://www.w3.org/1999/xhtml" >
<head id="Head1" runat="server">
    <title>Timed Test</title>
</head>
<body>
    <form id="form1" runat="server">
    <div>

    <p>
```

```
You have 5 seconds to answer the following question:
</p>

<asp:Label
    id="lblQuestion"
    Text="What was Aristotle's first name?"
    AssociatedControlID="txtAnswer"
    Runat="server" />
<br />
<asp:TextBox
    id="txtAnswer"
    Runat="server" />
<asp:CustomValidator
    id="valAnswer"
    Text="(You answered too slowly!)"
    OnServerValidate="valAnswer_ServerValidate"
    Runat="server"  />

<br /><br />

<asp:Button
    id="btnSubmit"
    Text="Submit"
    Runat="server" />

<asp:Button
    id="btnAgain"
    Text="Try Again!"
    CausesValidation="false"
    OnClick="btnAgain_Click"
    Runat="server" />

</div>
</form>
```

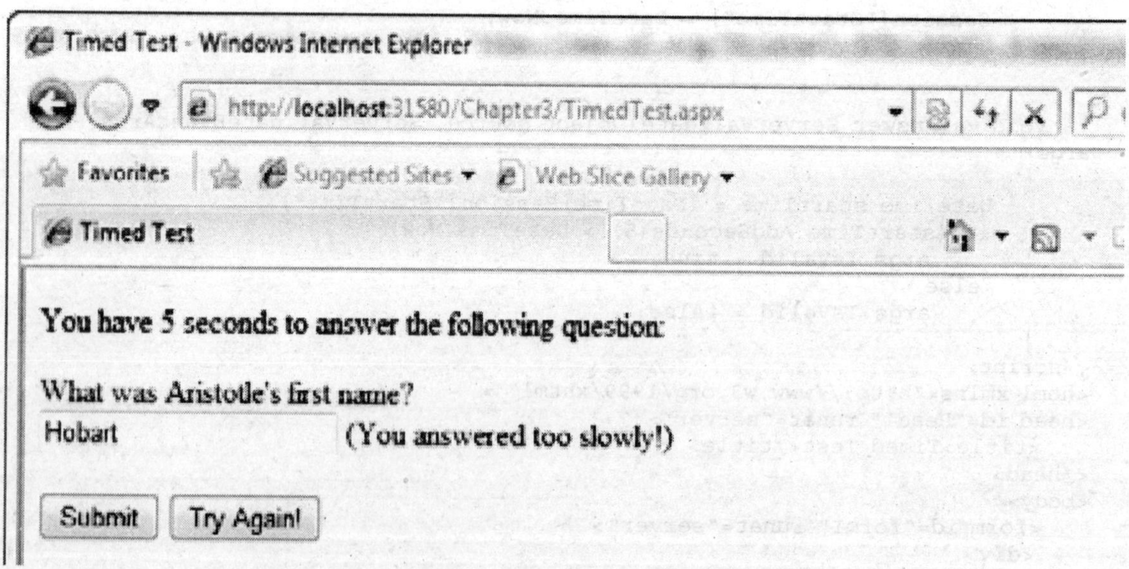

Performing validation against no particular field.

```
</body>
</html>
```

TimedTest.aspx

Using the VALIDATIONSUMMARY Control

The `ValidationSummary` control enables you to display a list of all the validation errors in a page in one location. This control is particularly useful when working with large forms. If a user enters the wrong value for a form field located toward the end of the page, the user might never see the error message. If you use the `ValidationSummary` control, however, you can always display a list of errors at the top of the form.

Each of the validation controls includes an `ErrorMessage` property. We have not been using the `ErrorMessage` property to represent the validation error message. Instead, we have used the `Text` property.

The distinction between the `ErrorMessage` and `Text` property is that any message that you assign to the `ErrorMessage` property appears in the `ValidationSummary` control, and any message that you assign to the `Text` property appears in the body of the page. Normally, you want to keep the error message for the `Text` property short (for example, `"Required!"`). The message assigned to the `ErrorMessage` property, on the other hand, should identify the form field that has the error (for example, `"First name is required!"`).

Note: If you don't assign a value to the `Text` property, the value of the `ErrorMessage` property displays in both the `ValidationSummary` control and the body of the page.

The page in next listing illustrates how you can use the `ValidationSummary` control to display a summary of error messages.

```
Code View: Scroll / Show All
<%@ Page Language="C#" %>
<!DOCTYPE html PUBLIC "-//W3C//DTD XHTML 1.0 Transitional//EN"
"http://www.w3.org/TR/xhtml1/DTD/xhtml1-transitional.dtd">
<html xmlns="http://www.w3.org/1999/xhtml" >
<head id="Head1" runat="server">
    <title>Show ValidationSummary</title>
</head>
<body>
    <form id="form1" runat="server">
    <div>

    <asp:ValidationSummary
        id="ValidationSummary1"
        Runat="server" />

    <asp:Label
        id="lblFirstName"
        Text="First Name:"
       AssociatedControlID="txtFirstName"
        Runat="server" />
    <br />
    <asp:TextBox
        id="txtFirstName"
        Runat="server" />
   <asp:RequiredFieldValidator
        id="reqFirstName"
```

```
        Text="(Required)"
        ErrorMessage="First Name is required"
        ControlToValidate="txtFirstName"
        Runat="server" />

    <br /><br />

    <asp:Label
        id="lblLastName"
        Text="Last Name:"
        AssociatedControlID="txtLastName"
        Runat="server" />
    <br />
    <asp:TextBox
        id="txtLastName"
        Runat="server" />
    <asp:RequiredFieldValidator
        id="reqLastName"
        Text="(Required)"
        ErrorMessage="Last Name is required"
        ControlToValidate="txtLastName"
        Runat="server" />

    <br /><br />

    <asp:Button
        id="btnSubmit"
        Text="Submit"
        Runat="server" />

    </div>
    </form>
</body>
</html>
```

ShowValidationSummary.aspx

If you submit the form in above listing without entering a value for the first and last name, validation error messages appear in both the body of the page and in the `ValidationSummary` control.

The `ValidationSummary` control supports the following properties:

- `DisplayMode`— Enables you to specify how the error messages are formatted. Possible values are `BulletList`, `List`, and `SingleParagraph`.
- `HeaderText`— Enables you to display header text above the validation summary.
- `ShowMessageBox`— Enables you to display a pop-up alert box.
- `ShowSummary`— Enables you to hide the validation summary in the page.

If you set the `ShowMessageBox` property to the value `True` and the `ShowSummary` property to the value `False`, you can display the validation summary only within a pop-up alert box. For example, the page in next listing displays a validation summary in an alert box.

```
Code View: Scroll / Show All
<%@ Page Language="C#" %>
<!DOCTYPE html PUBLIC "-//W3C//DTD XHTML 1.0 Transitional//EN"
"http://www.w3.org/TR/xhtml1/DTD/xhtml1-transitional.dtd">
<html xmlns="http://www.w3.org/1999/xhtml" >
<head id="Head1" runat="server">
```

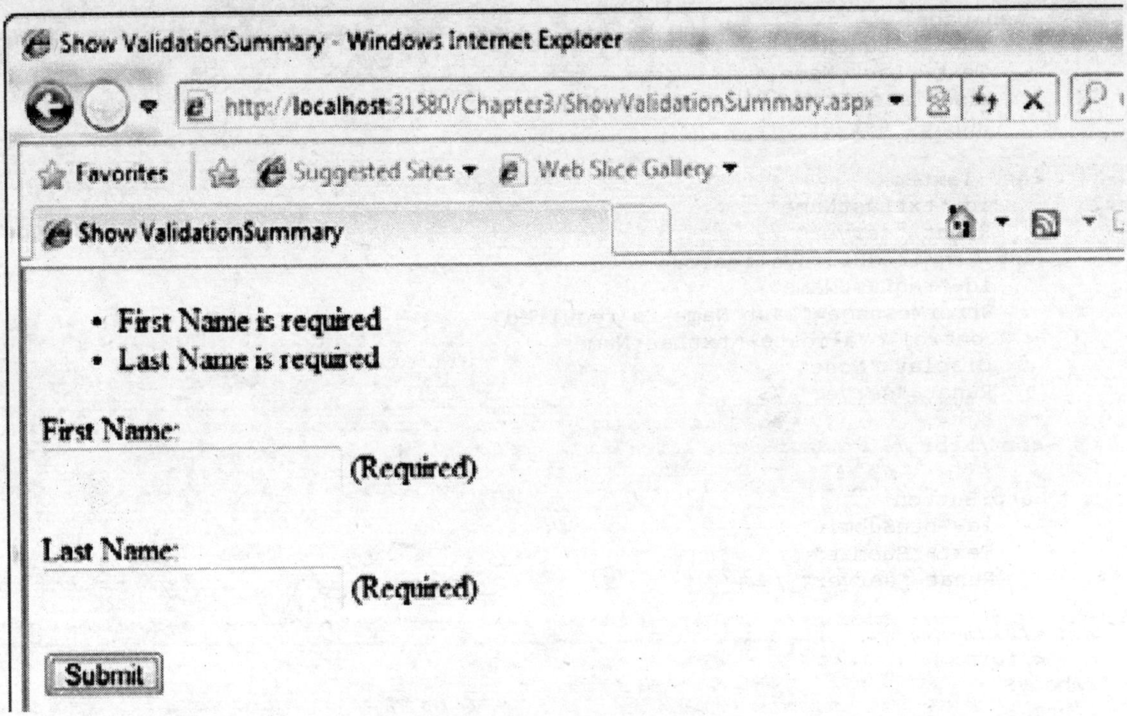

Displaying a validation summary.

```
    <title>Show Summary Popup</title>
</head>
<body>
    <form id="form1" runat="server">
     <div>

    <asp:ValidationSummary
        id="ValidationSummary1"
        ShowMessageBox="true"
        ShowSummary="false"
        Runat="server" />

     <asp:Label
        id="lblFirstName"
        Text="First Name:"
        AssociatedControlID="txtFirstName"
        Runat="server" />
     <br />
     <asp:TextBox
        id="txtFirstName"
        Runat="server" />
    <asp:RequiredFieldValidator
        id="reqFirstName"
        ErrorMessage="First Name is required"
        ControlToValidate="txtFirstName"
        Display="None"
        Runat="server" />

     <br /><br />
```

```
<asp:Label
    id="lblLastName"
    Text="Last Name:"
    AssociatedControlID="txtLastName"
    Runat="server" />
<br />
<asp:TextBox
    id="txtLastName"
    Runat="server" />
<asp:RequiredFieldValidator
    id="reqLastName"
    ErrorMessage="Last Name is required"
    ControlToValidate="txtLastName"
    Display="None"
    Runat="server" />

<br /><br />

<asp:Button
    id="btnSubmit"
    Text="Submit"
    Runat="server" />

</div>
</form>
</body>
</html>
```

ShowSummaryPopup.aspx

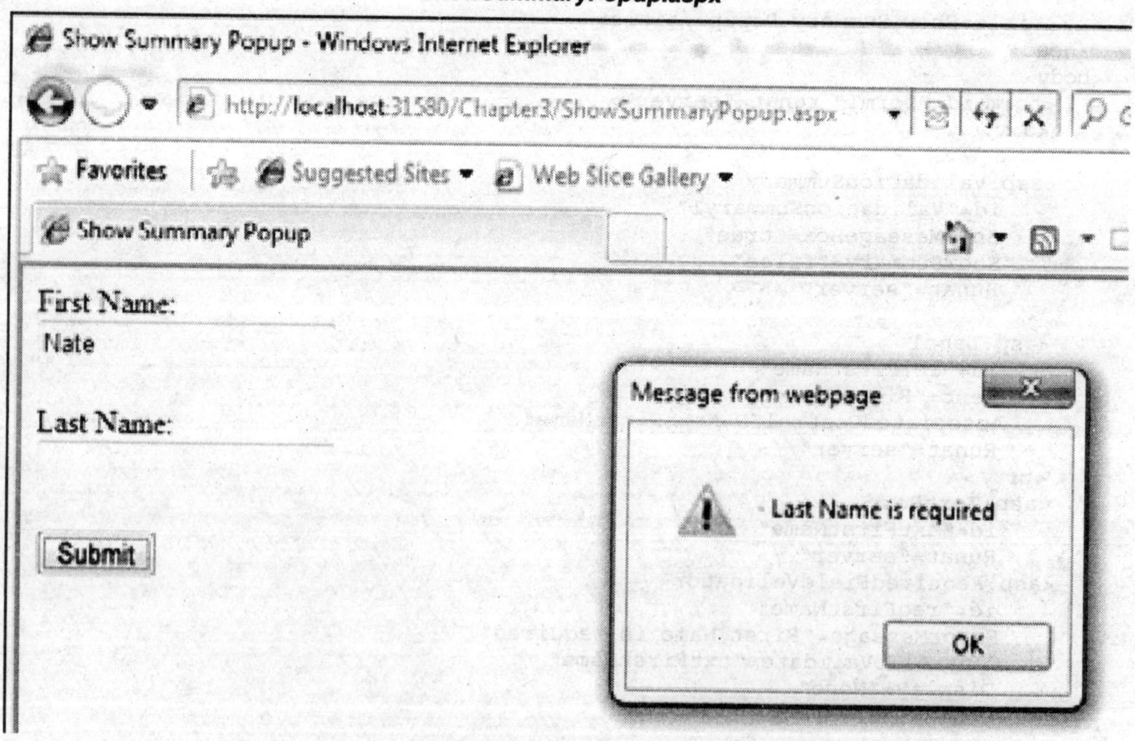

Displaying a validation summary in an alert box.

Both of the RequiredFieldValidator controls have their Display properties set to the value None. The validation error messages appear only in the alert box.

Creating Custom Validation Controls

In this final section, you learn how to create custom validation controls. We create two custom controls. First, we create a LengthValidator control that enables you to validate the length of an entry in a form field. Next, we create an AjaxValidator control. The AjaxValidator control performs validation on the client by passing information back to a custom function defined on the server.

You create a new validation control by deriving a new control from the BaseValidator class. As its name implies, the BaseValidator class is the base class for all the validation controls, including the RequiredFieldValidator and RegularExpressionValidator controls.

The BaseValidator class is a MustInherit (abstract) class, which requires you to implement a single method:

- EvaluateIsValid— Returns true when the form field being validated is valid.

The BaseValidator class also includes several other methods that you can override or otherwise use. The most useful of these methods follows:

- GetControlValidationValue— Enables you to retrieve the value of the control being validated.

When you create a custom validation control, you override the EvaluateIsValid() method and, within the EvaluateIsValid() method, you call GetControlValidationValue to get the value of the form field being validated.

Creating a LengthValidator Control

To illustrate the general technique for creating a custom validation control, in this section we create an extremely simple one. It's a LengthValidator control, which enables you to validate the length of a form field.

The code for the LengthValidator control is contained in next listing.

Code View: Scroll / Show All

```
using System;
using System.Web.UI;
using System.Web.UI.WebControls;

namespace myControls
{
    /// <summary>
    /// Validates the length of an input field
    /// </summary>
    public class LengthValidator : BaseValidator
    {
        int _maximumLength = 0;

        public int MaximumLength
        {
            get { return _maximumLength; }
            set { _maximumLength = value; }
        }

        protected override bool EvaluateIsValid()
        {
```

```
            String value =
 this.GetControlValidationValue(this.ControlToValidate);
            if (value.Length > _maximumLength)
                return false;
            else
                return true;
        }
    }
}
```

LengthValidator.cs

The above listing contains a class that inherits from the `BaseValidator` class. The new class overrides the `EvaluateIsValid` method. The value from the control being validated is retrieved with the help of the `GetControlValidationValue()` method, and the length of the value is compared against the `MaximumLength` property.

To use the class in above listing, you need to add the class to your application's `App_Code` folder by right-clicking the App_Code folder and choosing to add a new item. Any class added to this special folder is automatically compiled by the ASP.NET Framework.

The page in next listing uses the `LengthValidator` control to validate the length of a comment input field.

```
Code View: Scroll / Show All
<%@ Page Language="C#" %>
<%@ Register TagPrefix="custom" Namespace="myControls" %>
<!DOCTYPE html PUBLIC "-//W3C//DTD XHTML 1.0 Transitional//EN"
"http://www.w3.org/TR/xhtml1/DTD/xhtml1-transitional.dtd">
<html xmlns="http://www.w3.org/1999/xhtml" >
<head id="Head1" runat="server">
    <title>Show Length Validator</title>
</head>
<body>
    <form id="form1" runat="server">
    <div>

    <asp:Label
        id="lblComments"
        Text="Comments:"
       AssociatedControlID="txtComments"
        Runat="server" />
    <br />
    <asp:TextBox
        id="txtComments"
        TextMode="MultiLine"
        Columns="30"
        Rows="2"
        Runat="server" />
   <custom:LengthValidator
        id="valComments"
       ControlToValidate="txtComments"
       Text="(Must be less than 10 characters)"
       MaximumLength="10"
       Runat="server" />

    <br /><br />
```

```
    <asp:Button
        id="btnSubmit"
        Text="Submit"
        Runat="server" />

    </div>
    </form>
</body>
</html>
```

ShowLengthValidator.aspx

The `LengthValidator` is registered at the top of the page with the `<%@ Register %>` directive. If you need to use the control in multiple pages in your application, you can alternatively register the control in the `<pages>` section of your application's web configuration file.

Creating an AjaxValidator Control

In this section, we create an extremely useful control named the `AjaxValidator` control. Like the `CustomValidator` control, the `AjaxValidator` control enables you to create a custom server-side validation function. Unlike the `CustomValidator` control, however, the `AjaxValidator` control enables you to call the custom validation function from the browser.

The `AjaxValidator` control uses AJAX (Asynchronous JavaScript and XML) to call the server-side validation function from the client. The advantage of using AJAX is that no postback to the server is apparent to the user.

For example, imagine that you create a website registration form and you need to validate a User Name field. You want to make sure that the User Name entered does not already exist in the database. The `AjaxValidator` enables you to call a server-side validation function from the client to check whether the User Name is unique in the database.

The code for the `AjaxValidator` control is contained in next listing.

```
Code View: Scroll / Show All
using System;
using System.Web;
using System.Web.UI;
using System.Web.UI.WebControls;

namespace myControls
{
    /// <summary>
    /// Enables you to perform custom validation on both the client and
server
    /// </summary>
    public class AjaxValidator : BaseValidator, ICallbackEventHandler
    {
        public event ServerValidateEventHandler ServerValidate;

        string _controlToValidateValue;

        protected override void OnPreRender(EventArgs e)
        {
            String eventRef = Page.ClientScript.GetCallbackEventReference
                (
                    this,
                    "",
```

```
                "",
                ""
              );

            // Register include file
            String includeScript =
                Page.ResolveClientUrl("~/ClientScripts/AjaxValidator.js");
           Page.ClientScript.RegisterClientScriptInclude("AjaxValidator",
                 includeScript);

            // Register startup script
            String startupScript =
  String.Format("document.getElementById('{0}').evaluationfunction =
  'AjaxValidatorEvaluateIsValid';", this.ClientID);
           Page.ClientScript.RegisterStartupScript(this.GetType(),
  "AjaxValidator", startupScript, true);

            base.OnPreRender(e);
         }
         /// <summary>
         /// Only do the AJAX on browsers that support it
         /// </summary>
        protected override bool DetermineRenderUplevel()
         {
           return Context.Request.Browser.SupportsCallback;
         }

         /// <summary>
         /// Server method called by client AJAX call
         /// </summary>
         public string GetCallbackResult()
         {
            return
  ExecuteValidationFunction(_controlToValidateValue).ToString();
         }

         /// <summary>
         /// Return callback result to client
         /// </summary>
        public void RaiseCallbackEvent(string eventArgument)
         {
           _controlToValidateValue = eventArgument;
         }

         /// <summary>
         /// Server-side method for validation
         /// </summary>
         protected override bool EvaluateIsValid()
         {
            string controlToValidateValue =
  this.GetControlValidationValue(this.ControlToValidate);
           return ExecuteValidationFunction(controlToValidateValue);
         }

         /// <summary>
         /// Performs the validation for both server and client
         /// </summary>
```

```
        private bool ExecuteValidationFunction(String controlToValidateValue)
          {
              ServerValidateEventArgs args = new ServerValidateEventArgs
(controlToValidateValue, this.IsValid);
               if (ServerValidate != null)
                    ServerValidate(this, args);
               return args.IsValid;
          }

     }

}
```

AjaxValidator.cs

The control in above listing inherits from the `BaseValidator` class. It also implements the `ICallbackEventHandler` interface. The `ICallbackEventHandler` interface defines two methods called on the server when an AJAX request is made from the client.

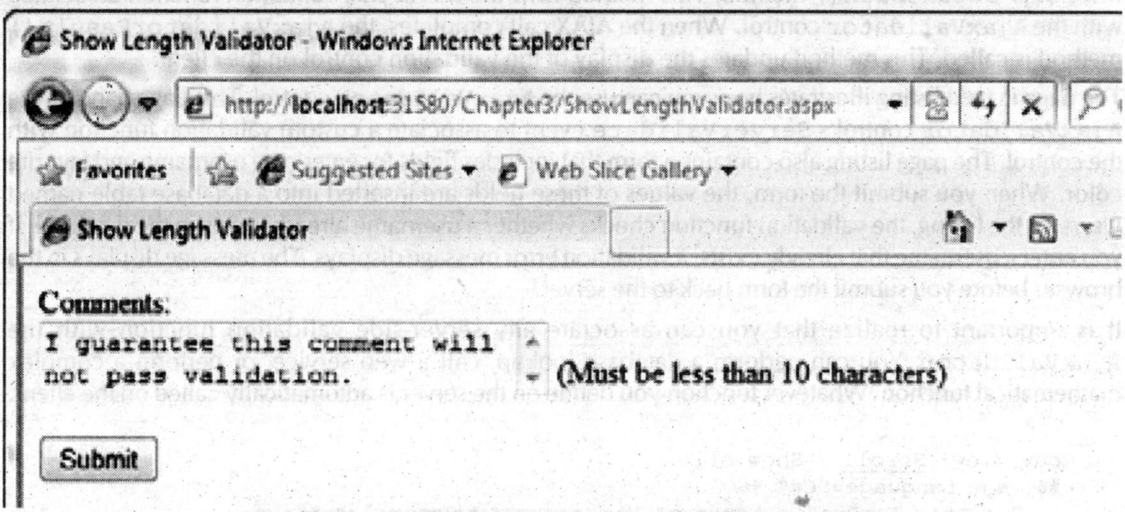

Validating the length of a field with the LengthValidator control.

In the `OnPreRender()` method, a JavaScript include file and startup script are registered. The JavaScript include file contains the client-side functions called when the `AjaxValidator` validates a form field on the client. The startup script associates the client-side `AjaxValidatorEvaluateIsValid()` function with the `AjaxValidator` control. The client-side validation framework automatically calls this JavaScript function when performing validation.

The JavaScript functions used by the `AjaxValidator` control are contained in next listing.

```
Code View: Scroll / Show All
// Performs AJAX call back to server
function AjaxValidatorEvaluateIsValid(val)
{
    var value = ValidatorGetValue(val.controltovalidate);
    WebForm_DoCallback(val.id, value, AjaxValidatorResult, val,
AjaxValidatorError, true);
     return true;
}

// Called when result is returned from server
```

```
function AjaxValidatorResult(returnValue, context)
{
    if (returnValue == 'True')
        context.isvalid = true;
    else
        context.isvalid = false;
   ValidatorUpdateDisplay(context);
}

// If there is an error, show it
function AjaxValidatorError(message)
{
    alert('Error: ' + message);
}
```

AjaxValidator.js

The `AjaxValidatorEvaluateIsValid()` JavaScript method initiates an AJAX call by calling the `WebForm_DoCallback()` method. This method calls the server-side validation function associated with the `AjaxValidator` control. When the AJAX call completes, the `AjaxValidatorResult()` method is called. This method updates the display of the validation control on the client.

The page in next listing illustrates how you can use the `AjaxValidator` control. This page handles the `AjaxValidator` control's `ServerValidate` event to associate a custom validation function with the control. The page listing also contains a form that includes fields for entering a username and favorite color. When you submit the form, the values of these fields are inserted into a database table named Users. In the listing, the validation function checks whether a username already exists in the database. If you enter a username that already exists, a validation error message displays. The message displays in the browser before you submit the form back to the server.

It is important to realize that you can associate any server-side validation function with the `AjaxValidator`. You can perform a database lookup, call a web service, or perform a complex mathematical function. Whatever function you define on the server is automatically called on the client.

```
Code View: Scroll / Show All
<%@ Page Language="C#" %>
<%@ Register TagPrefix="custom" Namespace="myControls" %>
<%@ Import Namespace="System.Data.SqlClient" %>
<%@ Import Namespace="System.Web.Configuration" %>
<!DOCTYPE html PUBLIC "-//W3C//DTD XHTML 1.0 Transitional//EN"
"http://www.w3.org/TR/xhtml1/DTD/xhtml1-transitional.dtd">
<script runat="server">

    /// <summary>
    /// Validation function that is called on both the client and server
    /// </summary>
    protected void AjaxValidator1_ServerValidate(object source,
ServerValidateEventArgs args)
    {
        if (UserNameExists(args.Value))
            args.IsValid = false;
        else
            args.IsValid = true;
    }

    /// <summary>
    /// Returns true when user name already exists
```

```
    /// in Users database table
    /// </summary>
    private bool UserNameExists(string userName)
    {
        string conString =
WebConfigurationManager.ConnectionStrings["UsersDB"].ConnectionString;
        SqlConnection con = new SqlConnection(conString);
        SqlCommand cmd = new SqlCommand("SELECT COUNT(*) FROM Users WHERE
UserName=@UserName", con);
        cmd.Parameters.AddWithValue("@UserName", userName);
        bool result = false;
        using (con)
        {
            con.Open();
            int count = (int)cmd.ExecuteScalar();
            if (count > 0)
                result = true;
        }
        return result;
    }

    /// <summary>
    /// Insert new user name to Users database table
    /// </summary>
    protected void btnSubmit_Click(object sender, EventArgs e)
    {
        string conString =
WebConfigurationManager.ConnectionStrings["UsersDB"].ConnectionString;
        SqlConnection con = new SqlConnection(conString);
        SqlCommand cmd = new SqlCommand("INSERT Users
(UserName,FavoriteColor) VALUES (@UserName,@FavoriteColor)", con);
        cmd.Parameters.AddWithValue("@UserName", txtUserName.Text);
        cmd.Parameters.AddWithValue("@FavoriteColor", txtFavoriteColor.Text);
        using (con)
        {
            con.Open();
            cmd.ExecuteNonQuery();
        }
        txtUserName.Text = String.Empty;
        txtFavoriteColor.Text = String.Empty;
    }
</script>
<html xmlns="http://www.w3.org/1999/xhtml" >
<head runat="server">
    <title>Show AjaxValidator</title>
</head>
<body>
    <form id="form1" runat="server">
    <div>

    <asp:Label
        id="lblUserName"
        Text="User Name:"
        AssociatedControlID="txtUserName"
        Runat="server" />
    <asp:TextBox
        id="txtUserName"
        Runat="server" />
```

```
        <custom:AjaxValidator
            id="AjaxValidator1"
            ControlToValidate="txtUserName"
            Text="User name already taken!"
            OnServerValidate="AjaxValidator1_ServerValidate"
            Runat="server" />

        <br /><br />
        <asp:Label
            id="lblFavoriteColor"
            Text="Favorite Color:"
            AssociatedControlID="txtFavoriteColor"
            Runat="server" />
        <asp:TextBox
            id="txtFavoriteColor"
            Runat="server" />

        <br /><br />
        <asp:Button
            id="btnSubmit"
            Text="Submit"
            Runat="server" OnClick="btnSubmit_Click" />

        </div>
        </form>
    </body>
    </html>
```

Listing ShowAjaxValidator.aspx

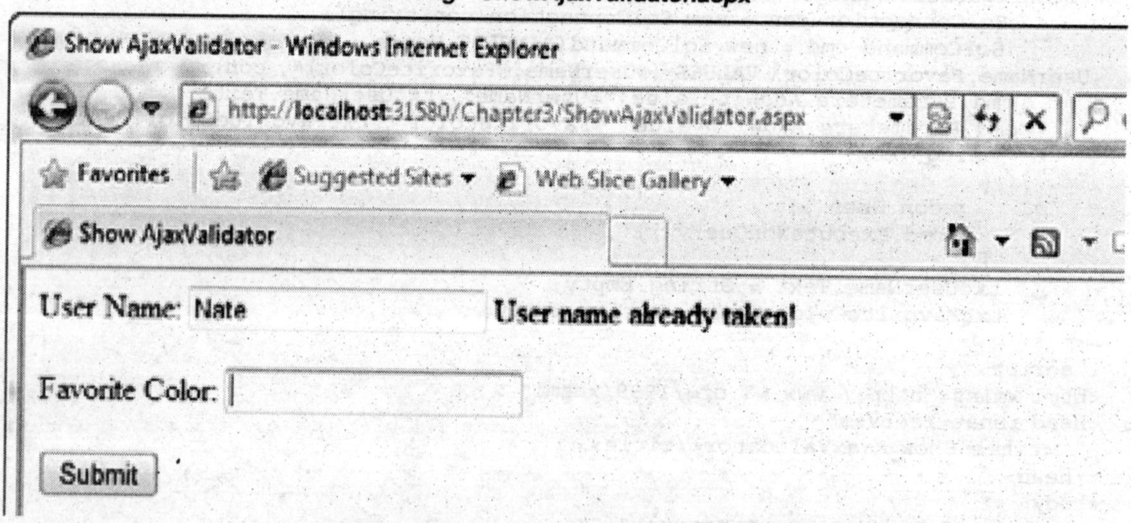

Using the AjaxValidator to check whether a username is unique.

CHAPTER 5

Designing Web Sites with Themes

In this chapter you will read about:

- Designing Websites with Themes.
- Applying Themes Dynamically.

Introduction

An ASP.NET Theme enables you to apply a consistent style to the pages in your website. You can use a Theme to control the appearance of both the HTML elements and ASP.NET controls that appear in a page. Themes are different than Master Pages. A Master Page enables you to share content across multiple pages in a website. A Theme, on the other hand, enables you to control the appearance of the content.

First, you learn how to create Skins, which enable you to modify the properties of an ASP.NET control that have an effect on its appearance. You learn how to create both Default and Named Skins. Next, you learn how to format both HTML elements and ASP.NET controls by adding Cascading Style Sheets (CSS) to a Theme, which enable you to control the appearance and layout of pages in a website in a standards-compliant manner.

You also learn how you can create Global Themes, which can be used by multiple applications located on the same server. You learn how to use Global Themes with both file systems and HTTP-based websites. Finally, you learn how to load Themes and Skins dynamically at runtime. You build a page that each user of a website can customize by skinning.

Creating Themes

You create a Theme by adding a new folder to a special folder in your application named App_Themes. Each folder that you add to the App_Themes folder represents a different Theme. If the App_Themes folder doesn't exist in your application, you can create it. It must be located in the root of your application.

Visual Web Developer Note

When using Visual Web Developer, you can create a new Theme folder by right-clicking the name of your project in the Solution Explorer window and selecting Add Folder, Theme Folder.

A Theme folder can contain a variety of different types of files, including images and text files. You also can organize the contents of a Theme folder by adding multiple subfolders to a Theme folder.

Following are the most important types of files in a Theme folder:

- Skin Files
- Cascading Style Sheet Files

In the following sections, you learn how to add both Skin files and CSS files to a Theme.

Be careful about how you name your Theme (the folder name). The contents of a Theme folder are automatically compiled in the background into a new class. Don't name a Theme with a class name that conflicts with an existing class name in your project.

Adding Skins to Themes

A Theme can contain one or more Skin files. A Skin enables you to modify any of the properties of an ASP.NET control that have an effect on its appearance.

For example, imagine that you decide that you want every `TextBox` control in your web application to appear with a yellow background color and a dotted border. If you add the file in next listing to the Simple Theme (the `App_Themes\Simple` folder), you can modify the appearance of all `TextBox` controls in all pages that use the Simple Theme.

```
<asp:TextBox
    BackColor="Yellow"
    BorderStyle="Dotted"
     Runat="Server" />
```

Simple\TextBox.skin

The Skin file in above listing is named `TextBox.skin`. You can name a Skin file anything you want. I recommend following a naming convention in which you name the Skin file after the name of the control that the Skin modifies.

A Theme folder can contain a single Skin file that contains Skins for hundreds of controls. Alternatively, a Theme can contain hundreds of Skin files, each of which contains a single Skin. It doesn't matter how you organize your Skins into files because everything in a Theme folder eventually gets compiled into one Theme class. The Skin file in last listing contains a declaration of a `TextBox` control. The `TextBox` control includes a `BackColor` property set to the value Yellow and a `BorderStyle` property set to the value Dotted.

The `TextBox` control includes a `Runat="Server"` attribute, but it does not include an `ID` attribute. You must always include a `Runat` attribute, but you can never include the `ID` attribute when declaring a control in a Skin.

You can't create a Skin that applies to the properties of a User Control. However, you can skin the controls contained inside a User Control.

The Skin is applied to every page to which the Simple Theme is applied. For example, the page in nexst listing uses the Simple Theme.

```
<%@ Page Language="C#" Theme="Simple" %>
<!DOCTYPE html PUBLIC "-//W3C//DTD XHTML 1.1//EN"
"http://www.w3.org/TR/xhtml11/DTD/xhtml11.dtd">
<html xmlns="http://www.w3.org/1999/xhtml" >
<head runat="server">
    <title>Show Skin</title>
</head>
<body>
    <form id="form1" runat="server">
    <div>

    <asp:TextBox
        Runat="server" />

    </div>
    </form>
</body>
</html>
```

ShowSkin.aspx

The page in above listing includes a `Theme` attribute in its `<%@ Page %>` directive. This attribute causes the Simple Theme to be applied to the page. When you open the page in above listing, the Label control appears with a yellow background color and dotted border. This is the background color and border specified by the Theme.

Only certain control properties are "themeable." In other words, you can create a Skin file that modifies only certain properties of a control. In general, you can use a Skin to modify properties that have an effect on a control's appearance but not its behavior. For example, you can modify the `BackColor` property of a `TextBox` control but not its `AutoPostBack` property.

By default, all control properties are themeable (can be modified in a Skin file). However, certain control properties are decorated with the `Themeable(False)` attribute, which disables theming.

Creating Named Skins

In the previous section, we created something called a Default Skin. A Default Skin is applied to every

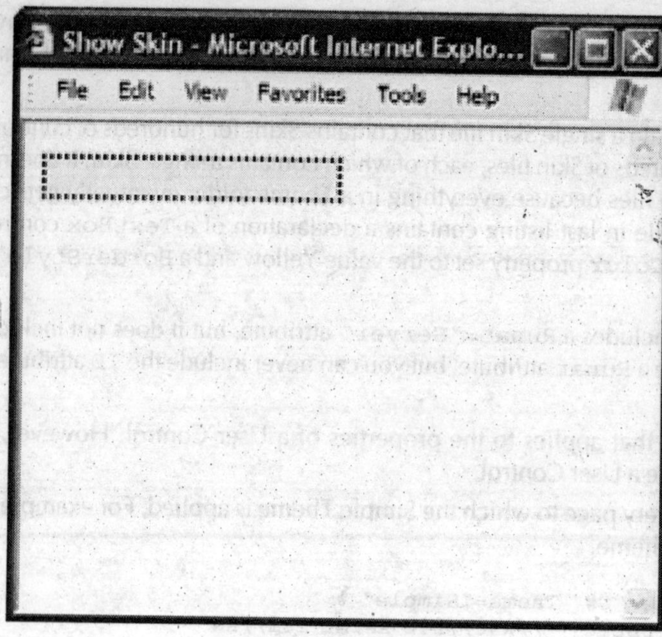

Using a TextBox Skin.

instance of a control of a certain type. For example, a Default Skin is applied to every instance of a `TextBox` control. You also have the option of creating a Named Skin. When you create a Named Skin, you can decide when you want to apply the Skin. For example, you might want required fields in a form to appear with a red border. In that case, you can create a Named Skin and apply the Skin to only particular `TextBox` controls.

The Skin in next listing contains both a Default Skin and a Named Skin for a `TextBox` control.

```
<asp:TextBox
    SkinID="DashedTextBox"
    BorderStyle="Dashed"
    BorderWidth="5px"
    Runat="Server" />

<asp:TextBox
    BorderStyle="Double"
    BorderWidth="5px"
    Runat="Server" />
```

Simple2\TextBox.skin

The first `TextBox` in above listing is an example of a Named Skin and includes a `SkinID` property. The `SkinID` property represents the name of the Named Skin. You use the value of this property when applying the Skin in a page. The file in above listing also includes a Default Skin for a `TextBox` control. The Default Skin does not include a `SkinID` property. If a `TextBox` control in a page is not associated with a Named Skin, the Default Skin is applied to the `TextBox`.

A Theme can contain only one Default Skin for each type of control. However, a Theme can contain as many Named Skins as you want. Each Named Skin must have a unique name. The page in next listing contains two `TextBox` controls. The first `TextBox` control includes a `SkinID` attribute. This attribute causes the Named Skin to be applied to the control. The second `TextBox`, on the other hand, does not include a `SkinID` property. The Default Skin is applied to the second `TextBox` control.

```
Code View: Scroll / Show All
<%@ Page Language="C#" Theme="Simple2" %>
<!DOCTYPE html PUBLIC "-//W3C//DTD XHTML 1.1//EN"
"http://www.w3.org/TR/xhtml11/DTD/xhtml11.dtd">
<html xmlns="http://www.w3.org/1999/xhtml" >
<head runat="server">
    <title>Show Named Skin</title>
</head>
<body>
    <form id="form1" runat="server">
    <div>

    <asp:TextBox
        id="txtFirstName"
        SkinID="DashedTextBox"
        Runat="server" />

    <br /><br />

    <asp:TextBox
        id="txtLastName"
        Runat="server" />

    </div>
    </form>
</body>
</html>
```

ShowNamedSkin.aspx

When you open the page in above listing, the first `TextBox` appears with a dashed border, and the second `TextBox` appears with a double border.

Using Named Skins.

Themes Versus StyleSheetThemes

When you apply a Theme to a page, the Skins in the Theme override any existing properties of the controls in the page. In other words, properties in a Skin override properties in a page.

For example, imagine that you create the Skin in next listing.

```
<asp:Label
    BackColor="Orange"
        Runat="Server" />
```

Simple3\Label.skin

The Skin in above listing sets the background color of all Label controls to the color Orange. Now, image that you apply the Skin in above listing to the ASP.NET page in next listing.

```
<%@ Page Language="C#" Theme="Simple3" %>
<!DOCTYPE html PUBLIC "-//W3C//DTD XHTML 1.1//EN"
"http://www.w3.org/TR/xhtml11/DTD/xhtml11.dtd">
<html xmlns="http://www.w3.org/1999/xhtml" >
<head runat="server">
    <title>Show Skin Theme</title>
</head>
<body>
    <form id="form1" runat="server">
    <div>

    <asp:Label
        id="Label1"
        Text="What color background do I have?"
        BackColor="red"
        Runat="server" />

    </div>
    </form>
</body>
</html>
```

ShowSkinTheme.aspx

The page in above listing includes a Label that has a `BackColor` property that is set to the value `Red`. However, when you open the page, the `BackColor` declared in the Skin overrides the `BackColor` declared in the page, and the Label displays with an orange background.

The default behavior of Themes makes it easy to modify the design of an existing website. You can override any existing control properties that have an effect on the appearance of the control.

However, there are situations in which you might want to override Skin properties. For example, you might want to display every Label in your website with an orange background color except for one Label. In that case, it would be nice if there were a way to override the `Skin` property.

You can override `Skin` properties by applying a Theme to a page with the `StyleSheetTheme` attribute instead of the `Theme` attribute. For example, the page in next listing uses the `StyleSheetTheme` attribute to apply the Simple3 Theme to the page.

```
<%@ Page Language="C#" StyleSheetTheme="Simple3" %>
<!DOCTYPE html PUBLIC "-//W3C//DTD XHTML 1.1//EN"
"http://www.w3.org/TR/xhtml11/DTD/xhtml11.dtd">
<html xmlns="http://www.w3.org/1999/xhtml" >
<head id="Head1" runat="server">
    <title>Show Skin Style Sheet Theme</title>
</head>
<body>
    <form id="form1" runat="server">
    <div>

    <asp:Label
        id="Label1"
        Text="What color background do I have?"
        BackColor="red"
        Runat="server" />
```

```
        </div>
        </form>
    </body>
    </html>
```

ShowSkinStyleSheetTheme.aspx

The `<%@Page %>` directive in above listing includes a `StyleSheetTheme` attribute. When you open the page in listing 6.7 in a web browser, the Label displays with a red background color instead of the orange background color specified by the Theme.

Disabling Themes

Every ASP.NET control includes an `EnableTheming` property. You can use the `EnableTheming` property to prevent a Skin from being applied to a particular control in a page. For example, the page in above next listing contains two `Calendar` controls. The second `Calendar` control has its `EnableTheming` property set to the value `False`.

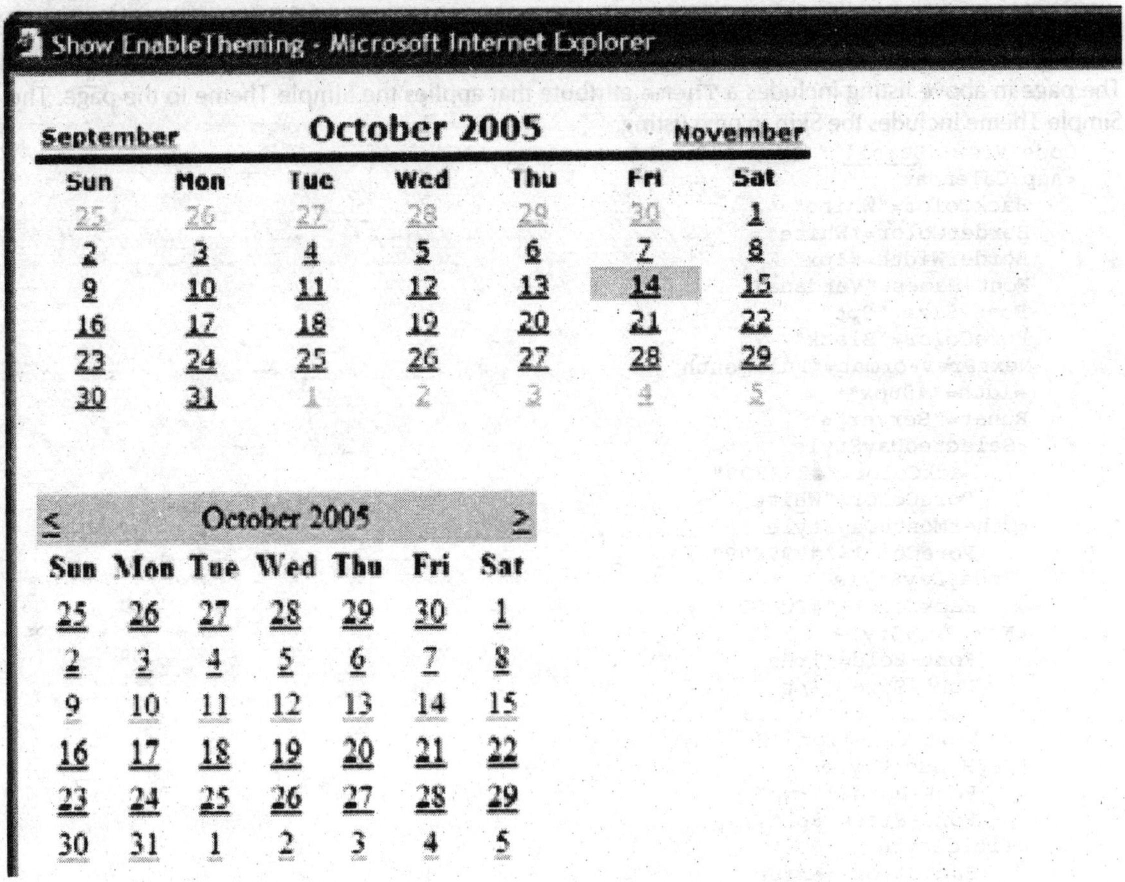

Disabling a Theme.

```
<%@ Page Language="C#" Theme="Simple4" %>
<html xmlns="http://www.w3.org/1999/xhtml" >
<head runat="server">
    <title>Show EnableTheming</title>
</head>
<body>
```

CHAPTER 5

```
    <form id="form1" runat="server">
    <div>

    <asp:Calendar
        id="Calendar1"
        Runat="server" />
    <br /><br />

    <asp:Calendar
        id="Calendar2"
        EnableTheming="false"
        Runat="server" />
    </div>
    </form>
</body>
</html>
```

ShowEnableTheming.aspx

The page in above listing includes a Theme attribute that applies the Simple Theme to the page. The Simple Theme includes the Skin in next listing.

```
Code View: Scroll / Show All
<asp:Calendar
    BackColor="White"
    BorderColor="White"
    BorderWidth="1px"
    Font-Names="Verdana"
    Font-Size="9pt"
    ForeColor="Black"
    NextPrevFormat="FullMonth"
    Width="400px"
    Runat="Server">
    <SelectedDayStyle
        BackColor="#333399"
        ForeColor="White" />
    <OtherMonthDayStyle
        ForeColor="#999999" />
    <TodayDayStyle
        BackColor="#CCCCCC" />
    <NextPrevStyle
        Font-Bold="True"
        Font-Size="8pt"
        ForeColor="#333333"
        VerticalAlign="Bottom" />
    <DayHeaderStyle
        Font-Bold="True"
        Font-Size="8pt" />
    <TitleStyle
        BackColor="White"
        BorderColor="Black"
        BorderWidth="4px"
        Font-Bold="True"
        Font-Size="12pt"
        ForeColor="#333399" />
</asp:Calendar>
```

Simple4\Calendar.skin

When you open the page in above listing in a web browser, the Skin is applied to the first `Calendar` control but not the second `Calendar` control.

Registering Themes in the Web Configuration File

Rather than add the `Theme` or `StyleSheetTheme` attribute to each and every page to which you want to apply a Theme, you can register a Theme for all pages in your application in the web configuration file. The Web.Config file in next listing applies the Site Theme to every page in an application.

```
<?xml version="1.0"?>
<configuration>
<system.web>

  <pages theme="Site" />

</system.web>
</configuration>
```

Web.Config

Rather than use the `theme` attribute, you can use the `styleSheetTheme` attribute to apply a Theme to the pages in an application. If you use the `styleSheetTheme` attribute, you can override particular Skin properties in a page. The web configuration file in listing 6.11 includes the `styleSheetTheme` attribute.

```
<?xml version="1.0"?>
<configuration>
<system.web>

  <pages styleSheetTheme="Site" />

</system.web>
</configuration>
```

Web.Config

After you enable a Theme for an application, you can disable the Theme for a particular page by using the `EnableTheming` attribute with the `<%@ Page %>` directive. For example, the page in next listing disables any Themes configured in the web configuration file.

```
<%@ Page Language="C#" EnableTheming="false" %>
<!DOCTYPE html PUBLIC "-//W3C//DTD XHTML 1.1//EN"
"http://www.w3.org/TR/xhtml11/DTD/xhtml11.dtd">
<html xmlns="http://www.w3.org/1999/xhtml" >
<head runat="server">
    <title>Disable Page Theme</title>
</head>
<body>
    <form id="form1" runat="server">
    <div>

    <asp:Label
        id="Label1"
        Text="Don't Theme Me!"
        Runat="server" />

    </div>
    </form>
```

```
</body>
</html>
```

DisablePageTheme.aspx

Adding Cascading Style Sheets to Themes

As an alternative to Skins, you can use a CSS file to control the appearance of both the HTML elements and ASP.NET controls contained in a page. If you add a CSS file to a Theme folder, the CSS is automatically applied to every page to which the Theme is applied. For example, the CSS in next listing contains style rules applied to several different HTML elements in a page.

Code View: Scroll / Show All

```
html
{
    background-color:gray;
    font:14px Georgia,Serif;
}

.content
{
    margin:auto;
    width:600px;
    border:solid 1px black;
    background-color:White;
    padding:10px;
}

h1
{
    color:Gray;
    font-size:18px;
    border-bottom:solid 1px orange;
}

label
{
    font-weight:bold;
}

input
{
    background-color:Yellow;
    border:double 3px orange;
}

.button
{
    background-color:#eeeeee;
}
```

App_Themes\StyleTheme\SimpleStyle.css

If you add the `SimpleStyle.css` file to a Theme named `StyleTheme` (a folder named StyleTheme in the `App_Themes` folder), the Cascading Style Sheet is applied automatically to the page in next listing.

Code View: Scroll / Show All

```
<%@ Page Language="C#" Theme="StyleTheme" %>
```

```
<!DOCTYPE html PUBLIC "-//W3C//DTD XHTML 1.1//EN"
"http://www.w3.org/TR/xhtml11/DTD/xhtml11.dtd">
<html xmlns="http://www.w3.org/1999/xhtml" >
<head id="Head1" runat="server">
   <title>Show Simple CSS</title>
</head>
<body>
   <form id="form1" runat="server">
   <div class="content">

   <h1>Registration Form</h1>

   <asp:Label
       id="lblFirstName"
       Text="First Name:"
      AssociatedControlID="txtFirstName"
       Runat="server" />
   <br />
   <asp:TextBox
       id="txtFirstName"
       Runat="server" />

   <br /><br />

   <asp:Label
   id="lblLastName"
   Text="Last Name:"
   AssociatedControlID="txtLastName"
   Runat="server" />
   <br />
   <asp:TextBox
       id="txtLastName"
       Runat="server" />

   <br /><br />

   <asp:Button
       id="btnSubmit"
       Text="Submit Form"
       CssClass="button"
       Runat="server" />

   </div>
   </form>
</body>
</html>
```

ShowSimpleCSS.aspx

The CSS is used to style several HTML elements in above listing. For example, the Style Sheet sets the background color of the page to the value Gray. It also centers the `<div>` tag containing the page content.

Because an ASP.NET control renders HTML, the Style Sheet also styles the HTML rendered by the ASP.NET `Label`, `TextBox`, and `Button` controls. An ASP.NET `Label` control renders an HTML `<label>` tag and the Style Sheet formats all `<label>` tags in bold. Both a `TextBox` control and a `Button` control render HTML `<input>` tags. The Style Sheet modifies the border and background color of the `<input>` tag.

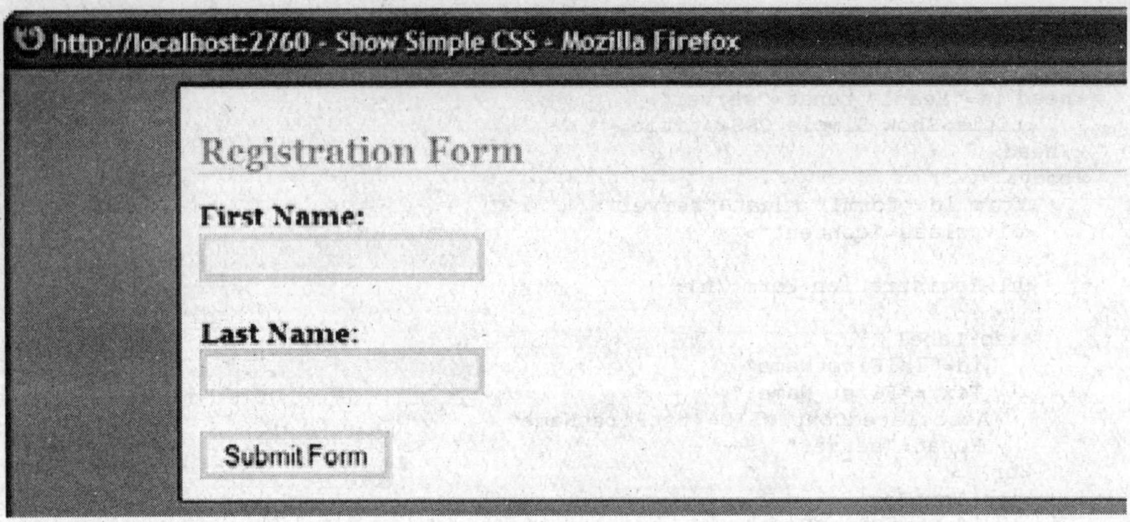

Styling with Cascading Style Sheets.

The `Button` control includes a `CssClass` attribute. By providing a control with a `CssClass` attribute, you can target a particular control (or set of controls) in a CSS. In this case, the background color of the `<input>` tag rendered by the Button control is set to the value `#eeeeee` (light gray). I recommend that you do all your web page design by using the method discussed in this section. You should place all your page design in an external CSS located in a Theme folder. In particular, you should not modify the appearance of a control by modifying its properties. Furthermore, you should avoid using Skin files.

The advantage of using Cascading Style Sheets is that they result in leaner and faster loading pages. The more content that you can place in an external Style Sheet, the less content must be loaded each time you make a page request. The contents of an external Style Sheet can be loaded and cached by a browser and applied to all pages in a web application. If, on the other hand, you modify the appearance of a control by modifying its properties, additional content must be rendered to the browser each time you make a page request. For example, if you modify a `Label` control's `BackColor` property, an additional `Style` attribute is rendered when the `Label` control is rendered.

Using Skins is no different than setting control properties. Skins also result in bloated pages. For example, if you create a Skin for a `Label` control, the properties of the Label Skin must be merged with each `Label` control on each page before the Label is rendered.

Adding Multiple Cascading Style Sheets to a Theme

You can add as many CSS files to a Theme folder as you need. When you add multiple Cascading Style Sheets to a Theme, all the Cascading Style Sheets are applied to a page when the Theme is applied to a page. The order in which an external Style Sheet is linked to a page can be important. For example, style sheet rules in one Style Sheet can override style sheet rules in another Style Sheet.

When you add multiple Style Sheets to a Theme, the style sheets are linked to a page in alphabetical order (in the order of the Style Sheet filename). For example, if the Theme contains three Style Sheet files named `ThemeA.css`, `ThemeB.css`, and `ThemeC.css`, the following three links are added to a page:

```
Code View: Scroll / Show All
<link href="App_Themes/Simple/ThemeA.css" type="text/css" rel="stylesheet" />
<link href="App_Themes/Simple/ThemeB.css" type="text/css" rel="stylesheet" />
<link href="App_Themes/Simple/ThemeC.css" type="text/css" rel="stylesheet" />
```

If you want to control the order in which Style Sheets are applied to a page, you need to follow a naming convention.

Changing Page Layouts with Cascading Style Sheets

Because you can use a Cascading Style Sheet to change the layout of a page, you can use a Theme to control page layout. For example, the page in next listing contains three `<div>` tags. By default, if you open the page, the contents of the `<div>` tags are stacked one on top of another.

```
Code View: Scroll / Show All
<%@ Page Language="C#" %>
<!DOCTYPE html PUBLIC "-//W3C//DTD XHTML 1.1//EN"
"http://www.w3.org/TR/xhtml11/DTD/xhtml11.dtd">
<html xmlns="http://www.w3.org/1999/xhtml" >
<head runat="server">
    <title>Show Layout</title>
</head>
<body>
    <form id="form1" runat="server">

    <div id="div1">
        First div content
        <br />First div content
        <br />First div content
        <br />First div content
        <br />First div content
    </div>

    <div id="div2">
        Second div content
        <br />Second div content
        <br />Second div content
        <br />Second div content
        <br />Second div content
    </div>

    <div id="div3">
        Third div content
        <br />Third div content
        <br />Third div content
        <br />Third div content
        <br />Third div content
    </div>

    </form>
</body>
</html>
```

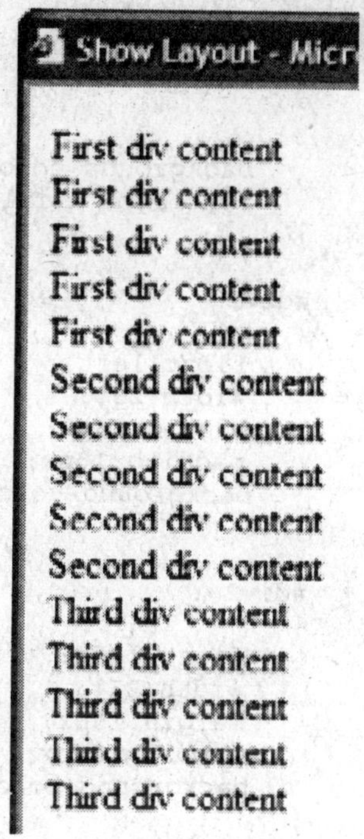

Page without Cascading Style Sheet.

ShowLayout.aspx

If you add the Cascading Style Sheet in next listing, you can modify the layout of the `<div>` tags. The Style Sheet in listing displays the `<div>` tags in three columns. (The Stylesheet floats each of the `<div>` tags.) You can appy this stylesheet to your page using the following line of code in the <head> tag:

```
<link href="float.css" type="text/css" rel="stylesheet" />
Code View: Scroll / Show All
html
{
```

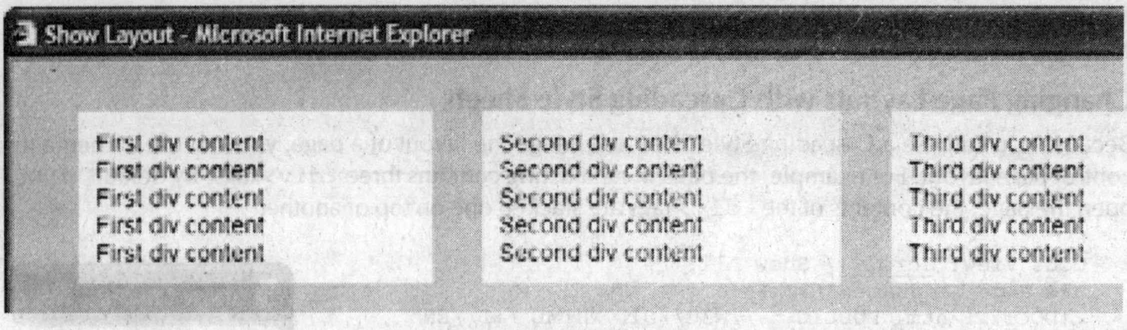

Using a floating layout.

```
    background-color:Silver;
    font:14px Arial,Sans-Serif;
}

#div1
{
    float:left;
    width:25%;
    margin:15px;
    padding:10px;
    background-color:White;
}

#div2
{
    float:left;
    width:25%;
    margin:15px;
    padding:10px;
    background-color:White;
}

#div3
{
    float:left;
    width:25%;
    margin:15px;
    padding:10px;
    background-color:White;
}
```

Float.css

Alternatively, you can position the `<div>` tags absolutely by using the `left` and `top` style properties. The Style Sheet in next listing reverses the order in which the three `<div>` tags are displayed.

The Cascading Style Sheets in this section work equally well with Internet Explorer, Firefox, and Opera.

```
Code View: Scroll / Show All
html
{
    background-color:Silver;
    font:14px Arial,Sans-Serif;
}

#div3
```

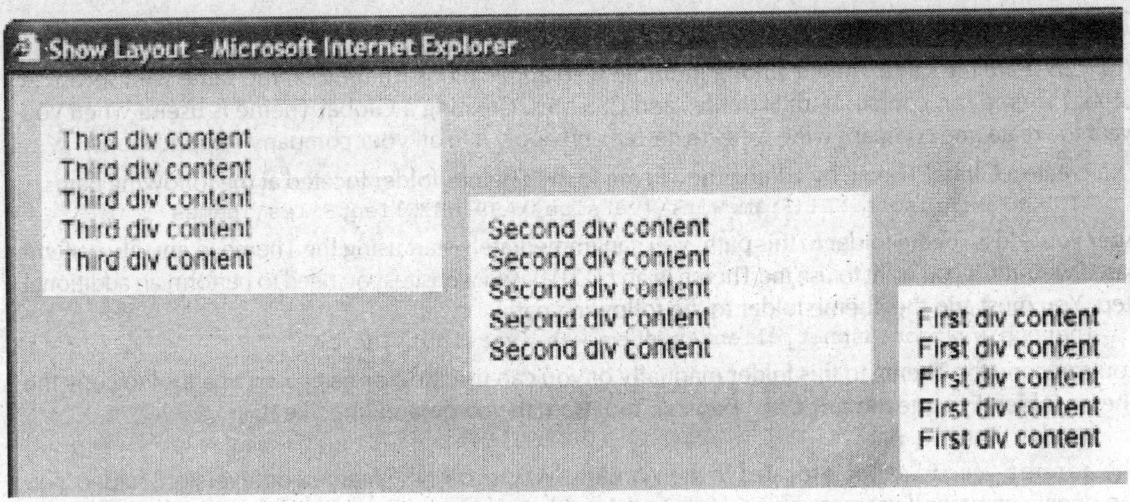

Using an absolute layout.

```
{
    position:absolute;
    left:15px;
    top:15px;
    width:200px;
    padding:10px;
    background-color:White;
}

#div2
{
    position:absolute;
    left:250px;
    top:65px;
    width:200px;
    padding:10px;
    background-color:White;
}

#div1
{
    position:absolute;
    left:485px;
    top:115px;
    width:200px;
    padding:10px;
    background-color:White;
}
```

Absolute.css

The point of this section is to demonstrate that Cascading Style Sheets are powerful. You can create elaborate website designs simply by creating the right Style Sheet. If you want to see some samples of some amazing website designs performed with Cascading Style Sheets, visit the CSS Zen Garden located at http://www.CSSZenGarden.com.

Creating Global Themes

You can share the same Theme among multiple web applications running on the same web server. A Global Theme can contain both Skin files and CSS files. Creating a Global Theme is useful when you want to create one companywide website design and apply it to all your company's applications.

You create a Global Theme by adding the Theme to the Themes folder located at the following path:

```
WINDOWS\Microsoft.NET\Framework\[version]\ASP.NETClientFiles\Themes
```

After you add a Theme folder to this path, you can immediately start using the Theme in any file system-based website. If you want to use the Theme in an HTTP-based website, you need to perform an additional step. You must add the Theme folder to the following path:

```
Inetpub\wwwroot\aspnet_client\system_web\[version]\Themes
```

You can copy the Theme to this folder manually or you can use the `aspnet_regiis` tool to copy the Theme folder. Execute the `aspnet_regiis` tool from the command line like this:

```
aspnet_regiis -c
```

The `aspnet_regiis` tool is located in the Windows\Microsoft.NET\Framework\[version] folder. You can open a command prompt and navigate to this folder to execute the tool. Alternatively, if you have installed the Microsoft .NET Framework SDK, you can execute the tool by opening the SDK Command Prompt from the Microsoft .NET Framework SDK program group.

Applying Themes Dynamically

You might want to enable each user of your website to customize the appearance of your website by selecting different Themes. Some website users might prefer a green Theme, and other website users might prefer a pink Theme. You can dynamically apply a Theme to a page by handling the Page `PreInit` event. This event is the first event raised when you request a page. You cannot apply a Theme dynamically in a later event such as the Page `Load` or `PreRender` events.

For example, the page in next listing applies either the Green Theme or the Pink Theme to the page depending on which link you click in the page body.

Selecting a Theme programmatically.

```
Code View: Scroll / Show All
<%@ Page Language="C#" %>
<!DOCTYPE html PUBLIC "-//W3C//DTD XHTML 1.1//EN"
```

```
"http://www.w3.org/TR/xhtml11/DTD/xhtml11.dtd">
<script runat="server">

    protected void Page_PreInit(object sender, EventArgs e)
    {
        if (Request["theme"] != null)
        {
            switch (Request["theme"])
            {
                case "Green":
                    Profile.userTheme = "GreenTheme";
                    break;
                case "Pink":
                    Profile.userTheme = "PinkTheme";
                    break;
            }
        }
        Theme = Profile.userTheme;
    }
</script>

<html xmlns="http://www.w3.org/1999/xhtml" >
<head runat="server">
    <title>Dynamic Theme</title>
</head>
<body>
    <form id="form1" runat="server">
    <div class="content">

    <h1>Dynamic Theme</h1>

    Please select a Theme:
    <ul>
    <li>
        <a href="DynamicTheme.aspx?theme=Green">Green Theme</a>
    </li>
    <li>
        <a href="DynamicTheme.aspx?theme=Pink">Pink Theme</a>
    </li>
    </ul>

    </div>
    </form>
</body>
</html>
```

DynamicTheme.aspx

A particular Theme is applied to the page with the help of the Theme property. You can assign the name of any Theme (Theme folder) to this property in the Page `PreInit` event, and the Theme will be applied to the page.

The selected Theme is stored in the `Profile` object. When you store information in the `Profile` object, the information is preserved across multiple visits to the website. So, if a user selects a favorite Theme once, the Theme is applied every time the user returns to the website in the future. The Profile is defined in the web configuration file in next listing.

```
<?xml version="1.0"?>
```

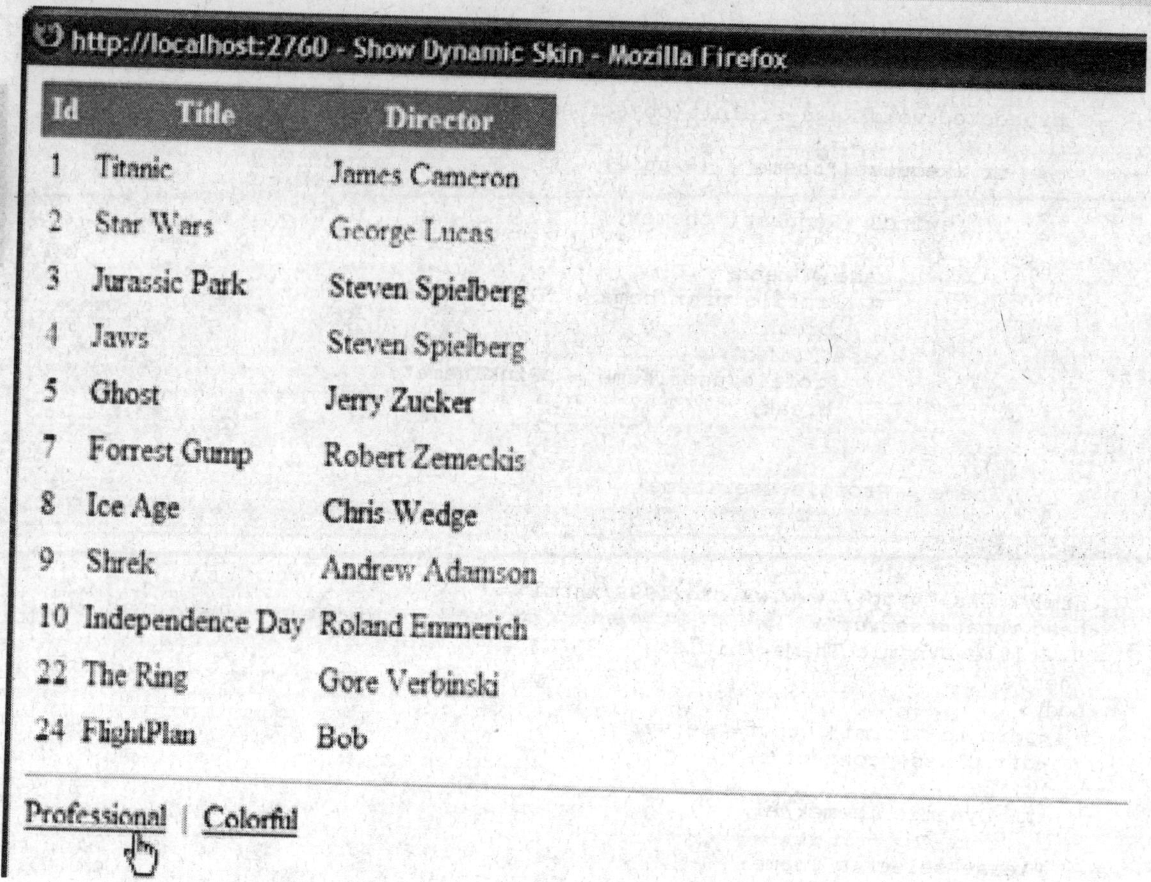

Applying a Skin programmatically.

```
<configuration>
  <system.web>
    <profile>
      <properties>
        <add name="UserTheme" />
      </properties>
    </profile>
  </system.web>
</configuration>
```

Web.Config

Because the control tree has not been created when the PreInit event is raised, you can't refer to any controls in a page. Hyperlinks are used in above listing to select a Theme. You could not use a `DropDownList` control because the `DropDownList` control would not have been created.

Applying Skins Dynamically

You can apply skins dynamically to particular controls in a page. In the Page `PreInit` event, you can modify a control's `SkinID` property programmatically. For example, the page in next listing enables a user to select a favorite skin for a `GridView` control. The `GridView` control displays a list of movies.

Code View: Scroll / Show All

```
<%@ Page Language="C#" Theme="DynamicSkin" %>
<!DOCTYPE html PUBLIC "-//W3C//DTD XHTML 1.1//EN"
"http://www.w3.org/TR/xhtml11/DTD/xhtml11.dtd">
<script runat="server">

    protected void Page_PreInit(object sender, EventArgs e)
    {
        if (Request["skin"] != null)
        {
            switch (Request["skin"])
            {
                case "professional":
                    grdMovies.SkinID = "Professional";
                    break;
                case "colorful":
                    grdMovies.SkinID = "Colorful";
                    break;
            }
        }
    }
</script>
<html xmlns="http://www.w3.org/1999/xhtml" >
<head runat="server">
    <title>Show Dynamic Skin</title>
</head>
<body>
    <form id="form1" runat="server">
    <div>

    <asp:GridView
        id="grdMovies"
        DataSourceID="srcMovies"
        Runat="server" />

    <asp:SqlDataSource
        id="srcMovies"
        ConnectionString="<%$ ConnectionStrings:Movies %>"
        SelectCommand="SELECT Id,Title,Director FROM Movies"
        Runat="server" />

    <hr />

    <a href="showdynamicskin.aspx?skin=professional">Professional</a>
     | 
    <a href="showdynamicskin.aspx?skin=colorful">Colorful</a>

    </div>
    </form>
</body>
</html>
```

ShowDynamicSkin.aspx

A hyperlink is used to select a particular Skin. The Skin is applied to the `GridView` in the `PreInit` event when a particular value is assigned to the `GridView` control's `SkinID` property. Of course, I don't recommend doing this. It makes more sense to use a CSS and modify a control's `CssClass` property. This alternative approach is demonstrated by the page in next listing.

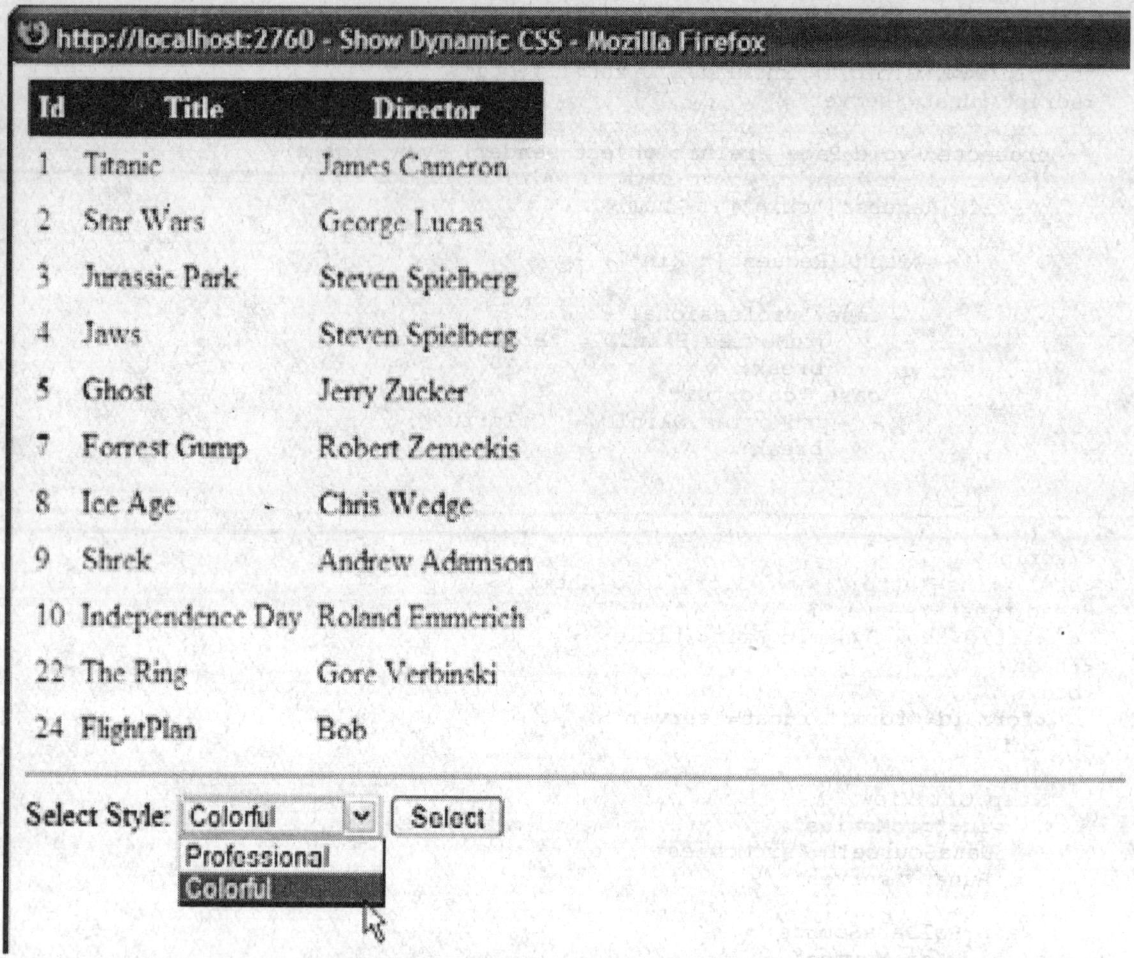

Modifying a CssClass programmatically.

Code View: Scroll / Show All

```
<%@ Page Language="C#" Theme="DynamicSkin" %>
<!DOCTYPE html PUBLIC "-//W3C//DTD XHTML 1.1//EN"
"http://www.w3.org/TR/xhtml11/DTD/xhtml11.dtd">
<script runat="server">

    protected void btnSubmit_Click(object sender, EventArgs e)
    {
        grdMovies.CssClass = ddlCssClass.SelectedItem.Text;
    }
</script>
<html xmlns="http://www.w3.org/1999/xhtml" >
<head id="Head1" runat="server">
    <title>Show Dynamic CSS</title>
</head>
<body>
    <form id="form1" runat="server">
    <div>

    <asp:GridView
```

```
        id="grdMovies"
        DataSourceID="srcMovies"
        HeaderStyle-CssClass="Header"
        AlternatingRowStyle-CssClass="Alternating"
        GridLines="none"
        Runat="server" />

    <asp:SqlDataSource
        id="srcMovies"
        ConnectionString="<%$ ConnectionStrings:Movies %>"
        SelectCommand="SELECT Id,Title,Director FROM Movies"
        Runat="server" />

    <hr />

    <asp:Label
        id="lblCssClass"
        Text="Select Style:"
        AssociatedControlID="ddlCssClass"
        Runat="server" />
    <asp:DropDownList
        id="ddlCssClass"
        Runat="server">
        <asp:ListItem Text="Professional" />
        <asp:ListItem Text="Colorful" />
    </asp:DropDownList>
    <asp:Button
        id="btnSubmit"
        Text="Select"
        Runat="server" OnClick="btnSubmit_Click" />

    </div>
    </form>
</body>
</html>
```

ShowDynamicCSS.aspx

Note that in this code sample, unlike the previous one, you can use a `DropDownList` and `Button` control to change the appearance of the `GridView` control when modifying the `CssClass` property. Because you can modify the `CssClass` property during any event before the page is rendered, you can handle the `Button Click` event to modify the value of the `CssClass` property.

Creating Global Themes

You can share the same Theme among multiple web applications running on the same web server. A Global Theme can contain both Skin files and CSS files. Creating a Global Theme is useful when you want to create one companywide website design and apply it to all your company's applications.

You create a Global Theme by adding the Theme to the Themes folder located at the following path:

```
WINDOWS\Microsoft.NET\Framework\[version]\ASP.NETClientFiles\Themes
```

After you add a Theme folder to this path, you can immediately start using the Theme in any file system-based website.

If you want to use the Theme in an HTTP-based website, you need to perform an additional step. You must add the Theme folder to the following path:

```
Inetpub\wwwroot\aspnet_client\system_web\[version]\Themes
```

You can copy the Theme to this folder manually or you can use the aspnet_regiis tool to copy the Theme folder. Execute the aspnet_regiis tool from the command line like this:

```
aspnet_regiis -c
```

The `aspnet_regiis` tool is located in the Windows\Microsoft.NET\Framework\[version] folder. You can open a command prompt and navigate to this folder to execute the tool. Alternatively, if you have installed the Microsoft .NET Framework SDK, you can execute the tool by opening the SDK Command Prompt from the Microsoft .NET Framework SDK program group.

CHAPTER 6

Overview of Data Access

In this chapter you will read about:

- Overview of Data Access.
- Using Programmatic DataBinding.
- Understanding Templates and DataBinding Expressions.
- Overview of SQL Server 2008 Express.

Introduction

Any web application worth writing involves data access. Now, you learn how to take advantage of the rich set of controls included in ASP.NET 4 Framework for working with data. You learn how to take advantage of the `DataBound` controls to display data in your ASP.NET pages. You also learn how to take advantage of the DataSource controls to represent different sources of data such as databases, XML files, and business objects.

Next, you are provided with an overview of Microsoft SQL Server 2008 Express, which is the royalty-free database included with Visual Web Developer. You learn how to connect to this database and use it for all your data access needs. Finally, we build a database-driven application, which illustrates how you can use many of the Data controls discussed in this chapter. We build an Employee Directory application.

Using DataBound Controls

You use `DataBound` controls to generate your application's user interface for working with data. The `DataBound` controls display and edit database data, XML data, or just about any other type of data you can imagine. There are three main types of `DataBound` controls: list controls, tabular `DataBound` controls, and hierarchical `DataBound`.

Working with List Controls

List controls display simple option lists. The ASP.NET 4 Framework includes the following five list controls:

- `BulletedList`— Displays a bulleted list of items. Each item can be displayed as text, a link button, or a hyperlink.
- `CheckBoxList`— Displays a list of check boxes. Multiple check boxes in the list can be selected.
- `DropDownList`— Displays a drop-down list. Only one item in the drop-down list can be selected.
- `ListBox`— Displays a list box. You can configure this control so that only one item in the list can be selected or multiple items can be selected.
- `RadioButtonList`— Displays a list of radio buttons. Only one radio button can be selected.

All five controls inherit from the same base `ListControl` class. This means that all these controls share a core set of properties and methods. The examples in this chapter rely on local databases. You can simply copy the database files (the `.mdf` files) from code examples found on the book's website. We'll discuss the SQL Server 2008 Express database engine that allows you to utilize these files later in the chapter.

The page in next listing illustrates how to use all five list controls to display the same set of database records.

```
Code View: Scroll / Show All
<%@ Page Language="C#" %>
<!DOCTYPE html PUBLIC "-//W3C//DTD XHTML 1.1//EN"
"http://www.w3.org/TR/xhtml11/DTD/xhtml11.dtd">
<html xmlns="http://www.w3.org/1999/xhtml" >
<head id="Head1" runat="server">
    <style type="text/css">
        .floater
        {
            float:left;
```

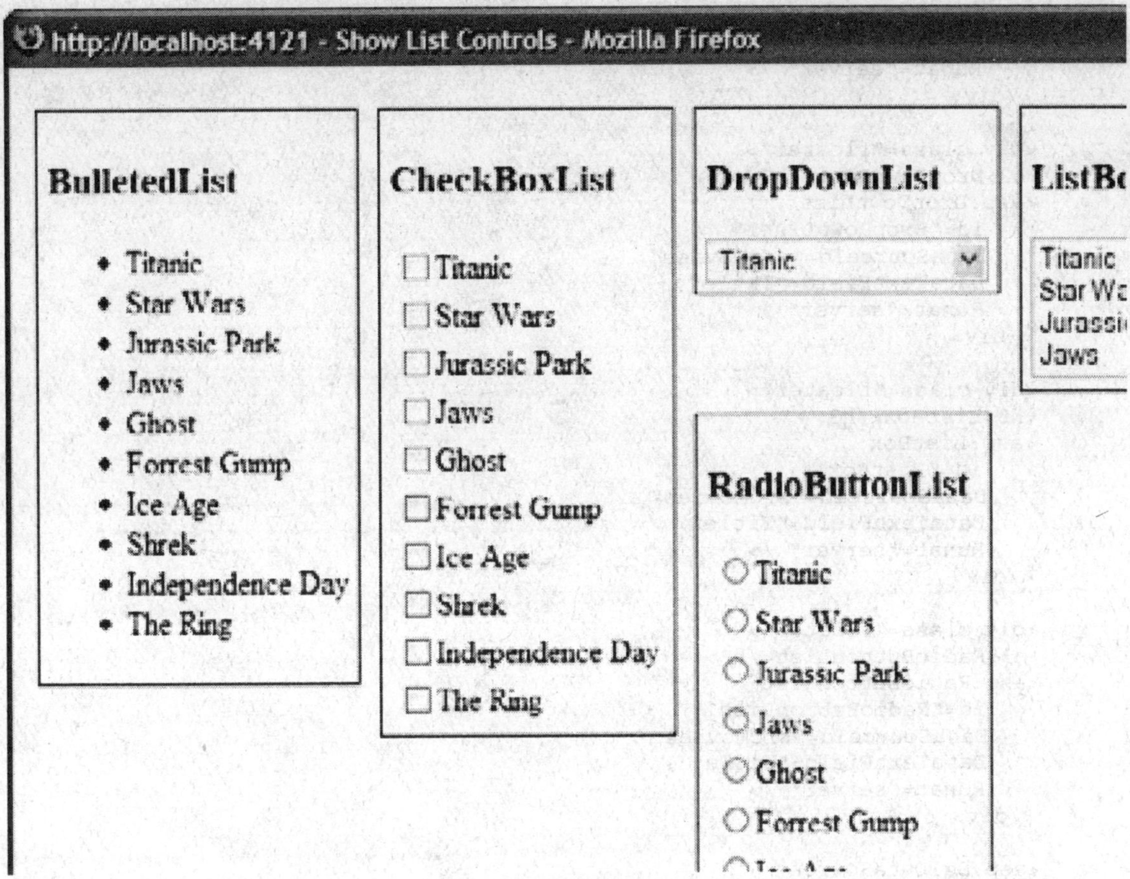

Using list controls.

```
            border:solid 1px black;
            padding:5px;
            margin:5px;
        }
    </style>
    <title>Show List Controls</title>
</head>
<body>
    <form id="form1" runat="server">

    <div class="floater">
    <h3>BulletedList</h3>
    <asp:BulletedList
        id="BulletedList1"
        DataSourceId="srcMovies"
        DataTextField="Title"
        Runat="server" />
    </div>

    <div class="floater">
    <h3>CheckBoxList</h3>
    <asp:CheckBoxList
        id="CheckBoxList1"
```

```
        DataSourceId="srcMovies"
        DataTextField="Title"
        Runat="server" />
    </div>

    <div class="floater">
    <h3>DropDownList</h3>
    <asp:DropDownList
        id="DropDownList1"
        DataSourceId="srcMovies"
        DataTextField="Title"
        Runat="server" />
    </div>

    <div class="floater">
    <h3>ListBox</h3>
    <asp:ListBox
        id="ListBox1"
        DataSourceId="srcMovies"
        DataTextField="Title"
        Runat="server" />
    </div>

    <div class="floater">
    <h3>RadioButtonList</h3>
    <asp:RadioButtonList
        id="RadioButtonList1"
        DataSourceId="srcMovies"
        DataTextField="Title"
        Runat="server" />
    </div>

    <asp:SqlDataSource
        id="srcMovies"
        ConnectionString="Data Source=.\SQLExpress;
            AttachDbFilename=|DataDirectory|MyDatabase.mdf;
            Integrated Security=True;User Instance=True"
        SelectCommand="SELECT Title FROM Movies"
        Runat="server" />

    </form>
</body>
</html>
```

ShowListControls.aspx

In above listing, each list control is bound to a `SqlDataSource` control which represents the contents of the Movies database table. For example, the `BulletedList` control is bound to the `DataSource` control like this:

```
<asp:BulletedList
  id="BulletedList1"
  DataSourceID="srcMovies"
  DataTextField="Title"
  Runat="server" />

<asp:SqlDataSource
  id="srcMovies"
```

```
    ConnectionString="Data Source=.\SQLExpress;
      AttachDbFilename=|DataDirectory|MyDatabase.mdf;
       Integrated Security=True;User Instance=True"
    SelectCommand="SELECT Title FROM Movies"
    Runat="server" />
```

The `BulletedList` control includes a `DataSourceID` attribute, which points to the ID of the `SqlDataSource` control. The `DataSourceID` attribute associates a `DataBound` control with a `DataSource` control.

Working with Tabular DataBound Controls

The tabular `DataBound` controls are the main set of controls that you use when working with database data. These controls enable you to display and, in some cases, modify data retrieved from a database or other type of data source.

Six tabular `DataBound` controls can be divided into two types: those that display multiple data items at a time and those that display a single data item at a time.

First, you can use any of the following controls to display a set of data items:

- `GridView`— Displays a set of data items in an HTML table. For example, you can use the `GridView` control to display all the records contained in the Movies database table. This control enables you to display, sort, page, select, and edit data.
- `DataList`— Displays a set of data items in an HTML table. Unlike the `GridView` control, more than one data item can display in a single row.
- `Repeater`— Displays a set of data items using a template. Unlike the `GridView` and `DataList` controls, a `Repeater` control does not automatically render an HTML table.
- `ListView`— Displays a set of data items using a template. Unlike the `Repeater` control, the `ListView` control supports sorting, paging, and editing database data.

You can use either of the following two controls to display a single data item at a time:

- `DetailsView`— Displays a single data item in an HTML table. For example, you can use the `DetailsView` control to display a single record from the Movies database table. This control enables you to display, page, edit, and add data.
- `FormView`— Uses a template to display a single data item. Unlike the `DetailsView`, a `FormView` enables you to use to layout a form by using templates.

The page in next listing illustrates how you can use each of the tabular `DataBound` controls.

```
Code View: Scroll / Show All
<%@ Page Language="C#" %>
<!DOCTYPE html PUBLIC "-//W3C//DTD XHTML 1.1//EN"
"http://www.w3.org/TR/xhtml11/DTD/xhtml11.dtd">
<html xmlns="http://www.w3.org/1999/xhtml" >
<head id="Head1" runat="server">
    <style type="text/css">
        .floater
        {
            float:left;
            border:solid 1px black;
            padding:5px;
            margin:5px;
        }
    </style>
    <title>Show Tabular Databound Controls</title>
```

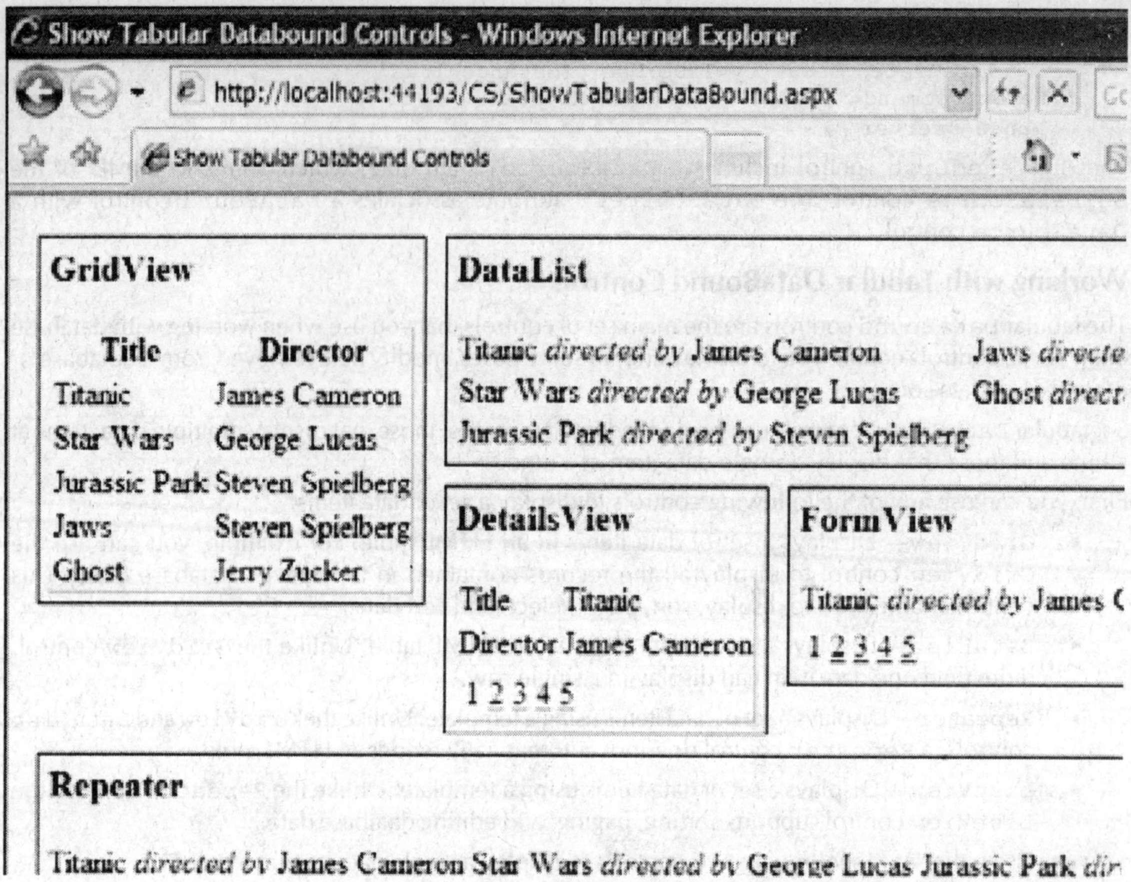

Figure Using tabular DataBound controls.

```
</head>
<body>
    <form id="form1" runat="server">

    <div class="floater">
    <h3>GridView</h3>
    <asp:GridView
        id="GridView1"
        DataSourceId="srcMovies"
        Runat="server" />
    </div>

    <div class="floater">
    <h3>DataList</h3>
    <asp:DataList
        id="DataList1"
        DataSourceId="srcMovies"
        RepeatColumns="2"
        Runat="server">
        <ItemTemplate>
        <%#Eval("Title")%>
        <i>directed by</i>
        <%#Eval("Director")%>
```

```
        </ItemTemplate>
    </asp:DataList>
    </div>

    <div class="floater">
    <h3>DetailsView</h3>
    <asp:DetailsView
        id="DetailsView1"
        DataSourceId="srcMovies"
        AllowPaging="true"
        Runat="server" />
    </div>

    <div class="floater">
    <h3>FormView</h3>
    <asp:FormView
        id="FormView1"
        DataSourceId="srcMovies"
        AllowPaging="true"
        Runat="server">
        <ItemTemplate>
        <%#Eval("Title")%>
        <i>directed by</i>
        <%#Eval("Director")%>
        </ItemTemplate>
    </asp:FormView>
    </div>
<br style="clear:both" />

    <div class="floater">
    <h3>Repeater</h3>
    <asp:Repeater
        id="Repeater1"
        DataSourceId="srcMovies"
        Runat="server">
        <ItemTemplate>
        <%#Eval("Title")%>
        <i>directed by</i>
        <%#Eval("Director")%>
        </ItemTemplate>
    </asp:Repeater>
    </div>

    <div class="floater">
    <h3>ListView</h3>
    <asp:ListView
        id="ListView1"
        DataSourceId="srcMovies"
        Runat="server">
        <LayoutTemplate>
        <div id="itemContainer" runat="server">
        </div>
        <asp:DataPager ID="pager1" PageSize="3" runat="server">
        <Fields>
            <asp:NumericPagerField />
        </Fields>
        </asp:DataPager>
        </LayoutTemplate>
```

```
        <ItemTemplate>
        <%#Eval("Title")%>
        <i>directed by</i>
        <%#Eval("Director")%>
        </ItemTemplate>
    </asp:ListView>
    </div>

    <asp:SqlDataSource
        id="srcMovies"
       ConnectionString="Data Source=.\SQLExpress;
          AttachDbFilename=|DataDirectory|MyDatabase.mdf;
          Integrated Security=True;User Instance=True"
       SelectCommand="SELECT TOP 5 Title,Director FROM Movies"
        Runat="server" />

    </form>
</body>
</html>
```

ShowTabularDataBound.aspx

For the moment, don't worry too much about formatting the controls. Each of the tabular `DataBound` controls supports an abundance of properties that modify the control's behavior and appearance.

Working with Hierarchical DataBound Controls

A hierarchical `DataBound` control can display nested data items. For example, you can use hierarchical `DataBound` controls to display the folder and page structure of your website, the contents of an XML file, or a set of master/detail database records. The ASP.NET 4 Framework includes two hierarchical `DataBound` controls:

- `Menu`— Displays data items in a static or dynamic menu.
- `TreeView`— Displays data items in a tree.

The page in first listing illustrates how you can use both the `Menu` and `TreeView` controls. Both controls are bound to an `XmlDataSource` control, which represents the XML file in second listing.

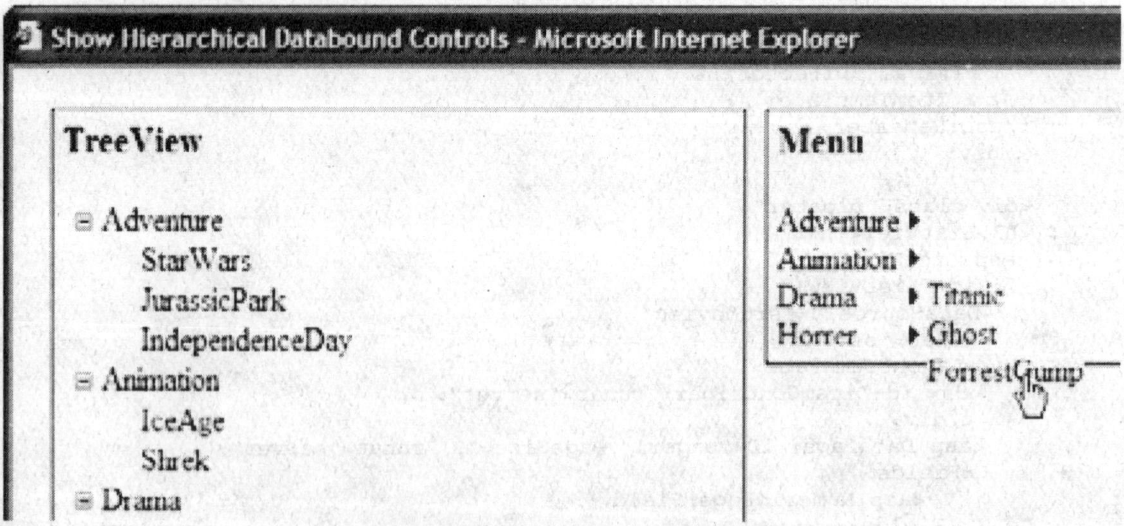

Using hierarchical DataBound controls.

```
Code View: Scroll / Show All
<%@ Page Language="C#" %>
<!DOCTYPE html PUBLIC "-//W3C//DTD XHTML 1.1//EN"
"http://www.w3.org/TR/xhtml11/DTD/xhtml11.dtd">
<html xmlns="http://www.w3.org/1999/xhtml" >
<head id="Head1" runat="server">
    <style type="text/css">
        .floater
        {
            float:left;
            width:45%;
            border:solid 1px black;
            padding:5px;
            margin:5px;
        }
    </style>
    <title>Show Hierarchical Databound Controls</title>
</head>
<body>
    <form id="form1" runat="server">

    <div class="floater">
    <h3>TreeView</h3>
    <asp:TreeView
        id="CheckBoxList1"
        DataSourceId="srcMovies"
        Runat="server" />
    </div>

    <div class="floater">
    <h3>Menu</h3>
    <asp:Menu
        id="BulletedList1"
        DataSourceId="srcMovies"
        Runat="server" />
    </div>

    <asp:XmlDataSource
        id="srcMovies"
        DataFile="~/Movies.xml"
        XPath="/movies/*"
        Runat="server" />

    </form>
</body>
</html>
```

ShowHierarchicalDataBound.aspx

```
<?xml version="1.0" encoding="utf-8" ?>
<movies>
  <Adventure>
    <StarWars />
    <JurassicPark />
    <IndependenceDay />
  </Adventure>
  <Animation>
    <IceAge />
```

```
      <Shrek />
    </Animation>
    <Drama>
      <Titanic />
      <Ghost />
      <ForrestGump />
    </Drama>
    <Horror>
      <Jaws />
      <TheRing />
    </Horror>
  </movies>
```

Movies.xml

Again, don't worry about the appearance of the `Menu` and `TreeView` controls in the page rendered by first listing. Both controls support a rich set of options for modifying the control's appearance.

Working with Other Controls

You can bind any control in ASP.NET Framework to the data items represented by a data source. Imagine, for example, that you want to display a photo gallery. In that case, you might want to bind a set of Image controls to a data source. You can bind any ASP.NET control to a data item by adding the control to a template. For example, the page in next listing automatically displays all the pictures in a folder named Photos.

Binding images to a data source.

Code View: Scroll / Show All

```
<%@ Page Language="C#" %>
<%@ Import Namespace="System.IO" %>
<%@ Import Namespace="System.Collections.Generic" %>
<!DOCTYPE html PUBLIC "-//W3C//DTD XHTML 1.1//EN"
"http://www.w3.org/TR/xhtml11/DTD/xhtml11.dtd">
<script runat="server">

    /// <summary>
    /// Bind photos to Repeater
    /// </summary>
```

```
    void Page_Load()
    {
        if (!Page.IsPostBack)
        {
            Repeater1.DataSource = GetPhotos();
            Repeater1.DataBind();
        }
    }

    /// <summary>
    /// Get list of photos from Photo folder
    /// </summary>
    public List<String> GetPhotos()
    {
        List<string> photos = new List<string>();
        string photoPath = MapPath("~/Photos");
        string[] files = Directory.GetFiles(photoPath);
        foreach (string photo in files)
            photos.Add("~/Photos/" + Path.GetFileName(photo));
        return photos;
    }

</script>
<html xmlns="http://www.w3.org/1999/xhtml" >
<head id="Head1" runat="server">
    <title>Show Photos</title>
</head>
<body>
    <form id="form1" runat="server">
    <div>

    <asp:Repeater
        id="Repeater1"
        runat="server">
        <ItemTemplate>
            <asp:Image
                id="Image1"
                Width="200px"
                ImageUrl='<%# Container.DataItem %>'
                Runat="server" />
        </ItemTemplate>
    </asp:Repeater>

    </div>
    </form>
</body>
</html>
```

ShowPhotos.aspx

The Repeater control contains an `ItemTemplate`, and the `ItemTemplate` contains an ASP.NET Image control. The `Image` control displays each of the photographs from the Photos folder.

Using DataSource Controls

You bind a `DataBound` control to a `DataSource` control. A `DataSource` control represents a particular type of data.

The ASP.NET 4 Framework includes the following six `DataSource` controls:

- `SqlDataSource`— Represents data retrieved from a SQL relational database, including Microsoft SQL Server, Oracle, or DB2.
- `LinqDataSource`— Represents a LINQ to SQL query.
- `AccessDataSource`— Represents data retrieved from a Microsoft Access database.
- `ObjectDataSource`— Represents data retrieved from a business object.
- `XmlDataSource`— Represents data retrieved from an XML document.
- `SiteMapDataSource`— Represents data retrieved from a Site Map Provider. A Site Map Provider represents the page and folder structure of a website.

The ASP.NET Framework contains two basic types of `DataSource` controls. The `SqlDataSource`, `AccessDataSource`, `LinqDataSource`, and `ObjectDataSource` controls all derive from the base `DataSourceControl` class. These controls can be used to represent tabular data. The `XmlDataSource` and `SiteMapDataSource` controls, on the other hand, derive from the base `HierarchicalDataSourceControl` control. These two controls can be used to represent both tabular and hierarchical data.

A `DataBound` control is associated with a particular data source control through its `DataSourceID` property. For example, the page in next listing contains a `GridView` control bound to a `SqlDataSource` control.

http://localhost:4121 - Bound GridView - Mozilla Firefox

Id	CategoryId	Title	Director	DateReleased
1	3	Titanic	James Cameron	6/21/1997 12:00:00 AM
2	1	Star Wars	George Lucas	6/1/1977 12:00:00 AM
3	1	Jurassic Park	Steven Spielberg	6/17/1993 12:00:00 AM
4	4	Jaws	Steven Spielberg	5/30/1975 12:00:00 AM
5	3	Ghost	Jerry Zucker	6/14/1990 12:00:00 AM
7	3	Forrest Gump	Robert Zemeckis	6/18/1994 12:00:00 AM
8	2	Ice Age	Chris Wedge	6/26/2002 12:00:00 AM
9	2	Shrek	Andrew Adamson	6/25/2001 12:00:00 AM
10	1	Independence Day	Roland Emmerich	6/20/1996 12:00:00 AM
11	4	The Ring	Gore Verbinski	6/26/2002 12:00:00 AM

Using the SqlDataSource control.

Code View: Scroll / Show All

```
<%@ Page Language="C#" %>
<!DOCTYPE html PUBLIC "-//W3C//DTD XHTML 1.1//EN"
"http://www.w3.org/TR/xhtml11/DTD/xhtml11.dtd">
<html xmlns="http://www.w3.org/1999/xhtml" >
<head id="Head1" runat="server">
    <title>Bound GridView</title>
</head>
<body>
```

```
    <form id="form1" runat="server">
    <div>

    <asp:GridView
        id="GridView1"
        DataSourceId="srcMovies"
        Runat="server" />

    <asp:SqlDataSource
        id="srcMovies"
        ConnectionString="Data Source=.\SQLExpress;
            AttachDbFilename=|DataDirectory|MyDatabase.mdf;
            Integrated Security=True;User Instance=True"
        SelectCommand="SELECT * FROM Movies"
        Runat="server" />

    </div>
    </form>
</body>
</html>
```

BoundGridView.aspx

Using ASP.NET Parameters with DataSource Controls

Many of the `DataSource` controls support ASP.NET parameters. You use ASP.NET parameters to modify the commands that a `DataSource` control executes. Different types of `DataSource` controls use ASP.NET parameters to represent different types of things. When you use ASP.NET parameters with a `SqlDataSource` control, the ASP.NET parameters represent ADO.NET parameters. In other words, they represent parameters used with SQL statements.

When you use parameters with the `ObjectDataSource` control, the ASP.NET parameters represent method parameters. They represent parameters passed to a particular method of a business object.

The `SqlDataSource`, `AccessDataSource`, `LinqDataSource`, and `ObjectDataSource` controls all support the following types of Parameter objects:

- `Parameter`— Represents an arbitrary static value.
- `ControlParameter`— Represents the value of a `control` or page property.
- `CookieParameter`— Represents the value of a browser cookie.
- `FormParameter`— Represents the value of an HTML form field.
- `ProfileParameter`— Represents the value of a `Profile` property.
- `QueryStringParameter`— Represents the value of a query string field.
- `SessionParameter`— Represents the value of an item stored in Session state.

For example, the page in next listing contains a `DropDownList`, `GridView`, and `SqlDataSource` control. The `DropDownList` displays a list of movie categories. When you select a new category, the `GridView` displays matching movies.

```
Code View: Scroll / Show All
<%@ Page Language="C#" %>
<!DOCTYPE html PUBLIC "-//W3C//DTD XHTML 1.1//EN"
"http://www.w3.org/TR/xhtml11/DTD/xhtml11.dtd">
<html xmlns="http://www.w3.org/1999/xhtml" >
<head id="Head1" runat="server">
    <title>Show Control Parameter</title>
```

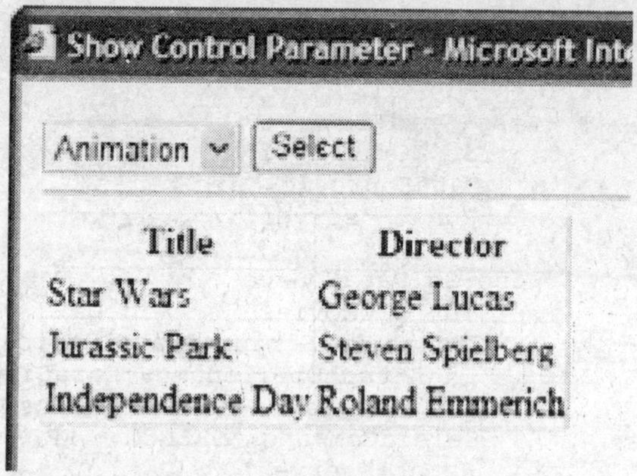

Using the ControlParameter object.

```
</head>
<body>
    <form id="form1" runat="server">
    <div>

    <asp:DropDownList
        id="ddlMovieCategory"
      DataSourceID="srcMovieCategories"
        DataTextField="Name"
        DataValueField="Id"
        Runat="server" />

    <asp:Button
        id="btnSelect"
        Text="Select"
        ToolTip="Select Movie"
        Runat="server" />

    <hr />

    <asp:GridView
        id="grdMovies"
        DataSourceID="srcMovies"
        Runat="server" />
    <asp:SqlDataSource
        id="srcMovieCategories"
       ConnectionString="Server=.\SQLExpress;
     Trusted_Connection=True;AttachDbFileName=|DataDirectory|MyDatabase.mdf;
        User Instance=True"
       SelectCommand="SELECT Id,Name FROM MovieCategories"
        Runat="server" />

    <asp:SqlDataSource
        id="srcMovies"
       ConnectionString="Data Source=.\SQLExpress;
           AttachDbFilename=|DataDirectory|MyDatabase.mdf;
           Integrated Security=True;User Instance=True"
       SelectCommand="SELECT Title,Director FROM Movies
            WHERE CategoryId=@Id"
        Runat="server">
        <SelectParameters>
            <asp:ControlParameter
                Name="Id"
                Type="int32"
               ControlID="ddlMovieCategory" />
        </SelectParameters>
    </asp:SqlDataSource>

    </div>
    </form>
</body>
</html>
```

ShowControlParameter.aspx

The SqlDataSource control includes a ControlParameter object. The ControlParameter represents the selected item in the DropDownList control. The value of the ControlParameter is used in the `SqlDataSource` control's `SelectCommand` to select movies that match the category selected in the `DropDownList` control.

Using Programmatic DataBinding

When you bind a `DataBound` control to a `DataSource` control, you can take advantage of declarative databinding. When you use declarative databinding, ASP.NET Framework handles all the messy details of deciding when to retrieve the data items represented by a `DataSource` control.

In certain situations, you want to handle these messy details yourself. For example, you might want to force a `GridView` control to refresh the data it displays after you add a new record to a database table. Or you might want to bind a `DataBound` control to a data source that can't be easily represented by one of the existing `DataSource` controls. In these situations, you want to use programmatic databinding.

Every `DataBound` control has a `DataSource` property and a `DataBind()` method. By using this property and method, you can programmatically associate a `DataBound` control with a data source. For example, the page in next listing displays a list of all the fonts installed on your computer .

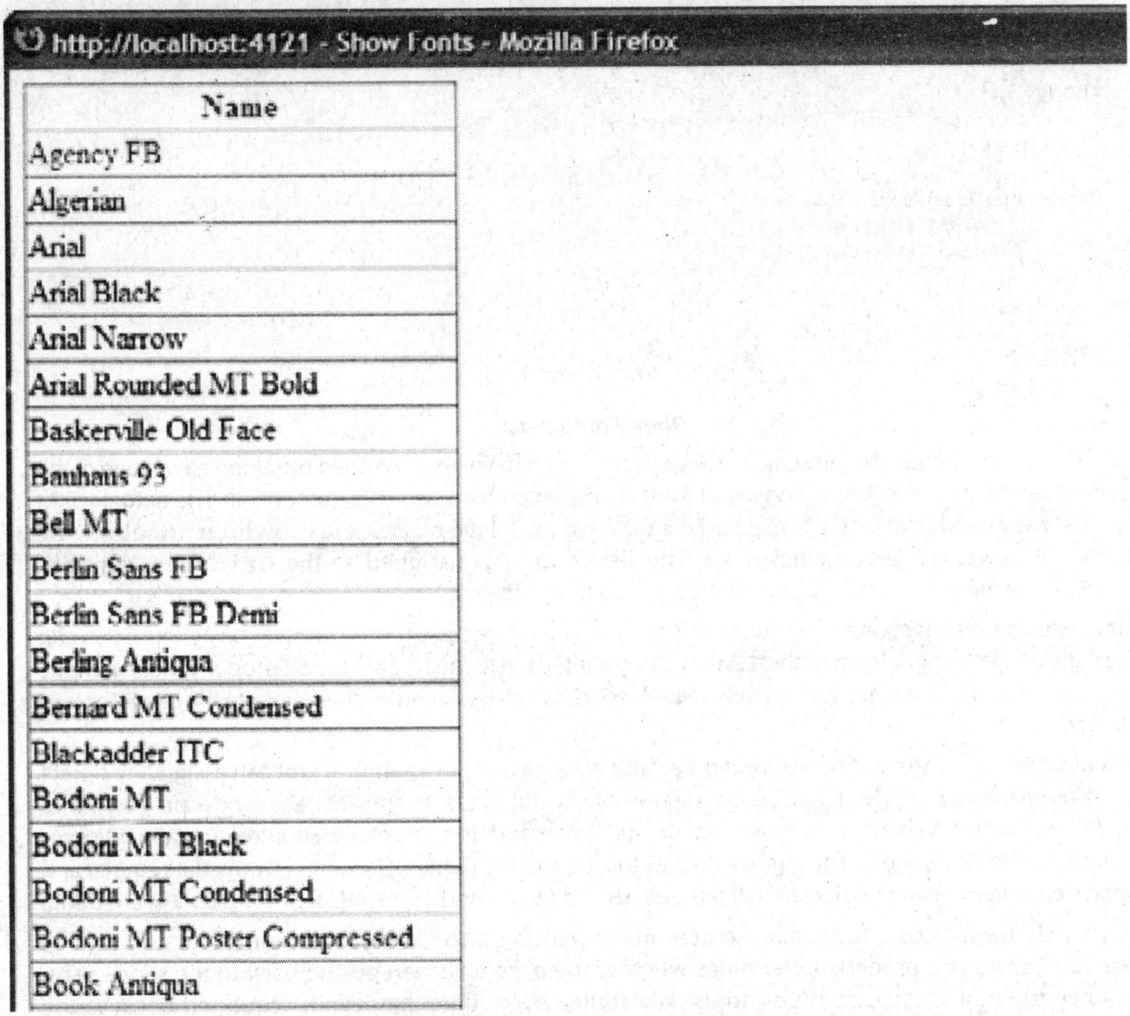

Figure Programmatic databinding.

```
Code View: Scroll / Show All
<%@ Page Language="C#" %>
<%@ Import Namespace="System.Drawing.Text" %>
<!DOCTYPE html PUBLIC "-//W3C//DTD XHTML 1.1//EN"
"http://www.w3.org/TR/xhtml11/DTD/xhtml11.dtd">
<script runat="server">

    void Page_Load()
    {
        if (!Page.IsPostBack)
        {
            InstalledFontCollection fonts = new InstalledFontCollection();
            GridView1.DataSource = fonts.Families;
            GridView1.DataBind();
        }
    }
</script>
<html xmlns="http://www.w3.org/1999/xhtml" >
<head id="Head1" runat="server">
    <title>Show Fonts</title>
</head>
<body>
    <form id="form1" runat="server">
    <div>

    <asp:GridView
        id="GridView1"
        Runat="server" />

    </div>
    </form>
</body>
</html>
```

ShowFonts.aspx

Note: The programmatic databinding in above listing could have been avoided by taking advantage of the `ObjectDataSource` control. The list of fonts is displayed by a `GridView` control. The actual list of fonts is retrieved from the `InstalledFontCollection` class (which inhabits the `System.Drawing.Text` namespace). The list of fonts is assigned to the `GridView` control's `DataSource` property, and the `DataBind()` method is called.

In above listing, a collection of fonts has been assigned to the `DataSource` property. In general, you can assign any object that implements the `IEnumerable` interface to the `DataSource` property. For example, you can assign collections, arrays, DataSets, DataReaders, DataViews, and enumerations to the `DataSource` property.

Particular `DataBound` controls support different data sources. For example, you can assign any object that implements the `IEnumerable` or `ITypedList` interface to the `DataSource` property of a `GridView` control. When you call the `DataBind()` method, the `GridView` control actually retrieves its data from the data source. The control iterates through all the items represented by the data source and displays each item. If you neglect to call the `DataBind()` method, the control never displays anything.

The `GridView` is bound to its data source only when the page is requested for the first time. The `Page.IsPostBack` property determines whether the page has been posted back to the server. You don't need to rebind the `GridView` to its data source every time the page is requested because the `GridView` uses View State to remember the data items that it displays.

You can't mix declarative and programmatic databinding. If you attempt to use both the `DataSource` and `DataSourceID` properties, you get an exception. On the other hand, you can call the `DataBind()` method even when you have declaratively bound a control to a `DataSource` control. When you explicitly call `DataBind()`, the `DataBound` control grabs the data items from its `DataSource` control again. Explicitly calling `DataBind()` is useful when you want to refresh the data displayed by a `DataBound` control.

Understanding Templates and DataBinding Expressions

Almost all the `DataBound` controls support templates. You can use a template to format the layout and appearance of each of the data items that a `DataBound` control displays. Within a template, you can use a DataBinding expression to display the value of a data item.

Using Templates

Every `DataBound` control included in ASP.NET 4 Framework supports templates with the sole exception of the `TreeView` control. The `Repeater`, `DataList`, `ListView`, and `FormView` controls all require you to use templates. If you don't supply a template, these controls display nothing. The `GridView`, `DetailsView`, and `Menu` controls also support templates, but they do not require a template.

For example, when you use the `Repeater` control, you must supply an ItemTemplate. The `Repeater` control uses the ItemTemplate to format each of the records that it displays. Next listing contains a `Repeater` control that formats each of the records from the Movies database table.

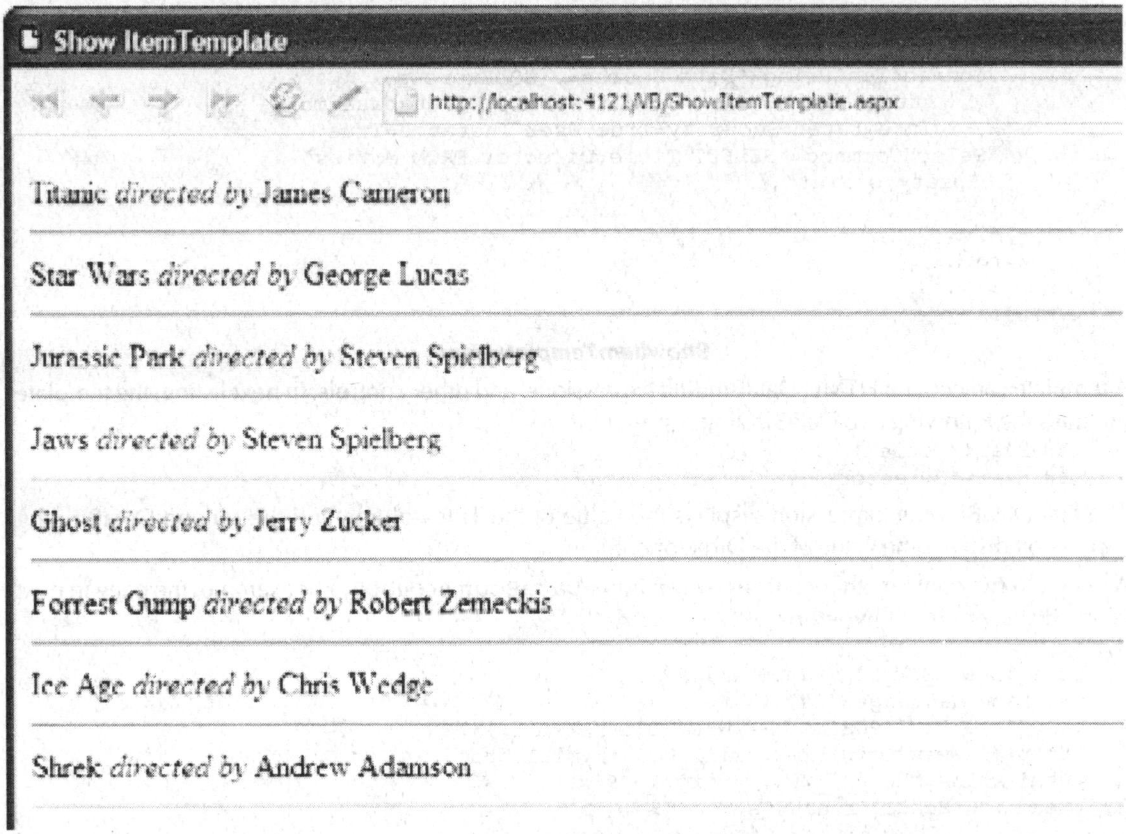

Using an ItemTemplate.

```
Code View: Scroll / Show All
<%@ Page Language="C#" %>
<!DOCTYPE html PUBLIC "-//W3C//DTD XHTML 1.1//EN"
"http://www.w3.org/TR/xhtml11/DTD/xhtml11.dtd">
<html xmlns="http://www.w3.org/1999/xhtml" >
<head id="Head1" runat="server">
   <title>Show ItemTemplate</title>
</head>
<body>
   <form id="form1" runat="server">
    <div>

    <asp:Repeater
        id="Repeater1"
       DataSourceId="srcMovies"
        Runat="server">
        <ItemTemplate>
        <%#Eval("Title")%>
        <i>directed by</i>
        <%#Eval("Director")%>
        <hr />
        </ItemTemplate>
    </asp:Repeater>


    <asp:SqlDataSource
        id="srcMovies"
       ConnectionString="Data Source=.\SQLExpress;
           AttachDbFilename=|DataDirectory|MyDatabase.mdf;
           Integrated Security=True;User Instance=True"
       SelectCommand="SELECT Title,Director FROM Movies"
        Runat="server" />

    </div>
    </form>
</body>
</html>
```

ShowItemTemplate.aspx

A template can contain HTML, DataBinding expressions, and other controls. In next listing, the template includes the following two DataBinding expressions:

```
<%# Eval("Title") %>
<%# Eval("Director") %>
```

The first DataBinding expression displays the value of the Title column and the second DataBinding expression displays the value of the Director column.

A template can contain other controls—even other DataBound controls. For example, the page in next listing displays a list of hyperlinks.

```
Code View: Scroll / Show All
<%@ Page Language="C#" %>
<!DOCTYPE html PUBLIC "-//W3C//DTD XHTML 1.1//EN"
"http://www.w3.org/TR/xhtml11/DTD/xhtml11.dtd">
<html xmlns="http://www.w3.org/1999/xhtml" >
<head id="Head1" runat="server">
   <title>Show Links</title>
</head>
```

```
<body>
    <form id="form1" runat="server">
    <div>

    <asp:Repeater
        id="Repeater1"
        DataSourceId="srcMovies"
        Runat="server">
        <ItemTemplate>

        <asp:HyperLink
            id="HyperLink1"
            Text='<%# Eval("Title") %>'
            NavigateUrl='<%# Eval("Id",
"Details.aspx?id={0}") %>'
            runat="server" />
        <br />

        </ItemTemplate>
    </asp:Repeater>
```

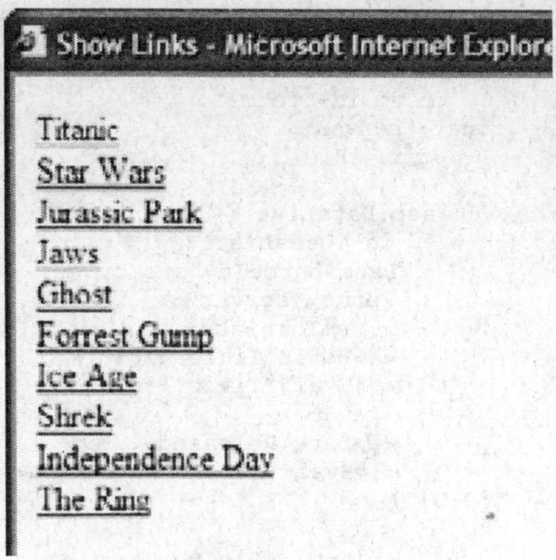

Figure Displaying a list of hyperlinks.

```
    <asp:SqlDataSource
        id="srcMovies"
        ConnectionString="Data Source=.\SQLExpress;
            AttachDbFilename=|DataDirectory|MyDatabase.mdf;
            Integrated Security=True;User Instance=True"
        SelectCommand="SELECT Id, Title FROM Movies"
        Runat="server" />

    </div>
    </form>
</body>
</html>
```

ShowLinks.aspx

In above listing, a HyperLink control displays for each item from the data source. The HyperLink control displays the movie title and links to a details page for the movie.

Using DataBinding Expressions

A DataBinding expression is a special type of expression not evaluated until runtime. You mark a databinding expression in a page by wrapping the expression in opening `<%#` and closing `%>` brackets.

A DataBinding expression isn't evaluated until a control's DataBinding event is raised. When you bind a `DataBound` control to a `DataSource` control declaratively, this event is raised automatically. When you bind a `DataSource` control to a data source programmatically, the DataBinding event is raised when you call the `DataBind()` method.

For example, the page in next listing contains a `DataList` control that contains a template that includes two DataBinding expressions.

```
Code View: Scroll / Show All
<%@ Page Language="C#" %>
<!DOCTYPE html PUBLIC "-//W3C//DTD XHTML 1.1//EN"
"http://www.w3.org/TR/xhtml11/DTD/xhtml11.dtd">
<html xmlns="http://www.w3.org/1999/xhtml" >
<head id="Head1" runat="server">
```

```
        <title>Show DataList</title>
  </head>
  <body>
      <form id="form1"
  runat="server">
      <div>

      <asp:DataList
          id="DataList1"
          DataSourceId="srcMovies"
          Runat="server">
          <ItemTemplate>
          <b>Movie Title:</b>
          <%#Eval("Title")%>
          <br />
          <b>Date Released:</b>
          <%#Eval("DateReleased",
  "{0:D}") %>
          <hr />
          </ItemTemplate>
      </asp:DataList>

      <asp:SqlDataSource
          id="srcMovies"
          ConnectionString="Data
  Source=.\SQLExpress;
              AttachDbFilename=|
  DataDirectory|MyDatabase.mdf;
              Integrated
  Security=True;User Instance=True"
          SelectCommand="SELECT
  Title,Director,DateReleased FROM
  Movies"
          Runat="server" />

      </div>
      </form>
  </body>
  </html>
```

ShowDataList.aspx

Using databinding expressions.

The first DataBinding expression displays the title of the movie and the second DataBinding expression displays the date the movie was released.

Both DataBinding expressions call the `Eval()` method. The `Eval()` method is a protected method of the `Page` class. Behind the scenes, the `Page.Eval()` method calls the static (shared) `DataBinder.Eval()` method. If you want to be verbose, instead of using the `Eval()` method, you could use the following two expressions:

```
<%# DataBinder.Eval(Container.DataItem, "Title") %>
<%# DataBinder.Eval(Container.DataItem, "DateReleased", "{0:D}" ) %>
```

In ASP.NET version 1.x, you had to use `DataBinder.Eval()` when displaying data items in a template. However, Microsoft took pity on programmers after ASP.NET 2.0 and provided us with the shorter syntax.

As an alternative, you can improve the performance of your DataBinding expressions by casting the data items to a particular type like this:

```
<%# ((System.Data.DataRowView)Container.DataItem)["Title"] %>
```

The second DataBinding expression in above listing includes a second parameter. The `Eval()` method, optionally, accepts a format string. You can use the format string to format values such as dates and currency amounts. In above listing, the format string formats the DateReleased column as a long date.

Format strings use format specifiers such as the D format specifier when formatting strings. You can find a list of format specifiers by looking up Formatting Types in the index of the Microsoft .NET Framework SDK documentation.

You can call other methods than the `Eval()` method in a DataBinding expression. For example, the DataBinding expression in next listing calls a method named `FormatTitle()` to format the movie titles.

```
Code View: Scroll / Show All
<%@ Page Language="C#" %>
<!DOCTYPE html PUBLIC "-//W3C//DTD XHTML 1.1//EN"
"http://www.w3.org/TR/xhtml11/DTD/xhtml11.dtd">
<script runat="server">

    public string FormatTitle(Object title)
    {
        return "<b>" + title.ToString().ToUpper() + "</b>";
    }

</script>
<html xmlns="http://www.w3.org/1999/xhtml" >
<head id="Head1" runat="server">
    <title>Format Movie Titles</title>
</head>
<body>
    <form id="form1" runat="server">
    <div>

    <asp:Repeater
        id="Repeater1"
        DataSourceId="srcMovies"
        Runat="server">
        <ItemTemplate>
        <%# FormatTitle(Eval("Title")) %>
        <hr />
        </ItemTemplate>
    </asp:Repeater>

    <asp:SqlDataSource
        id="srcMovies"
        ConnectionString="Data Source=.\SQLExpress;
            AttachDbFilename=|DataDirectory|MyDatabase.mdf;
            Integrated Security=True;User Instance=True"
        SelectCommand="SELECT Title FROM Movies"
        Runat="server" />

    </div>
    </form>
</body>
</html>
```

FormatMovieTitles.aspx

The `FormatTitle()` method is defined in the page in above listing. This method formats each of the titles displayed by the `Repeater` control by making each title bold and uppercase.

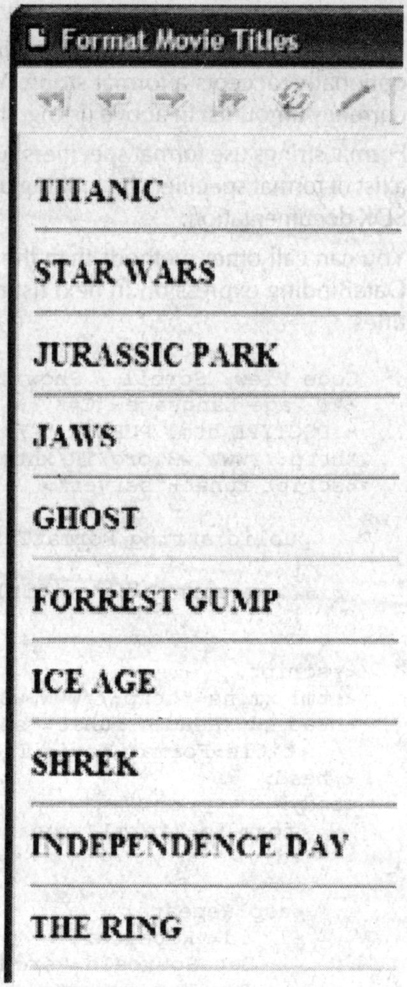

Formatting movie titles.

Using Two-Way DataBinding Expressions

The ASP.NET Framework actually supports two types of templates and two types of DataBinding expressions. The ASP.NET Framework supports both one-way DataBinding expressions and two-way DataBinding expressions. Up to this point, we have used one-way DataBinding expressions exclusively. In a one-way DataBinding expression, you use the DataBinding expression to display the value of a data item. You use the `Eval()` method to display the value of a one-way DataBinding expression.

In a two-way DataBinding expression, you not only can display the value of a data item, you also can modify the value of a data item. You use the `Bind()` method when working with a two-way DataBinding expression. For example, the page in next listing contains a `FormView` control that includes a template for editing a movie record in the Movies database table.

```
Code View: Scroll / Show All
<%@ Page Language="C#" %>
<!DOCTYPE html PUBLIC "-//W3C//DTD XHTML 1.1//
EN"
"http://www.w3.org/TR/xhtml11/DTD/xhtml11.dtd">
<html xmlns="http://www.w3.org/1999/xhtml" >
<head id="Head1" runat="server">
    <title>Show FormView</title>
</head>
<body>
    <form id="form1" runat="server">
    <div>

    <asp:FormView
        id="FormView1"
        DataKeyNames="Id"
        DataSourceId="srcMovies"
        DefaultMode="Edit"
        AllowPaging="true"
        Runat="server">
        <EditItemTemplate>
        <asp:Label
            id="lblTitle"
            Text="Title:"
           AssociatedControlID="txtTitle"
            Runat="server" />
        <asp:TextBox
            id="txtTitle"
           Text='<%#Bind("Title")%>'
            Runat="server" />
        <br />
        <asp:Label
            id="lblDirector"
```

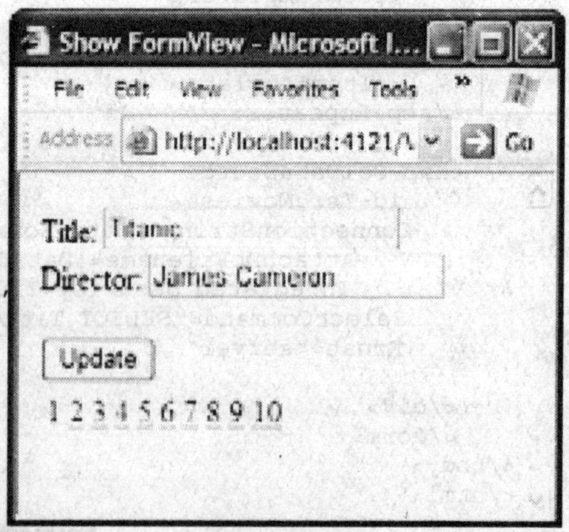

Editing a movie.

```
            Text="Director:"
            AssociatedControlID="txtDirector"
            Runat="server" />
        <asp:TextBox
            id="txtDirector"
            Text='<%#Bind("Director")%>'
            Runat="server" />
        <br />
        <asp:Button
            id="btnUpdate"
            Text="Update"
            CommandName="Update"
            Runat="server" />
        </EditItemTemplate>
    </asp:FormView>

    <asp:SqlDataSource
        id="srcMovies"
        ConnectionString="Data Source=.\SQLExpress;
            AttachDbFilename=|DataDirectory|MyDatabase.mdf;
            Integrated Security=True;User Instance=True"
        SelectCommand="SELECT Id, Title,Director,DateReleased FROM Movies"
        UpdateCommand="UPDATE Movies SET Title=@Title,
            Director=@Director WHERE Id=@Id"
        Runat="server" />

    </div>
    </form>
</body>
</html>
```

ShowFormView.aspx

The `FormView` contains an `EditItemTemplate`. The `EditItemTemplate` contains three `TextBox` controls. Each `TextBox` control has a two-way DataBinding expression assigned to its Text property. The DataBinding expressions associate the `TextBox` control properties with the properties of the data item being edited. When you click the Update button, any changes you make to the Text properties are updated in the Movies database table.

Overview of SQL Server 2008 Express

Microsoft SQL Server 2008 Express is the version of SQL Server bundled with Visual Web Developer. You can also download this database engine from the Microsoft website (http://www.microsoft.com/express/Database/). SQL Server Express is used for almost all the database examples in this book.

Features of SQL Server Express

One of the most important features of SQL Server 2008 Express is that it is a royalty-free database engine. You can download it and use it for free in your applications. You also can distribute the database in commercial applications that you produce for others without paying royalties to Microsoft.

Microsoft SQL Server 2008 Express uses the same database engine as the full retail version of SQL Server 2008. However, because it is a free product, Microsoft has limited some of its features to encourage you to upgrade to the full version of SQL Server 2008. First, unlike the full version of SQL Server 2008, a SQL Server Express database can be no larger than 4 gigabytes. Furthermore, SQL Server Express is limited to using 1 gigabyte of RAM. Also, SQL Server Express uses only a single processor even when used on a multiprocessor server.

SQL Server Express also does not support several of the advanced features of the full version of SQL Server 2008. For example, it doesn't support Analysis Services, Notification Services, English Query, Data Transformation Services, or OLAP.

However, SQL Server Express does not have a Workload Governor. The performance of a SQL Server Express database is never throttled. This means that you can use SQL Server Express for small websites without worrying about performance limitations. Finally, like the full version of SQL Server 2008, SQL Server Express supports the Common Language Runtime. In other words, you can use C# or Visual Basic .NET to create stored procedures, triggers, user-defined functions, and user-defined types.

SQL Server 2008 Express Management Tools

You can use three tools to create new database objects when using SQL Server 2008 Express. You can use Database Explorer in Visual Web Developer, Microsoft SQL Server Management Studio Express, and SQLCMD utility.

The Database Explorer included in Visual Web Developer provides you with a user-friendly interface for working with database objects.

Alternatively, you can use Microsoft SQL Server Management Studio Express. You can download Management Studio from the Microsoft site at http://www.microsoft.com/sqlserver/2008/en/us/express.aspx. This tool enables you to browse database objects and execute SQL queries.

Finally, SQL Server 2008 Express includes a command-line tool named SQLCMD. You can use the SQLCMD tool to fire off SQL queries from the Command Prompt. This alternative is the most painful, but it works.

You use SQLCMD by opening a command prompt and connecting to your database with the following command:

```
SQLCMD -S .\SQLExpress
```

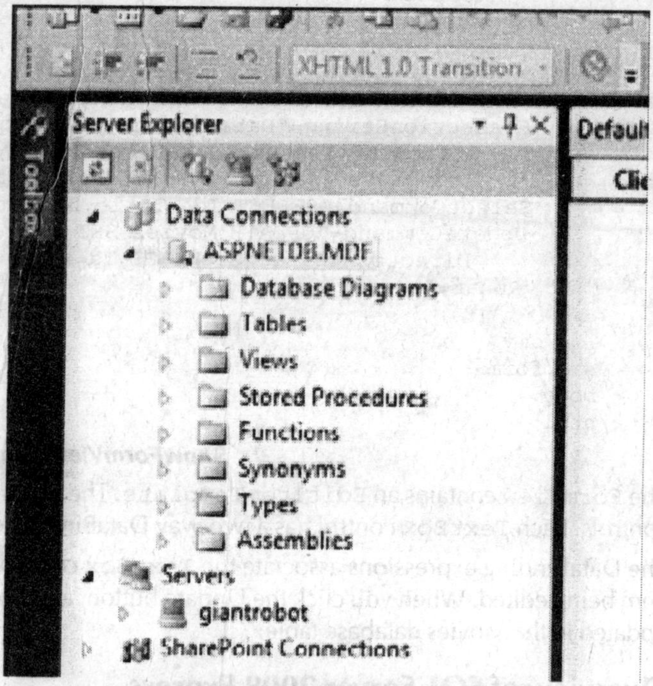

The Database Explorer window in Visual Web Developer.

CHAPTER 7

Questions

In this chapter you will read about:

- Various questions based on the topics read in the chapters of the book.

Chapter 1 — Introduction to ASP.NET 4.0

1. What do you understand by the various ASP.NET controls?
2. What are HTML controls?
3. Describe the various HTML controls.
4. e cri e t e ariou ASP.NET age .

2

1. Describe the ways of using Literal Controls.
2. How would you use the following:

   TextBox Control
   CheckBox Control
   RadioButton Control
   Button Control
   LinkButton Control
   ImageButton Control
   Client Scripts with Button Controls
   Image Controls
   ImageMap Controls
   Panel Controls

Chapter 3 — Using the Navigation Controls

1. What do you understand by Site Maps?
2. How would you use the Menu Controls?
3. Describe the use of TreeView Controls.
4. How would you build a SQL Hierarchical Data Source Controls?

Chapter 4 — Using Validation Controls

1. How would you use Validation Controls?
2. How would you use the following controls?

   RequiredFieldValidator Control
   RangeValidator Control
   CompareValidator Control
   RegularExpressionValidator Control
   CustomValidator Control
   ValidationSummary Control
3. How would you create a Custom Validation Control?

Chapter 5 — Designing Web Sites with Themes

1. How would you create Themes?

2. Describe the process of disabling themes.
3. How would you apply Themes Dynamically?
4. Describe the process of applying Skins Dynamically.

Chapter 6 — Overview of Data Access

1. How would you use Programmatic DataBinding?
2. What do you understand by Templates and DataBinding Expressions?
3. Describe the various features of SQL Server Express.
4. Which are the SQL Server 2008 Express Management Tools?

This page is intentionally left blank